Kohlhammer

Michal Opatrný

The Good Samaritan – A Public Theology for Helping Professions

W. Kohlhammer Verlag

1. Edition 2026

All rights reserved
© W. Kohlhammer GmbH, Stuttgart
Production: W. Kohlhammer GmbH, Heßbrühlstr. 69, 70565 Stuttgart
product safety: produktsicherheit@kohlhammer.de

Print:
ISBN 978-3-17-045733-1

E-Books:
pdf: ISBN 978-3-17-045734-8
epub: ISBN 978-3-17-045735-5

Any links in this book do not constitute an endorsement or an approval of any of the services or opinions of the corporation or organization or individual. W. Kohlhammer GmbH bears no responsibility for the accuracy, legality or content of the external site or for that of subsequent links.
All rights reserved. This book or parts thereof may not be reproduced in any form, stored in any retrieval system, or transmitted in any form by any means—electronic, mechanical, photocopy, recording, microfilm/microfiche or otherwise—without prior written permission of W. Kohlhammer GmbH, Stuttgart, Germany.

Contents

Preface 7

1. **The Good Samaritan story** 15
1.1 The story of the Good Samaritan and the reasons for focusing on it ... 16
1.2 The story of the Good Samaritan: characters and plot 19
1.3 The story of the Good Samaritan: how to approach it (*public theology*) .. 35
    1.3.1 Public theology 36
    1.3.2 Theology of Christian caritas and diakonia as public theology .. 38
    1.3.3 Public theology, social sciences, and social matters 41
    1.3.4 Public theology and intelligibility of religious language 43
1.4 Who is my neighbour – a question for public theology 45

2. **Modern Allegorical Interpretations** 47
2.1 Economic interpretations 49
2.2 Methodological Interpretations 51
2.3 Pastoral Interpretations 60
2.4 Diaconal exegesis 66

3. **Exegesis of the Samaritan story and criteria for evaluating the allegorical interpretations** 71
3.1 Notes on parables as a literary genre 72
3.2 The Gospel according to Luke 78
3.3 The Good Samaritan in contemporary exegetic literature 83
3.4 Commentary on individual verses in *Lk* 10:25–37 90
3.5 Unsurpassable criteria for caritas and diakonic interpretations of the text 105

4. **What's left of the story? The public message of the parable** 114
4.1 Hermeneutical key to and of mercy 115
4.2 Modern allegory and the hermeneutic key to and of the parable 119
    4.2.1 Economic interpretations 119
    4.2.2 Methodological interpretations 122
4.3 The public message of the parable 125

5. **What's left of the story for Christian caritas and diakonia?** 130

5.1	Cultic and praxeological messages of the parable	132
	5.1.1 Caritas and diakonia in the spirit of the parable as public theology *par excellence*	132
	5.1.2 Practical implications	137
5.2	The missionary message of the parable	140
	5.2.1 Missionary and public messages of the Samaritan's story	142
	5.2.2 Missionary message of the parable in the post-secular environment.	144
	5.2.3 Practical implications	146

Instead of a conclusion, the Samaritan's story continues 150

References 152

Preface

When I started preparing this book, I remembered my first Children's Bible and its cover. There was not a picture of the Lord Jesus with children on it, or Jesus crucified or resurrected. On the cover there was a scene depicting the story of the Good Samaritan. At the front, the Samaritan was leaning towards a beaten traveller while a priest and a Levite were disappearing in the distance, having passed by the unfortunate ambushed person at a distance. My mother even took this Bible with us on a trip to what was then Yugoslavia (now Croatia), where I suspect it had been printed and then smuggled into Czechoslovakia. And thus I had a three times smuggled Bible. Although my younger siblings inherited it in a rather worn state and it has fallen apart long ago, the memory of the cover with the Samaritan is one of my earliest memories. Today I dare to say that it belonged also to my most important memories. As early as in my childhood, the image of Christianity, as presented in Luke's Gospel, became close to me. The story of the Samaritan is one of its focal points, a kind of *anthropo*-logical rather than the *Theo*-logical Parable of the Merciful Father, otherwise known as the Parable of the Prodigal Son.

Regardless of my personal memories and Christian faith, it is also true that the Samaritan's story, more than many other Biblical passages, has had an indisputable appeal to its listeners and readers since the beginning of Christianity. The so-called Samaritan's Dilemma[1] (Goodman, Herzberg, 2020) shows the term 'Samaritan' in the sense of help without borders, help without reflection, etc. '*Samaritanism*, benevolence helping people in need, trying to relieve their grief through aid and donations, may have negative rather than positive consequences. First, on the beneficiaries of such help. Indeed (...) helping people may contribute to maintaining them in a state of poverty, dependent on aid and assistance (Marciano, 2022).' In economics, the word 'Samaritan' is also used for different thought experiments and games, usually unrelated to the original story (Basu, 2022). The so-called '911 Good Samaritan Law' in the USA also marked immunity for people who report to rescue services the drug overdoses of others (Reader, Walton, Linder, 2022). With the story of the Good Samaritan, both sides, *pro-choice* and *pro-life*, argue in the abortion controversy (Blackshaw, 2021). For example, the story is also an important resource for Christian medical ethics (Cavanaugh, 2020). Considering the covid-19 pandemic, a new interpretation of the Good Samaritan story arises because it faces discrimination and solidarity with the wea-

---

[1] The term comes from Buchan, J. M. (1975). The Samaritan's Dilemma: Altruism, Morality and Economic Theory. New York: Russell Sage Foundation (König, Hofmann 2017, p. 27).

kest. Moreover, the story deals with the situation where the foreigner is the neighbour, and the neighbour becomes the dangerous other (Chamburuka, Gusha, 2020).

Pope John Paul II wrote in his letter *Salvifici doloris*, on the Christian meaning of human suffering, that 'the parable of the Samaritan of the Gospel has become *one of the essential elements of moral culture and universally human civilization*' (1984). His successor Benedict XVI reminded us in his encyclical on hope *Spe salvi* that the beauty and depth of the Good Samaritan parable again and again spontaneously affects even those who do not profess Christianity (Benedict XVI, 2007b). Pope Francis then draws attention to Jesus speaking about the helping Samaritan precisely because in his time the Samaritans were a group despised by the Jews due to their different religious practice and tradition (Francis, 2016).

> The parable shows us how a community can be rebuilt by men and women who identify with the vulnerability of others, who reject the creation of a society of exclusion, and act instead as neighbours, lifting up and rehabilitating the fallen for the sake of the common good. (Francis, 2020, 67)

According to Francis (2016), Jesus shows that, despite this, the Samaritan's heart was so generous as to act for the good of the other according to the will of God who desires mercy and not sacrifice (*Mk* 12:33), who desires mercy and not condemnation of others. It is clear from this brief insight into the main documents of the denominational tradition to which I am affiliated that in the last almost fifty years each of the Roman pontiffs wanted to comment on the parable in one of their important documents. And this is precisely because the parable in its literary material connects the theme of helping others in need with the theme of otherness, and cultural, social, and religious tension, and thus it is widely understandable even outside the space of sharing the Christian faith. Further, another reason is that all of this relates to the person of Christian God. Faith in God should be manifested by the kind of conduct that Jesus talks about when telling the story of the good Samaritan who helped the ambushed traveller.

Gaining a brief yet actual overview of Samaritans is possible thanks to the comprehensive article of Mattew Chalmers (Chalmers, 2021), with more detail than in the books of Reinhard Pummer (Pummer, 2016) or the team of Jan Dušek (Dusek, 2018). The use of different metaphors related to the story of the Good Samaritan in today's public communication and politics is interestingly described in Spencer's Political Samaritan (Spencer, 2017). In addition is important to emphasize, the current Samaritans living in West Bank do not understand themselves as Samaritans. They call themselves 'Israelite Samaritans' (Chalmers, 2021) (Pummer, 2016).

Personally, I must admit that this is precisely the reason for this biblical passage being among the most fascinating for me, in which – as it seems to me - the true essence and meaning of the Christian faith is most revealed. My earliest childhood memories, my parents' religious upbringing, and my later study of theology as well as my interest in the social sciences eventually meet in the Samaritan's story. This was ultimately the reason why I decided to dedicate this work to him. I wrote 'work' because I have to admit that I could not simply write a book about the Samaritan. The very study of the Bible and other literature on this theme gave me meaning in itself – it was meaningful work for me. On the other hand, it was this study that was increasingly pushing me to try to write the book – a book where I work on bringing the parable closer also to 'non-Bible readers', that is, to those who are not Christians, who are other than Christians, who might perceive from Christians even a kind of tension towards them. Because the Samaritan's story is a story about helping those in need, this intention is concentrated on readers from among the helping professions. My academic work has led me to the environment of social sciences, and social work in particular. The book is therefore primarily intended for social workers. But I am convinced that other helping professions can quite easily apply its conclusions to their own areas of interest also.

The book is therefore intended also for those who have never read or heard anything about the Good Samaritan parable – to people involved in helping professions, whether as social workers, heads of social services organisations, or in any other field. The book aims at introducing in steps to them how Jesus Christ's thinking is shown in one of the parables in the *Gospel according to Luke* regarding human need and regarding how people should approach the need of others, how they should react to it, how they should deal with it. The book therefore departs from some of those plausibilities that Christians commonly associate with this parable. At the same time, it also aims at addressing preconceptions that are directed either against the parable itself or against Christian caritas and diakonia.[2] By analysing the Samaritan's story, I want to show that this often regards prejudice and especially preconceptions which find the justification (more than in the Bible or in this parable) in the unquestioned adoption of these problematic plausibilities by Christians, that is, in the actions of Christians, churches, and helping organisations, and in some inconsistent or even dubious interpretations of the parable.

Thus, it can be said that the intention of this book is nothing other than seeking the answer to the question as to whether theology can bring its own theory for helping practice, to which a specific method or a specific procedure in providing help might be connected. This theological theory and method are sought in the Christian kerygma – in the core of its message summarised by the Gospels. As I have already written, for me personally and professionally, the core of the Gospel messages is concentrated in the story of the Good Samaritan – in a story about one's need, otherness, and tension, as well as a story about the change that, according to God, man should undergo. In order for such a theory and method to be an actual theory and an actual method for helping practice, it must be useful not only for Christians, not only for the philanthropic projects of churches, not only for Christian caritas and diakonia, but it must be useful for social work and other helping professions in general. Thus, if I

---

2   Regarding the terminology, I use *caritas* for the Catholic concept of Christian philanthropy and *diakonia* for Protestant one. For the helping organisation and social services providers running typically in Europe by churches I use *Caritas* for the Catholic and *Diakonia* for the Protestant organisation. The terms *diacona, diaconic* I use only as the general term for the task of the Church to serve the poor and needy and in the sense of *diaconate* as the Church ministry.

want to bring the parable and its message closer to 'non-Bible readers', in my opinion this is only possible by showing its suitability and usefulness for helping professions. So, in the first chapter the book addresses three topics introducing the story of the Good Samaritan to the reader together with the way I intend to work with it here. First of all, I elaborate here in more detail the reasons for taking this parable into account, and why it should be taken into account in relation to the current conception of helping professions or social work. It is therefore a deepening and systematic addressing of the plan I described in preceding paragraphs. I do not bring the Samaritan story closer to the readers by quoting it or by retelling it, as theologians usually do when speaking to a wider that Christian audience. Instead, I have chosen the path supported by visual arts which has been inspired many times by the Good Samaritan story. Thus, I present to the readers reproductions of various works of art with my brief description, which, of course, is not a historical artistic analysis of them but is intended to help 'non-Bible readers' become familiar in steps with the Samaritan's story and its key moments. Only then, in the first chapter, do I address how I want to approach this matter in the book. My approach to the subject of the Good Samaritan parable is based on the approach of so-called *public theology* which intends to address theological material in a way that is understandable and also applicable to a wider than merely Christian public. Approaching the Good Samaritan story from the field of public theology is not surprising. Spencer, for example, recently did so in his book *The Political Samaritan*, where he compares especially the use of allusions to the story in statements of British politicians with the religious and theological understanding and interpretation of the message of the Good Samaritan's parable (Spencer, 2017). In my understanding, the approach of public theology significantly overlaps with the approach of Catholic pastoral theology which I understand as so-called practical theology. By this I mean the theology of the practice of the entire Church or the theology of the pastoral conduct of all Christians towards the world – towards secular society, nature, the state and politics, etc. This takes place in the sense of how the Second Vatican Council's (1962–1965) Pastoral Constitution on the Church in Today's World *Gaudium et Spes* talks about these topics.

The second chapter focuses on current interpretations of the parable in the context of contemporary theological reflection of Christian caritas and diakonia. I divide it into four parts following the ways of how these interpretations can also be classified. Some of them focus on the matter of financing charity organisations established by churches because the parable can be understood as a certain stimulus also for this topic. This therefore regards the parable's economic interpretations. The second group is methodological interpretations addressing the above-mentioned question of whether the parable offers a method of help for helping practice and, if yes, what kind. Further, pastoral interpretations are concerned with what the parable says about the aforementioned pastoral relationship of churches to the world, or for pastoral activities in church communities such as parishes, congregations, church communities, etc. The issue is included here of the relationship between church communities and church helping organisations. The final part is dedicated to so-called diaconical exegesis, being more complex approaches to the parable's matter which are rooted in the focus on helping people in need while subordinating all other conclusions to this.

The comprehensive third chapter creates a counterpoint to the second chapter. While the second chapter describes so-called modern allegories, that is, contemporary interpretations of the parable approaching it as an inspiration for contemporary caritas, diakonical, and pastoral practice, the third chapter summarises the state of the biblical exegetical discussion. Without thinking that I have exhausted the entire current state of exegetical knowledge of the parable, respectively of the *Gospel according to Luke*, I strive for the parable interpretation based on literature that employs standard scientific methods for researching biblical texts. These are based on textual criticism, historiography, and archaeology, with their mutual combination and criticism. Thanks to this, it is possible to gain a fairly contoured idea regarding who for and with what intention the author wrote the text of the parable (respectively, of the whole Gospel), how old the text is, to what facts and preconceptions of his contemporaries he alludes, and thus what the core of his message is. Thanks to this, it is possible to formulate in the third chapter the so-called public message of the parable, that is, one which, in the sense of public theology, is intended to aim also outside the environment of Christian churches. Then it is also possible to formulate criteria for how to interpret the parable for the needs of current helping practice in a way not contradicting the current state of scientific – exegetical – knowledge about the *Gospel according to Luke* and the parable of the Good Samaritan.

The following two chapters are devoted to the interpretations of the parable for the needs of current helping practice with regard to the exegetical state of knowledge. In a sense, this book has two different conclusions here. The first of these two chapters focuses on the parable's public message and its application for the helping professions. It therefore forms a theological theory and a method of helping practice (respectively, of social work) based on the public message of the parable. The other is devoted to Christian caritas and diakonia, however in a wider sense than merely Christian helping organisations. It again works with the parable's public message asking what form the caritas and diaconal practice of churches and individual Christians should have with regard to this.

Since the Good Samaritan story has become a kind of general cultural heritage of the Christian faith, as already mentioned, its specific internal plausibility can be assumed. However, at the same time this led to the fact that the whole story was sometimes accepted and applied uncritically and thoughtlessly, trivialised into a simple ethical appeal, and accepted as an uncritically meaningless motive for 'good conduct' (Haslinger, 2009, p. 247). It is precisely such approaches that this book aims to confront, respectively, aims to offer their alternative as a rational-critical view of the parable. As I have already stated, its method thus consists in a combination of the approach of public theology and Catholic practical theology, which I describe in more detail in the first chapter. Both of these approaches are united by the interest in the world as a theological concept, that is, the world as a cultural and social environment outside the church, which is concentrated in the secular way of life in the contemporary society. However, both Catholic practical theology and public theology do not perceive the Church and theological thinking as opposites of this 'world' but as its part. This consequently means that society, the cultural and social environment, is the context of theological thinking and ecclesial life. Although this might be a completely banal statement, for example, for the social sciences, it does not have to be so in theology when it is approached as a normatively conceived science, let alone, for example, in Catholic Church documents which are theological texts of their own kind. In this sense, the approach of public theology and Catholic practical theology are innovative currents within theological thinking which consciously and deliberately aims at combining the current concept of the humanities and social sciences influenced by positivism with theological hermeneutics. The first chapter discusses this problem in detail and also places it in the context of contemporary thinking about Christian charity. These have a lot in common with the Samaritan story while being also the subject of theological reflection in the fields of the *caritas theory* (in German, Caritaswissenschaft) in Catholic theology and the *diakonics* (in German, Diakonik) in Protestant theology, which have the majority of the features of public theology.

Due to this approach, it is therefore not possible to address the current state of knowledge on the topic of the book only in one chapter. There is no longer-term debate in this sense about the public message of the Good Samaritan parable. The current state of knowledge in connection with the book topic is thus captured in the first three chapters. In addition to the chosen approach, to which the first chapter is devoted, this regards the parable's contemporary allegories addressed in the second chapter, and the state of exegetical knowledge about the parable in the third chapter. Indeed, if in the fourth and fifth chapters I wanted to consider what the public message of the parable is for contemporary helping practice (especially for social work) and what it means for Christian charity, it was necessary to inquire what the state of knowledge is regarding the approach of public theology, what interpretations of the parable already exist in relation to current helping practice, and what the state of knowledge is about the parable based on the methods of contemporary exegesis.

As I have already indicated and as is described in detail in the first chapter, my approach will be ecumenical to a significant extent. Although my theological home is Catholic pastoral theology, I aim at taking into account the point of view of the Catholic theory of caritas as well as of Protestant diakonics. After all, the very approach of public theology is in principle ecumenical because the denominational differences among Christians and their theological thinking prove to be marginal regarding the claim to make theology publicly beneficial to secular society. Likewise, biblical matter and biblical exegesis allow the research of the parable by both Catholic and Protestant biblical scholars to be taken into account.

The parable of the Good Samaritan offers a practical model for conduct for Christians of various denominations and also for all people. It is a model with radical requirements with its part being the acceptance or rejection of other models of conduct (Fitzmyer, 1970–1985, p. 883). If I were asked to summarise this practical Samaritan's model of help in one word, I would describe it with the word *mercy*. Aware of how controversial this term is in relation to the helping professions, it is precisely the story of the Good Samaritan – as its name suggests in some languages – which defines mercy in its own original way. Communist regimes in Europe, such as the one I was born into in the second half of the last century, sought to eradicate mercy since 1917 as a 'dangerous relic' of the bourgeois-capitalist organisation of society. In their view, mercy humiliated people. In reality, however, this meant that the individual meant absolutely nothing to these regimes, being for them a productive force, a procreative force, a military force. Therefore, after 1989, mercy was rediscovered in the former communist countries experiencing an unprecedented flowering that fascinated people in the so-called West (Bopp, 1998, p. 16). Later, however, it became apparent that even this newly awakened mercy needed to be transformed into professional approaches of helping professions. This was hard to accept for many helping people in the post-communist countries, and many left the helping professions while even more underwent education, training, internships abroad, etc., and became professionals. This very experience shows that the mercy of the Merciful Samaritan is possible and that it is even one of the prerequisites of professionalism. Why this is so and how it is possible, I will try to explain on the following pages of this book. I will be glad if the readers of this book accept the invitation to seek this mercy in the Samaritan's story.

This intention of mine was possible only thanks to the generosity of the Humboldt Foundation (Alexander von Humboldt-Stiftung, Berlin) providing for me a stipend for a six-month study stay at the Albert-Ludwigs-Universität Freiburg in southern Germany. Moreover, the Humboldt Foundation generously supported the publication of this book, for which I am truly grateful.

In addition to the foundation, I would like to thank also my friend Klaus Baumann for this opportunity, who, being a professor at the theological faculty in Freiburg, has focused on the issues of Christian caritas and diakonia for a long time. I truly appreciate that I was able to be a part of his workplace, which is the oldest of its kind in the world. The preparation and publication of this book would also not have been possible without the kind help and support of colleagues from the University of South Bohemia in České Budějovice, Czech Republic. I should also like to extend my heartfelt gratitude to Mrs Martina Nicolson and Mr Stuart Nicolson, whose kind assistance in the refinement of both language and style proved most invaluable throughout the preparation of this manuscript. Among the academics, special thanks belongs to my sister Marie, who focuses on the history of church art at Charles University in Prague, and with whom I was able to consult my questions connected with the first chapter of this book. Above all, however, I would like to take this opportunity to thank my family, my children Tereza, Tomáš, and Kristina, and my wife Eva for their support and for going to Freiburg with me.

1. The Good Samaritan story

The biblical story of the Good Samaritan has been imprinted in the discourse of helping professions but also, and above all, in ordinary language. A measure of the unparalleled fame of this parable is the fact that the expression 'to be a good Samaritan' is synonymous with the phrase 'to help somebody'. The term 'Samaritan' began to refer to spontaneous help based on the emotional state of the helper; however, such help also means help without rational reflection and therefore being uninformed. Expressions such as 'do not try to be a Samaritan' or 'are you a Samaritan or what, trying to save the whole world?' do not refer so much to the biblical story itself as to the person who wants to help. When someone is called a 'Samaritan' in this sense it means he is helping 'in a hot-headed way': he is 'committing good' and giving more than the needs of the one receiving help, and such a 'Samaritan' is interested in quietening down his own compulsive need to help. It is obvious that the result of such an approach is not only *non-help* but also the helping person causing harm to himself. In this context, the so-called *Samaritan's dilemma* (see above) was described, referring to the emotionally founded motivation to help which ends with the physical and mental ruin of the helping person.

Such an understanding of the word Samaritan responds to the fact that this biblical story has always been considered a norm, a source of motivation, or even a guide to philanthropy (Fitzmyer, 1970–1985, p. 885). The parable of the good – in some languages the merciful – Samaritan who, unlike others, helped the ambushed person lying by the road, echoed in more than just the ordinary language and the historical development of helping professions. It also was, of course, a topic for theology and art where it gained great popularity (Bovon, 1989, p. 143). The depiction of the Samaritan story is one of the images telling biblical history, thus, for example, the story's motif is not used as an image evoking prayer. It is the artistic introduction of the whole story. However, it is used rarely in the 'Bible of the poor', being the pictures of biblical stories in sacred buildings' frescoes. It tends to be used on windows and on the outside of sacred buildings, and also on secular buildings (for example, on town halls such as in Ulm, Germany). In addition, depictions of the parable can also be found in liturgical books (Metzsch, 1998, pp. 76–77) and in modern and de facto secular art. As the parable had been an inspiration for many artists, it is possible to introduce the Good Samaritan story in this chapter using its artistic depictions.

The controversial interpretations that the story allows, as was previously mentioned, will be set aside for the time being with subsequent chapters focusing on them. As the titles of the fourth and fifth chapters suggest, these will discuss that which remains of the Good Samaritan story after its application interpretations are critically taken into account for the purposes of Christian caritas and diakonia, and pastoral care (see ▸ Chapter 2) with regards to its hermeneutic analysis using biblical exegesis (▸ Chapter 3). Sufficient space will be given to possible interpretations of the story and its various interpretations regarding helping professions in general and Christian caritas and diakonia in particular.

Therefore, the first chapter will initially focus on a brief explanation of the reasons for concentrating on this story nowadays (▸ Chapter 1.1) even though it is an ancient literary work of religious character, and in what sense such a story is inspiring for helping professions. It will also significantly regard ridding the story of the most banal prejudices. The first chapter will continue with a presentation of the Samaritan's story (▸ Chapter 1.2). There, I do not wish merely to resort to its simple quotation or, on the contrary, to its paraphrases, of which there are many. Instead, I have decided to present the characters and the plot of the story with regards to the postmodern era, that is, using briefly commented upon visual examples of fine arts, for which the story has always been an inspiration. The third part of the first chapter will be more comprehensive because I intend to focus on the way of approaching the Good Samaritan story in today's postmodern times as to be beneficial for helping professions and especially social work (▸ Chapter 1.3). There, I justify the chosen theoretical points of departure and methodology of the whole book, thus it is a somewhat dry academic chapter. Also, I aim at showing that the approach called *public theology* is appropriate for grasping the theme and message of the parable in a way so as to be understandable for helping professions as well as for non-Christians or non-practising Christians. In successive steps, I clarify what this approach consists of, how it regards Christian caritas, diakonia, and their reflection, what the relationship is between theology and social sciences (respectively, social work) within public theology, and also the fact that the main topic and problem that public theology seeks to address is the question of the intelligibility of religious language in the public (and thus primarily non-religious) environment. Finally, I return to the neuralgic question of the Good Samaritan parable 'Who is my neighbour?' to present it as a question that is chiefly of public theology (▸ Chapter 1.4), thus linking the subject of the parable with the matters of public theology.

1.1 The story of the Good Samaritan and the reasons for focusing on it

If we want to answer the question of why the story of the Good Samaritan should be worth the interest of someone other than practising Christians or scientists researching ancient literature, we must ask what makes it special and specific. For this reason, it is first necessary to become acquainted, at least in general terms, with the historical and social context of the story itself and its interpretations. So to speak, we have to absorb the atmosphere of the environment of its taking place because in understanding the text, the processing of information is complete only when we take into account the text itself and also the affective and cognitive motives of the text's authors and recipients (Theis, 2005, pp. 112–113). Thus, for understanding the text it is, above all, necessary to emphasise that the phrase Good (or Merciful) Samaritan should evoke the paradox that the person who is standing on the margins can be good and, respectively, that the evil person is not the one who is considered bad. This also evokes the idea that good is done by the one who is considered to be bad (Bovon, 1989, pp. 81 and 89). The text of the story and the whole *Gospel according to Luke*, of which it is a part, thus works with the underlying motif of conflict between Samaritans and Israelites: Samaritans were considered by Israelites to be heretics and schismatics unfaithful in the interpretation of the Torah (that is, they were committing a heresy), who have an alternative Torah (Pummer, 2016) and carry out their own religious practice on *Mount Garazim*, being in competition with the Jerusalem Temple practice (that is, they were in schism).

However, the context for such an old story does not merely consist in the historical circumstances in which it originated and how Jesus' contemporaries understood it. Similarly, it is also given by the tradition of its interpretation, that is, by the history of its interpretations, where earlier interpretations have always influenced later ones; those later either developed them or defined themselves in contrast with the older ones. In the history of Christianity from antiquity to modern times, the parable has been predominantly read Christologically: since the time of the ancient Church Fathers, the figure of the helping Samaritan was considered an allegory of Jesus Christ who is helping man. During his journey through life, he was attacked and beaten by demons and sin, represented in the story by robbers. It is obvious that the paradox intended by the author that good is carried out by the one who is considered bad was one of the reasons for such a relecture (rereading) of the parable. The issue of solidarity and aid, approached in such a provocative way, remains controversial to this day for many religious people as well as religious authorities. Thus, less attention than deserved was received by the anthropological-ethical reading of the text as a statement about a person and about the way to act so that in situations where he encounters the obvious need of another he acts well and in as best a way as possible. However, it would be a mistake to completely omit the allegorical interpretation tradition. As will be shown in detail in the third chapter, allegorical interpretations of biblical texts have a long history and the real break away from them began only with the Protestant theology of the 19th century, while in the Catholic theology it was even later. Given that such an interpretation of the Bible has influenced Christian thought and theology for a long time, and also given that it was an authentic interpretation of biblical texts at the time, it cannot be simply said that allegories are merely erroneous interpretations, a dead end of human knowledge. For, the genre of parable always allows for several different interpretations. Therefore, it is possible as well as legitimate to read the Good Samaritan story also Christologically, that is, as an allegory – as an image of Jesus and his mercy, as an invitation to faith in merciful Christ (Benedict XVI, 2007a, p. 143); this is to be done without excluding or invalidating the interpretation which works with affective and cognitive motifs of the ancient text author, and of its first readers and listeners who were in his mind during the writing. Additionally, the fourth chapter will show that modern application interpretations of the parable, which have an ethical-anthropological character and are therefore conceived as guides to caritas and diakonia conduct (see ▸ Chapter 2), constitute a not insignificant part of modern or postmodern allegories of the parable. Understanding the issue of allegorical interpretations can therefore be useful also for current reading of the story and is also necessary to assess its current allegories, whether or not they are relevant to exegetical findings.

However, all the tensions and paradoxes associated with the Good Samaritan story are not resolved. Although, thanks to this story, love of neighbour and mercy or help to those in need in general constitute one of the central themes of Christian faith, at the same time this opens up a brand-new field for criticism and controversy. It is precisely the issue of mercy that has made the word 'Samaritan' an expression for *non-help*. Christianity and Christian churches thus find themselves under a double tension because of mercy: on the one hand, they are ascribed a specific meaning because they can solve unresolved need through the concept of mercy, while on the other hand they are considered obsolete institutions precisely because of their concept of mercy in religion. In addition, the theme of mercy is often not sufficiently developed by Christian churches, and when it somewhat is, they use it relatively inconsistently. Until the publication of Pope Francis' document on love in the family *Amoris laetitia* (2016), an example of the inconsistent work regarding mercy was often given as the merciless approach of the Catholic Church towards the civilly remarried couples where one or both spouses had originally entered a sacramental (ecclesiastical) marriage that was civilly divorced. For the theme of this book, however, a more fitting example is the involvement of ecclesial organisations (such as Catholic Caritas, Evangelical Diakonia, or smaller local organisations) in social service systems. Although these are independent helping organisations that are only set up by the churches, the churches consider them to be part of the churches and use them to justify their own existence with regards to the society and the state. At the same time, they do not take into account at all that this form of social help is also criticised as a new form of exercise of power and oppression (Bopp, 1998, pp. 16–17): the term mercy is thus often used as a theological expression which is so general as to be comprehensible to everyone in order to justify the contribution of churches to society. However, the 'exercise of mercy' is entrusted to a professional organisation of social services which is established by the church, which however is financed primarily from public funds, from donors, and from the environment outside the church. Thus, mercy refers to the provision of social services and social work services, which is subsequently criticised by the churches themselves as an overly secular conception of help. In the end, the practice that emphasises helping without limits (including the self-sacrifice of the helping person) in the name of love of neighbour impersonates the ideal manifestation of Christian mercy. That means that the churches demand precisely such a practice which tends to be criticised as 'committing good', often using the word 'Samaritan' in its figurative and critical sense. However, such a practice has much more in common with the motives for the relecture (rereading) of the Samaritan's story which is unable to bear the paradox that good is done by the one who is not considered good, rather than with the biblical story itself.

In the New Testament, it is difficult to find a strict requirement of self-sacrifice connected to the relationship between love of neighbour and love of oneself, that is, the requirement that makes the suppression of love for oneself into the *sine qua non* condition for love of neighbour. The Samaritan's story is a good example of this (Hoffmann, 2002, pp. 128–129) – although even the Samaritan is in some way exposed to danger when he stops at the ambushed one to help him (for more details, see Chapter 3). Help described in the tenth chapter of the *Gospel according to Luke* is limited: '"The Samaritan's dilemma" does not take place. In helping, the Samaritan does not spend all his time, he does not spend all his money, he does not get ruined financially or personally to present the necessary – exemplary – provision of help' (König, Hofmann, 2017, p. 34). The interpreters of the parable in history were aware of this, with the anthropological-ethical account of the story of charitable conduct and mercy often having the same importance as its allegorical account of Jesus Christ's mercy. Therefore, it is pointless to pit Christological and anthropological-ethical interpretations against each other. The story can also be interpreted, as Bernhard of Clairvaux suggested in the Middle Ages, that while God's love must be without measure and boundaries, the love of neighbour and thus also compassion have boundaries applicable 'as to one's own self' – that is, no more and no less (Bernhard z Clairvaux, 1990, p. 75). In this sense, the story of the Good Samaritan is an allegory of Christ who loves man without measure and boundaries, as well as an anthropological-ethical example of how people should act well and in the best possible way. And this is precisely what this book aims at addressing with regard to helping professions.

In addition, there is an important message for Christians included here, that their charitable mission extends to people outside the Church: 'The parable of the Good Samaritan remains a measuring scale of the universality of love which should be applied to the person in need we have met *"by chance"* (cf. *Lk* 10:31), regardless of who this person is' (Benedict XVI, 2006, 25). This aspect of the story, and in fact other purely Christian implications of the Good Samaritan parable cannot be simply overlooked or set aside thus this book will address them as appropriate.

1.2 The story of the Good Samaritan: characters and plot

The Good Samaritan story is a parable, being a key genre used in Bible books, especially the Gospels. The genre of the parable itself is addressed in detail in Chapter 3.1. Here, as a preliminary note, it suffices to bring up that every parable in the New Testament is part of a situation or particular episode in the whole Gospel narrative. In short, parables are not just collected stories told by Jesus Christ. Similarly, the parable of the Good Samaritan responds to a specific situation that arose around Jesus at that point. However, as there is only a small number of artistic depictions of the story including this situation, for some people it may be a completely unknown context of the parable. Actually, this is the decisive impulse for Jesus to tell the parable. Without such a broader storyline, there would be no reason for telling it at all. Hans Georg Anniès expressed this framework in his painting (▸ Fig. 1). It is primarily Jesus and his listeners who, according to their expressions, either assent to him or determine themselves against him. Between them, in a circle, the very story that Jesus is telling is taking place – he is pointing to it with his hand. To the left there is a figure who, through his facial expression and folded hands, shows that he is trying to resist Jesus' story. This is Jesus's opponent, a Scribe – an expert on the Torah, the Law of Moses, who tried to catch out Jesus with his questions. But he doesn't at all like Jesus' answer in the form of the Good Samaritan story. Besides Jesus, this is the second main character of the whole situation – Jesus' *sparring partner*. In their dialogue, the story of the Good Samaritan acts as if being inserted while at the same time it is the key episode of the whole biblical passage.

Fig. 1: Hans Georg Anniès, Der Barmherzige Samariter (1968)

In Anniès' image, we see that Jesus' account of the Samaritan has affected the Scribe so much that he took a defensive stance. But the beginning of the whole situation was rather the opposite. The Scribe sought to put Jesus in a difficult position when asking how one can attain eternal life with God. However, this was a completely banal question, to which every thirteen-year-old Jewish boy must have known the answer because it was the so-called greatest commandment: to love God and to love one's neighbour as oneself. Therefore, he who loves God and his neighbour will attain eternal life. But Jesus did not answer the question, instead he asked the Scribe – who was an expert – what he himself read in the Law of Moses. And the Scribe, as an expert, could not fail to answer, quoting from the Torah that it is necessary to love God and to love one's neighbour as oneself. As the initiative was now on the side of Jesus, who thus took authority over the whole situation, he was able to praise the Scribe for answering correctly. This was, of course, a bitter-comic situation because the Scribe was praised for what he must have known at the age of 13 before beginning to study the Law of Moses as an expert. Furthermore, Jesus answered his first question that he would gain eternal life when he loves God and his neighbour as himself. In fact, he repeated the Scribe's own answer to confirm it to him and ensured him that he himself knew very well what he had actually asked him.

In the end, the Scribe put his own self into a difficult situation. He proved himself to be a fool because the whole situation came across as if he was asking about matters he should have known about long ago and well. In order to extract himself out of this extremely unpleasant situation, he asked who he should consider to be his neighbour. The third chapter will explain in detail that such a question was not unusual at the time, rather the opposite. The Scribe was therefore still trying to save himself from the embarrassing situation he had gotten himself into so he asked the question that was the subject of expert disputations between leading rabbis and law experts. However, he did not gain control over the situation but rather, on the contrary, improved the position of Jesus who then cut the Gordian knot of the whole issue of one's neighbour when responding clearly and concisely to the Scribe through the parable of the Good Samaritan. In principle, it can be assumed that Jesus responded to the Scribe in such a wise and clever way as to make space in their dialogue for the narration of the Good Samaritan parable.

Jesus began his story by talking about a man going from Jerusalem to Jericho and being attacked. While this figure of a traveller is not at all described in detail, the geographical context of the story is emphasised. Jesus' listeners associated the reference to the journey from Jerusalem to Jericho with the descent through the rocky desert from the mountains of Judah to the level of the Dead Sea, descending even below the level of the Mediterranean Sea. Such a geographical context also entails specific climatic conditions making the rocky desert route even more challenging. There were however other reasons why it was called the bloody path. The main and most serious danger was posed by robbers for whom the terrain offered long-term shelter as well as a number of hidden spots suitable for ambush. Historical fine arts have not at all taken this geographical context into account, rather presenting the situation as an ambush in deep forest as was common in Europe. They also focused on the figure of the one ambushed, who was portrayed in the Renaissance and Baroque styles as a strong man of whom no one would think to be an ambush victim succumbing to robbers (Metzsch, 1998, p. 85), as he is, for example, in the painting by Jan Wijnants (▸ Fig. 2). In the manner of a verso and recto, such a depiction of the figure of the ambushed expressed what the reader or listener of the *Gospel according to Luke* in ancient Palestine associated with the geographical context: no one can completely avoid all situations of potentially finding oneself in need and relying on the help of others. Also, the reader would make the association that it does not at all matter who the one in need of help is – which the story expresses by not describing the traveller at all; however, the fine arts portrayed him as a strong man who must have been worth attacking.

Fig. 2: Jan Wijnants, Parable of the Good Samaritan (1670)

Jesus tells the information about the ambush, literally, in one breath together with a minimalist description of the traveller and an important reference to the place where the incident took place. This is important to remember because the robbers who committed the ambush are not specified in any way either. All of this expresses that it was a common situation – everyone knew that there were ambushes taking place on the difficult route from Jerusalem to Jericho and that this could happen to anyone who set out on this road.

Likewise, Jesus' listeners and readers of the *Gospel according to Luke* could not be surprised when a priest[1] and then a Levite appeared on the way of the ambushed

---

1 The Jewish priesthood has no connection to the Christian priesthood. While a Christian priest at Mass acts as an *alter Christus* – another Christ – in doing what Jesus Christ did at the Last Supper, the task of the priests in the Jerusalem Temple was to offer sacrifices (crops, cattle) to thank God for what he gave to man. Thus, these priests are not related to the current Jewish rabbis either as the Jerusalem Temple has been destroyed for almost two thousand years, which means this priesthood is not being exercised.

person who was left to his own fate by the robbers. In Jericho by the Dead Sea and its surroundings, members of the Israeli tribe of Levi lived, being the only ones authorised to carry out services in the Jerusalem Temple. Therefore, the priests and their Levites helpers often travelled here as they took turns in the Temple service on the Temple Mount in Jerusalem. Both of the travellers avoided the ambushed when they passed by despite seeing him well, as Jesus emphasised. No more is said about them and their motives as to why they did not help the ambushed. Furthermore, it was possible to speculate about this, as will be shown in the second and third chapters and as the fine arts also show. In Fig. 3 from the Golden Gospels of Henry III, the priest and the Levite are depicted with a stole, being a symbol of Christian priests and deacons – the older priest has the stole over his shoulders as a Christian priest or bishop and also has a staff resembling a bishop's or abbot's crozier, while the younger Levite has the stole over one shoulder like a Christian deacon. They are similarly depicted in the illuminations in the Gospels of Henry the Lion (▸ Fig. 4), where the priest has a chasuble and miter as a Christian bishop turning away from the ambushed and removing his hands from him while the Levite is dressed in a dalmatic as a Christian deacon blessing the ambushed from a safe distance while the Samaritan is taking care of him (Kuder, 2015, pp. 171–172).

Fig. 3: The Golden Gospels of Henry III (1043–1046)

Fig. 4: The Gospels of Henry the Lion (ca. 1188)

Thus, since the Middle Ages or even earlier times, Christian clerics were seen in the figures of the priest and the Levite spoken of in the Gospel. This expresses a critique of clericalism, respectively, it criticises the departure of the Christian clergy from human need and help to the poor, the sick, and the excluded. Given that these are illuminations from the Gospels, it is clear that the tension between the ideal of the Gospel and the practice of the Church has long been present in the matters of caritas and diakonia.

Fig. 5: unknown author, Parable of the Good Samaritan (ca. 1490–1510)

However, it was more than Christian clergy that became the object of the criticism that might be expressed by the parable. In the image from the cathedral in Lübeck by an unknown author (▸ Fig. 5), the priest and the Levite are depicted as university masters leading a learned debate about the whole 'case'. According to the characters' clothing, the painting dates back between the years 1490 and 1510. This regards a critique of vain intellectual and rhetorical exercises in the face of human need. Given that this panel painting was found by chance after a 1943 bombing (Metzsch, 1998), it is difficult to determine whether its author referred only to the conditions of the time. However, this is an actualisation that has retained its significance to this day, when even academic work in the field of helping professions might become a vain rhetorical and intellectual exercise that creates a safe barrier – apartheid – against the need of others (Staub-Bernasconi, 2018). However, the parable itself is (also and above all) the critique of vain intellectual exercises used by Jesus to answer the question posed by the Scribe and by the Jewish theologians and intellectuals of the time, namely, who is and who is not a neighbour.

To answer, Jesus used both the figure of the Samaritan, who comes to the scene of the ambush after the priest and the Levite, and also the way he acts in the story. In the fine arts, we can find two very significant ways of the Samaritan's depiction reflecting two basic approaches to the analysis and interpretation of the text in history. The Samaritan either resembles Christ in the so-called *allegorical* interpretations (▸ Fig. 6) or is depicted with a turban (▸ Fig. 5), that is, as a Muslim – a foreigner, an unbeliever – within the socio-historical context of the parable in so-called *anthropological-ethical* interpretations.

Fig. 6: Codex Purpureus Rossanensis (third quarter of the 6th cent.)

The Syrian *Codex Purpureus Rossanensis* leaves the reader in no doubt with whom to identify the Samaritan when his representation bears all the attributes of Christ, especially the halo with a cross. Like Christ, the Samaritan tends to the beaten traveller here and transports him to the inn paying the innkeeper in advance for further care. He is assisted by an angel holding a chalice. The illumination thus refers to conclusions of Christological allegorical interpretations that it is the Sacraments – here especially the Eucharist – which serve Christ to help man beaten by sin (Kuder, 2015, pp. 178–179). Then, the inn is the Church to where Christ entrusts the assaulted man, and the innkeeper is, in the logic of such an interpretation, a representative of the Church – a cleric administering the Sacraments. In the case of this codex, however, this is not expressed in any symbolic way.

The Samaritan is perceived differently in anthropological-ethical interpretations that read the parable as a response to the question of what one should do to act well and as best as possible. They emphasise his care which is reflected in most artistic representations by him leaning over the ambushed and carefully tending to him, or lifting him up onto his animal with significant effort (Noll, 2015, pp. 344–345) (▸ Fig. 7). Elsewhere, the Samaritan is also portrayed as a merchant or simply a wealthy man (▸ Fig. 4) so that it is clear that help can be provided by those healthy and not in need (Metzsch, 1998, p. 7). The depiction of the Samaritan with a turban (▸ Fig. 5 and Fig. 7), that is, as a Muslim, shifts the original meaning this figure had for the first readers and listeners of the *Gospel according to Luke*. Although the Israelites were not particularly fond of the Samaritans, this was a conflict of denominational nature rather than a tension between various religions. This means that the core of their dispute was the various interpretations of the Law of Moses – as Chapter 3 describes in detail – and this also means that faithfulness to the Law of Moses was, on the contrary, what was uniting them. The Samaritan as a Muslim thus radicalises the original statement of the Gospel, emphasising its foreignness to the level of a dangerous enemy of another faith. But this also radicalises the message contained by the parable. The authors of the artistic depictions of the Samaritan's story thus want to communicate that even a hated enemy, who is considered the embodiment of all evil, may act correctly.

Fig. 7: Eugène Delacroix, The Good Samaritan (1849–1851)

However, the portrayal of the Samaritan as a Muslim may also be related to the inspiration of medieval European medicine in comparison with the then much more advanced Arab medicine (Metzsch, 1998, pp. 82–85). Thus, suddenly, the Samaritan becomes a role model for a professional who knows exactly how and what to do when he finds the beaten traveller lying by the road.

In comparison with other parables, the Samaritan story perhaps too specifically described what the Samaritan did when he arrived at the scene of the ambush and saw the half-dead traveller. In his painting, Luca Giordano captured the care for disinfecting and treating wounds with wine and oil, which Jesus explicitly mentioned in the parable, as well as the Samaritan's concern whether the ambushed was still actually alive (▸ Fig. 8); the ancient parable expressed this in a great detail in comparison with this particular genre's general description of aid. Similarly, Delacroix (▸ Fig. 7) shows the event following the first aid when the Samaritan lifts the ambushed onto his mule to transport him to the safety. At the same time, he emphasises the suffering of the ambushed and the Samaritan's commitment as being a kind of opposites – the more the ambushed suffers, the more effort the Samaritan puts in; however, the transport of the ambushed to the safety, which the parable also explicitly mentions, is a much older motif used since the Middle Ages – see Figs. 3 to 6 (Noll, 2015, pp. 344–345).

Fig. 8:   Luca Giordano, The Good Samaritan (1650)

The detailed description of care for the ambushed one in the parable was probably the inspiration for the artistic depictions of the parable which were expressing the reality of the helping ones together with the criticism of those not helping. The first indication may be the portrayal of the Samaritan as a Muslim, that is, as an expert who could teach a lot about medicine to undeveloped medieval Europeans. However, the burden of caring for the sick and infirm, as well as for the poor, has historically been a woman's task. That is why female characters are gradually beginning to be used in the artistic depictions of the parable. The paintings thus express what ancient readers and listeners of the parable were able to understand through the detailed description: the Samaritan helped the ambushed as carefully and well as only women can. Thus, in Max Liebermann's painting from 1911 (▸ Fig. 9) we can see a woman helping the Samaritan similarly to an angel helping Christ in the early medieval Codex Purpureus Rossanensis (▸ Fig. 6). However, the one leaning further down in the codex is Christ while at Liebermann's it is the woman, which thus enables the possibility of the interpretation that even though the man exerts more effort, the woman symbolises the Samaritan (Noll, 2015, pp. 345–346).

Fig. 9: Max Liebermann, The Good Samaritan (1911)

A similar motif may be found in the work of the Czech painter Jan Zrzavý, where the figure of the Samaritan is clearly identifiable, however it resembles a woman rather than a man (▸ Fig. 10). While the ambushed is curled up on the Samaritan's knees, he treats his numerous wounds. The composition thus resembles a mother taking care of her own child. The Samaritan's face, eyes, mouth, and especially the hair evoke it being a woman. Additionally, long hair as a characteristic feature of femininity has its opposite in the spring gushing from a rock and it seems as if the Samaritan's care was life-giving as water is in the middle of a rocky desert.

Fig. 10: Jan Zrzavý, The Good Samaritan, 1914-1915[1]

---

1 Photo © National Gallery Prague 2025; Copyright © 2025, Jan Zrzavý, National Gallery Prague.

However, the story of the Samaritan does not end halfway; he does not stop after the initial help, that is, at the level of the most necessary help demanded by the situation. It has already been mentioned that after the treatment, he places him on his beast (▸ Fig. 7). Thus, the ambush victim is ready to be transported to safety, this being the inn to where the Samaritan transports him safely (▸ Fig. 11). As already indicated, allegorical interpretations associated this inn with the Church and her care for the people through the sacraments. Later anthropological-ethical interpretations perceived it as the centre of social services (see Chapter 2) while current biblical exegesis notes the original Greek term for the inn used in the Gospel which could be described in colloquial terms such as a tavern or even a dive (Chapter 3). However, Jesus' story pays only little attention to the inn itself. Much more important to him is the situation that thus arises.

Fig. 11: Rembrandt, The Good Samaritan (after 1633)

The Samaritan in the inn continues caring for the ambushed one. When he then sets out on his further journey, he asks the innkeeper to continue the care and therefore pays him a certain deposit (Figs. 4, 6, 11 and 12). In allegorical interpretations this was understood as a promise of Christ's support for the Church while in the fine arts, the innkeeper was often depicted as a monarch who was the patron of the work thus expressing his concern for social politics (Kuder, 2015, pp. 176–179). In this sense, it may be said that even today's allegorical understanding of the inn as a centre of social services has a long history. More important, however, is the Samaritan's concluding remark that on his return he will reimburse the innkeeper for his care if the current deposit is not sufficient. The parable thus expresses that the Samaritan's care is truly complex, including the first aid – in the immediate need, comprising of more than a mere transport to safety – and also the future of the ambushed.

Fig. 12: Gospels of Otto III (ca. 1005)

The narration ends with the Samaritan's advance payment to the innkeeper for the care of the ambushed. However, Jesus follows it up with a question that could have provoked an even stronger disapproval of the Law expert than we can see in Anniès's painting (▸ Fig. 1). Jesus asks who in the story became the neighbour for the victim. The Law expert in his answer is thus forced to point to the Samaritan, doing this with a periphrasis when he says that it was the one who treated him mercifully. In fact, this is expressed in all works of art encapsulating the parable – whether the Samaritan helps the ambushed on the road or transports him or entrusts him to the care of the innkeeper, it always expresses what the Law expert answers to Jesus, that he acted mercifully, as a neighbour. It is from here that the title of the story is derived in some languages as the parable about the *merciful* Samaritan.

Jesus confirms the Scribe's answer by asking him to do so. In doing so, the Scribe answered his own question as to who his neighbour was, and Jesus further reminded him that being a neighbour primarily means acting like a neighbour. This is expressed in an interesting way by Overbeck's picture named Christ in the House of Mary and Martha (▸ Fig. 13). It primarily depicts the following scene from the *Gospel according to Luke* (10:38–42),[2] where Jesus comes to the house of two sisters and while Martha waits on Jesus, Mary sits at his feet listening to him. Martha eventually turns to Jesus to invite Mary also to take part in the care for the visitor. But Jesus answers her, '"Martha, Martha," the Lord answered, "you are worried and upset about many things, but few things are needed – or indeed only one. Mary has chosen what is better, and it will not be taken away from her"' (*Lk* 10:41–42). In Overbeck's painting, a frame containing these verses hangs on the wall above Jesus. The author thus shows that active conduct according to God's will, concern for the other (Lat. *vita activa*), and spiritual life (Lat. *vita contemplativa*) are closely related. Through the window, one can also see the Samaritan (with a turban) treating the wounds of the ambushed person while the priest and the Levite are leaving.

This picture within the picture thus refers to the fact that the words addressed to Martha do not exclude *vita activa* – acting according to God's will, merciful acting, acting as a neighbour, which was introduced in the previous story of the Good Samaritan. Even Overbeck's statement is preserved that he created the painting in this sense (Noll, 2015, pp. 342–343). As will be shown in detail in Chapter 3, this context of the Samaritan story is very important. It points to the necessary level of balance between living and acting according to God's will (*vita activa*) and spiritual life (*vita contemplativa*). We can therefore read it as an important addition to the Samaritan story, as a final warning that the helping person must not make the help to be the end

---

2   As Jesus and his disciples were on their way, he came to a village where a woman named Martha opened her home to him. She had a sister called Mary, who sat at the Lord's feet listening to what he said. But Martha was distracted by all the preparations that had to be made. She came to him and asked, 'Lord, don't you care that my sister has left me to do the work by myself? Tell her to help me!' 'Martha, Martha,' the Lord answered, 'you are worried and upset about many things, but few things are needed—or indeed only one. Mary has chosen what is better, and it will not be taken away from her.'

in itself, and to the point that it would eventually lead to its his own destruction. Just as the Samaritan continues on his way, anyone who feels the urgency of the situation to act as a neighbour must be able to carry on his other duties. Also, orientation in spiritual matters (or simply a certain reflective distance from practice and everyday issues) is as important for life as it may be important in a certain situation to act mercifully as a neighbour.

Fig. 13: Johann Friedrich Overbeck, Christ in the House of Mary and Martha (1805)

1.3 The story of the Good Samaritan: how to approach it (*public theology*)

It has certainly not escaped the readers' attention that I have not yet quoted the parable of the Good Samaritan in this book. In previous parts, it was possible to become acquainted with the paraphrase of this biblical story and, especially, with its expressions in the fine arts. As I indicated in the Introduction, this book wants to grasp the theme of the Good Samaritan in a way that will be understandable for the helping professions – not just for Christians in the helping professions. It is my goal, which I hope to be able to achieve at least a little, to present the topic so that it can be understood even by *non-readers of the Bible*.

Such an approach and ambition of the text are possible only because, in the new millennium, religion has gradually returned to public discourse (Graham, 2017, pp. 282–285). But religious views of the world today are given in a different way than before. They have become part of a liberal discourse: the reason why religion has the right to speak in public is not because it claims the truth but because it *also* has the right – like many others – to comment on the matter (Bradstock, 2012, pp. 153–154). Therefore, today, the representatives of Christianity, its various denominations, and of other religions can promote their conservative agenda against liberal democracy or liberalism in general, paradoxically, thanks to the generally liberal setting of public debate. The liberal setting of social discourse gives them the right to express themselves as well as the right to be heard. However, they are fighting against Hydra – as they understand liberalism – which has given them a hearing and attention. In such a way, however, struggles become futile, like struggles with Hydra, and ultimately marginalise the fighters themselves and their voices. The fighters assume that the louder they speak the more people hear them (which is true) and the better their message is communicated (which however is not true) (Elliot, 2007, p. 296). If this book aspires to grasp the Samaritan's story in a way that is comprehensible, understandable, and usable even for *non-readers of the Bible* in helping professions, this is not done in order to *ipso facto* claim the truth as a theological text. On the contrary, it relies on the possibility of freely addressing this matter for the discourse of helping professions as well as on the persuasiveness of the story itself.

Such an approach is often called public theology. Therefore, in this chapter, public theology will be briefly described regarding the clarification of this book's methodology. This chapter will therefore be more of a 'dry scientific' theological chapter which is intended to clarify the legitimacy of, and to justify the appropriateness of, approaching the Good Samaritan parable in the spirit of *public theology*. In steps, I would like to clarify what public theology is (▸ Section 1.3.1), how it pertains to the theological reflection of Christian philanthropy (▸ Section 1.3.2) and of social issues in general (▸ Section 1.3.3), and how public theology in this sense responds to secularity and its arguments in order to make it clear that the fundamental issue is the problem of the intelligibility of the religious language, of religious faith, and religion in general (▸ Section 1.3.4). All of these will be approached with the view of the neuralgic question regarding the Good Samaritan parable: Who is my neighbour (▸ Chapter 1.4)?

1.3.1 Public theology

The theoretical-theological background of my approach to the topic is the Catholic concept of practical theology and especially the approach called *public theology*, in German *Öffentliche Theologie*, in Czech *veřejná teologie*. Catholic practical theology emphasises, among other things, the understanding and interpretation of non-ecclesial discourse in theology (Opatrný, 2013) and the comprehensibility of theological expressions in the extra-ecclesial space: 'With the help of the Holy Spirit, it is the task of the entire People of God, especially pastors and theologians, to hear, distinguish and interpret the many voices of our age, and to judge them in the light of the divine word, so that the revealed truth can always be more deeply penetrated, better understood and set forth to greater advantage' (*Gaudium et spes,* 1965). The approach called *public theology* is then ecumenical in nature and is understood in a broader way. The term first appeared in the 1970s as a reaction to the sociological term *civil religion.* In contrast to the descriptive term civil religion, *public theology* generally assumes that various religions and specifically religious communities, respectively theology as a rational reflection of their faith, are to be beneficial for the wide society (Cady, 2014, p. 294). Unlike the older so-called *political theology*, public theology understands pluralism not as fate, but as the fruit of Christianity. It therefore participates in social discourse without requiring a privileged status for its own views, which would then be prescribed with the help of state power or legislation to all citizens (Körtner, 2017, pp. 41–42). Public theology seeks to influence the general society at various levels for the common good (Cartledge, 2016, 161–165) and therefore, within public theology, we must speak of authority non-authoritatively and of tradition non-traditionalistically – without challenging the concept of authority in Christian denominations, being the *Magisterium*[3] or *sola scriptura*[4] (Peters, 2018, pp. 159–160). Thus, while for me, Catholic practical theology is my environment and my specialisation, which I use as my foundation, public theology is the approach through which I want to grasp, analyse, and interpret the theme of the Good Samaritan story for helping professions.

If public theology is to be a rational reflection upon the Christian faith that benefits society, it cannot be at the same time a mere moralising arbitrator to judge and define what society is and should be. It is therefore necessary to clarify – both in general and with regard to the topic of the book – what such a theology actually regards and with what and whom its public aspect is concerned (Paeth, 2016, pp. 462–463).

---

3   This is the so-called teaching office of the Catholic Church pertaining to the Pope and with him to the bishops regarding the interpretation of the faith and morals of the Church.

4   In Latin 'Scripture only', which is the principle of the Protestant tradition considering the Scripture, that is, the Bible, to be the sole authority and norm.

The classic distinction of the Catholic theologian David Tracy states that *public theology* is public in three ways:

- regarding the academic public;
- regarding the ecclesiastical public;
- in the sense of its social public.

It must have affirmative as well as critical relationships with each of its publics because it is always bound by loyalty to the other two publics as well. Without such a loyalty, it would lose its most important loyalty – loyalty to God (Körtner, 2017, p. 41) – thus it would cease to be theology. In the postmodern period, however, everything public is also global, pluralistic, and, above all, secular (Paeth, 2016, pp. 469–480). And it is the encounter of secular public with religious thought and practice that causes the need for public theology – rational reflections on faith in the public interest: Islamist terrorism eventually caused Islamic theologians to be asked what they were actually teaching. In the United States, the disgust of some Protestants is evident due to their rejection of the evolution science, opposition to gender equality and racial justice, or LGBTQ rights (Peters, 2018, p. 162). In Europe we could similarly speak of and consider the Catholic tradition and the politically and ecclesiastically conservative agenda of certain local churches, local leaders, and authors who encounter Russia's imperial ambitions and propaganda (Snyder, 2018). Christianity, in the eyes of other people, gains the flavour of wickedness, racism, and arrogant condemnation of others, thus, 'Theologians, among others, have a responsibility to confirm, disconfirm, or modify this existing public image. What is called for by this situation is apologetic theology' (Peters, 2018, p. 162).

Although the apologetic approach is not alien to public theology, within its discourse it is not identical with classical apologetics.[5] Classic apologetic theologians understood themselves as those who prove the Christian faith and rationally interpret the doctrine of faith to people outside the Church. The mission of public theology somewhat differs. It does not necessarily seek to convince the other person and gain converts. More modestly, public theology shows that Christian symbols and doctrine are useful to humanity for its own self-understanding (Peters, 2018, p. 163). Thus, apologetic public theology transfers the questions asked in society to the field of theological tradition where answers are sought. The advantage of such an approach is that it is committed to the interest in public life and problems of people. On the contrary, its risk is the adoption of cultural and social patterns of thought without further examination as to whether and to what extent they are (or are not) compatible with Christianity, risking in the end the loss of the prophetic character of theology. However, the apologetic approach is not the only characteristic of public

---

5   Apologetics was a theological discipline that sought to rationally (philosophically) defend the reasons for the Christian faith. In Catholic theology, after the Second Vatican Council, it was replaced by fundamental theology, a field that focuses on the rational reflection of the fundaments (lat. *fundamentum*) of Christian faith. The term apologetics has thus been released for its new – modified – or figurative use.

theology. The secular context can also lead to a completely opposite reaction, that is, to the approach of the profession of faith in which the Christian tradition, individual denominations, and local communities stand (partially) in opposition to the broad social and cultural context of modern secular society. The advantage is the provocative prophetic edge on which such a theology is founded. The disadvantage is the loss of understanding for other disciplines, the inability to communicate with them about what theology is, and thus the inability to hear prophetic voices outside the Christian tradition. It is therefore desirable to synthesise the apologetic approach and the approach of the profession of faith, which is a synthetic approach that ensures that Christian theology remains rooted in the traditions and narratives of the Christian community while being deeply engaged in contemporary cultural discussions without privileging the Christian tradition or using it as a trump card to stop the discussion (Paeth, 2016, 480–483).

1.3.2 Theology of Christian caritas and diakonia as public theology

The so-called *caritas theory* (in German *Caritaswissenschaft*) from the Catholic environment together with *the diakonics* (in German *Diakonik*) and *diakonia theory* (in German *Diakoniewissenschaft*) from the Protestant environment are examples *par excellence* of such a synthesis of apologetic theology and that of profession of faith which aspires in public interest to be the intellectual reflection upon Christian faith. In Germany, both intellectual currents were established during the first half of the 20th century as new theological disciplines focusing on the topics of caritas and diakonia. They gradually defined themselves and were shaped especially with regards to practical and pastoral theology and theological and social ethics, including social teaching of the Catholic Church (Opatrný, 2020). Regardless of the denomination, both disciplines are connected in their fundamental character of being a dialogical platform for academic dialogue between theology and social work or a socio-scientific conception of other helping professions. For this, they adopt the methods from social sciences combining them with classical theological hermeneutics (Baumann, 2018).

Both denominational intellectual currents of Christian philanthropy were a form of reaction to secularisation. Although the original conception of Catholic caritas theory had significant features of the above-described approach of the profession of faith (Maurer, 1998), nowadays both currents are, in the main stream of their discourses as well as in the common ecumenical discourse, significantly synthetic through the organic combination of the apologetic approach bringing to theology the themes and issues from the environment of helping professions,[6] and of the approach of the profession of faith; thus they offer an alternative and criticism to some trends,

---

[6] An example of this is the professional ethics that almost all helping professions have developed; however only a small development took place in pastoral professions and their roles in helping professions and as leaders of religious communities.

theories, and to practical aspects in helping activities (Opatrný, 2010).[7] So, theological reflection upon Christian practice of caritas and diakonia becomes an essential part of public theology which aims at working on the contribution of Christianity for a more humane and socially just organisation of human society.

Thus, caritas theory and the diakonics are one of the early forms – if not the first form – of public theology because the intention of public theology has not been to provide a broader and greater social influence for theology and religion but to adopt such forms of thinking which are convincing – at least potentially – for those outside the religious community (Cady, 2014, p. 295). We can therefore consider them a *sui generis* public theology because in Western society theology has always had a general public character. In the last century, its public character began to be analysed and examined in more detail as the social and cultural context of theological thinking changed. However, the significance of theology for the humane and socially just organisation of human society has not changed (Paeth, 2016, pp. 461–462); contrariwise, it is necessary to exert even more effort in theological thinking: this is a matter for caritas theory and the diakonics, and also is the intention of this book.

Further active actors in *public theology* are organisations such as Catholic Caritas organisations and Protestant Diakonias accredited as public social service providers, or other Christian helping organisations, parishes, churches and communities, and last but not least, situations and places where caritas or diakonic help is offered and implemented. This takes place not only in the sense of them partaking in public discourse and actively entering this, but also by them being a *place* where public theology can be learned (in German *Lernort*) (Körtner, 2017, p. V). Therefore, if the character of the Church and Christianity is to be one of service – as exemplified, for instance, in the Catholic context by Pope Francis during his pontificate – then this implies that any theology and practice devoted to caritas or diakonia must also be a form of public theology. When it focuses on the fundamental ideological pillar of Christian caritas and diakonia, being the Good Samaritan story, it regards supporting reflexivity in helping professions with regards to religious literacy and promoting reconciliation of religious and other values in post-secular cooperation for the common good (Graham, 2017, pp. 278–279).[8]

Such an approach is proving to be very important in the environment of Central and Eastern Europe which has experienced forced atheisation and has shared most of the secularisation processes with Western Europe. Although we can consider the USA to be a secular country, for example, where the separation of church and state applies even though the majority of the population practices their religion and (especially some) churches have great influence on politics, or the United Kingdom, where there is an official national church but most people do not practice their religion and the

---

7   An example of this is the Christian option for the poor, that is, the preference of those who suffer the greatest need. This is an old principle which has its foundations in the Good Samaritan parable and was applied, for example, in Latin America in the so-called theology of liberation.

8   For more information regarding the problem of religious literacy, see ▸ Chapter 1.3.4.

church does not have any significant influence on politics, truly secular countries are those where there is no state church or religion and where the majority of the population does not practice the religion; among these, we can classify New Zealand (Bradstock, 2012, p. 140) and the Czech Republic, where I come from, together with some other Central and Eastern European countries. However, regarding such 'purely' secular countries, it is not true that society is strictly secular, politics is value-neutral, and that religion has no influence on them.[9] The ways of thinking and conduct corresponding to intellectual processes and ways of acting within religions or churches, in fact, also appears in the secular countries of Central Europe – even though it is not explicitly named, let alone realised consciously and out of conviction (Hamplová, 2013). A very good example is the so-called *democracy without attributes* currently promoted by the establishment (Pehe, 2020); this is not a neutral concept ethics-wise although its promoters are striving to create such an impression. Conservative religious thinkers who have found allies in various populists for advancing their agenda thus also argue against liberal democracy. Although this seems to be a kind of postmodern 'alliance of the throne and the altar', it is in fact a pragmatic alliance in which Christians risk the remnants of their credibility. In a democracy without attributes, the divorce takes place between the protection of individual freedom and democracy which becomes so-called conservative socialism (Michéa, 2013) or even so-called Christian fascism (Snyder, 2018). Conservative socialism, like economic rationalism (neoliberal economy), appears primarily as certain forms of public spirituality that need to be criticised – precisely and especially by theology because it regards a society-wide philosophy or ideology, respectively, a culture expressing certain beliefs and attitudes (Darragh, 2010, pp. 396–397). Such criticism does not arise in the case of populist allies from the side of conservative religious thinkers even though they perceive the problematic nature of some aspects of populist rule disagreeing with it in many ways. They prefer to sacrifice their criticism to the chimeras of their influence possessed in such a context. In some countries, theologians such as Tomáš Halík (Pongratz-Lippitt, 2020) and Tomáš Petráček (Petráček, 2020) in the Czech Republic have thus carried out such direct critique of conservative socialism and economic rationalism. Another way of criticising problematic forms of public spirituality may also be the pursuit of post-secular reconciliation of religion and other values and the strengthening of religious literacy; this takes place through and is founded on social issues, as public theology does in general and caritas theory or the diakonics do specifically, together with other theological disciplines.

In my country, being the exceptionally secular Czech Republic (Pew Research Center, 2017), caritas theory and the diakonics became established as a platform through which it has been possible to build and accredit the study of social work at theological faculties (Opatrný - Šimr, 2023). Study programmes such as social and caritas work, pastoral work and the diakonics, and ethics in social work (Opatrný, 2020) have beco-

---

9 Examples are *pro-life* and *pro-choice* stances, both of which attribute moral status to another person – *pro-choice* only to the mother, *pro-life* to the mother and the child; this means that neither is ethically neutral (Bradstock 2012, pp. 145–147).

me an opportunity to integrate theological thinking into a topic that is an example *par excellence* of post-secular cooperation for the common good. At the same time, however, this also regards the support and development of religious literacy in the environment of helping professions. The following is true regarding most students of social work at theological faculties, actually being the case of more than merely the Czech Republic or the former East Germany: 'most non-religious people consider themselves to have no religion and with losing their affiliation to the church they have also lost access to religion' (Körtner, 2017, p. 36).

As our book comes from this cultural milieu of Europe, it is necessary to emphasise its intention to perceive public themes precisely through the prism of the diakonics and caritas theory as *sui generis* public theology. At the same time, however, this book regards also public theology growing from the Christian diaspora.[10] As such, it is not focused only on the specifics of Central and Eastern Europe. Due to the detraditionalisation and deinstitutionalisation of religion, the experience of intensive diaspora and the ongoing theological reflection of Christian caritas and diakonia in its context is becoming an inspiration for public theology also in other cultural and historical contexts; this takes place not '... as an expression of withdrawal from the secular world, but as encouragement to mingle with this world and to witness by word and deed to the gospel of God's love, its agape[11] and caritas[12]' (Körtner, 2017, p. 54).

1.3.3 Public theology, social sciences, and social matters

Public theology, which seeks to reconcile religious and other values and to improve religious literacy through social themes, on which they are being founded, thus necessarily enters the field of social sciences. This occurs because, like the social sciences, it is aware of and reflects upon its contextual determination, and also because it focuses on the topics that social sciences consider to be their domain – partly because theology originally (with some minor exceptions)[13] did not focus on them at all.

However, since the time when the social sciences established themselves apart from philosophy, there has been a constant tension between religion together with theology and the social sciences. This tension is not founded merely in the social sciences as such but previously in the modern philosophical streams from which the

---

10 Diaspora here refers to the small and dispersed number of practicing Christians in a certain territory and/or a certain culture so that people do not experience their faith as part of the culture in which they live.
11 In Biblical Greek, this refers to love in the sense of friendly, helping love; it is love that does not require the same intensity of the relationship from the other person. (Author's comment.)
12 The term *caritas* is the Latin translation of Greek *agape*. It was used already in *Vulgata*, the first ancient translation of the Bible into Latin. (Author's comment.)
13 It was, for example, Spanish philosopher, theologian, and lawyer Dominican Francisco de Vitoria (Vitoria, Nys, Bate, Simon, Wright 1917), who was critical of the Conqista in South America at the turn of the 15th and 16th centuries.

social sciences arose. Therefore, despite its various historical and cultural-political developmental stages,[14] it is primarily a construct that ignores the reality of the various levels at which the postulates of theology and social sciences are compared regarding social help and human need (Allen, 2017, p. 230). Thus, paradigmatic and syntagmatic levels of theology and social sciences are commonly compared – their ontological points of departure and their key narratives are:

- While the ontological point of departure of theology, which focuses on social problems and need, is love (see *caritas*) and service (see *diakonia*), for social sciences it is epistemic justice.[15]
- The key narrative of theology by which justice is promoted is the horizon of the Kingdom of God, that is, the eschatological fulfilment of history that can be anticipated and approached through neighbourly love and selfless service, while in the social sciences it is social conflict and class struggle (Allen, 2017, p. 231).

There are different views on how to overcome this permanent tension. These differ from each other mainly in whether they see the solution in the ontological level or at the opposite end, that is, in the practical level.

An example of a solution that relies on the ontological level is the concept of social work as an action theory according to Silvia Staub-Bernasconi. She distinguishes between practical, applied, and ontological-ethical levels of theories of social work. While the practical level concerns techniques and procedures for working with the client, the applied level provides a theoretical explanation of why and how the particular communication technique is effective (that is, for example, psychological explanation) or why the situation arose in practice (that is, for example, sociological explanation); the ontological-ethical level then says whether the theoretical explanation is reasonable, good, and the best one (Staub-Bernasconi, 2018). Naturally, theology can be easily applied to this intellectual model as well (Opatrný, 2020). At the ontological-ethical level of social work as an action theory, the philosophical starting points of the social sciences belonging to the applied level (that is, ontological starting points and ethical issues of psychology, sociology, law, etc.) meet other philosophical theories and theology. If theology is effective on this level of argumentation, it subsequently influences applied and practical levels, respectively, it provides for them an ontological justification for situations from practice and an ethical evaluation of practice and its theoretical explanation on the applied level.

The completely opposite approach relies on overcoming the tension between theology and social sciences in general – that is, not merely social work – at the level of helping practice, that is, to practice addressing social issues and need:

---

14   Allen here refers mainly to the influence of Anglican theology on social politics in Great Britain; analogically we could consider the influence of Catholic theology, respectively, Catholic Social Thought, on social politics in Germany, Italy, etc. (Ebertz, 2011).
15   That is, justice, which, in order to be fulfilled, is interested in examining and knowing the problem.

a key social scientific problem with Christian charity is that the privileged that practice charity are largely unreflexive about the manner in which it buttresses their privilege and maintains oppression. Conversely critical social science requires its practitioners to be reflexive about the manner in which their own privileged standpoints infuse their episteme and understanding of the oppressed, i. e. they are required to exhibit epistemic humility. (Allen, 2017, p. 231)

The theological view on human need and social problems, however, at the level of practice leads to charity in the sense of pro-existence and thus to the confirmation of the privileges of all people (that is, being a person who is for others) which has similar normative consequences for practice as the epistemic humility of the social sciences. Charity pro-existence thus leads to a personalistic conception of human life, to simple life, to hospitality and service, and to *voluntary poverty* (or modesty). The epistemic humility of social sciences leads to the option for the marginalised, to participatory research, and to understanding the concept of help as a co-solution to social problems and need by those helping, by clients, and the community or society. In both cases, therefore, a common narrative arises in the sense of abandonment of power and domination in favour of strengthening social justice, strengthening the oppressed, and reducing social problems. The view of theology and social sciences is thus connected in the cross-narrative of 'being with' the marginalised and 'being for' them, which, however, cannot consist of mere words but demands radical practice on both sides (Allen, 2017, pp. 233–234).

1.3.4 Public theology and intelligibility of religious language

The fact that the aspects described above took several pages to show the relationship of Christianity and theology towards social and other public topics points to another important matter of public theology. It is the search for a solution to the problem of intelligibility of religious language, respectively, the interpreting function of any theology that aspires to be public – to be a rational reflection upon faith in the public interest. If religion has the opportunity and space to express itself in public discourse, it is also necessary for representatives of religion and theologians to be able to translate its language into the general language of public discourse – while maintaining the question of what shared public discourse is. It will only be when all voices which are present there are treated with respect that all voices will resound there as well. This, in turn, requires the ability to speak one's own religious language – to share the values and beliefs of religion (Bradstock, 2012, pp. 153–154). If in the postmodern period everything public is secular at the same time, it becomes not only a task but also a part of the very essence of public theology to promote mutual comprehensibility and understanding between public affairs and religion. However, having this nature – being the task and the essence – public theology is associated with a double problem, respectively, this nature breaks down into two different tasks similar to active and passive interpreting between two different languages. The combination of renewed vitality of religion and persistent and irreconcilable secularism raises the need for a debate on religious literacy: 'There is need for greater understanding of and knowledge about religion, in all aspects of public life' (Graham, 2017, 285–286). This is the first task of public theology, comparable to active interpretation into a foreign language. The second task of public theology, similar to passive interpretation into the mother tongue, consists in ways to preserve the theological meaning in the face of public lack of understanding (Cartledge, 2016, p. 163). Actually, the latter task is only an internal problem of theology regarding the development of theological thinking and the language in which it is expressed, while the earlier one is also a cultural problem which as such is a public matter.

Religious literacy is not only a question of individual education, it is also a prerequisite for responsible and effective citizenship, being a prerequisite for the development of civil society:

> We cannot make good political judgements without it; and once more, that is something that extends across the spheres of local, national and international politics. In the case of the US, for example, religious literacy might enable greater understanding of the beliefs of one's next-door neighbour, or how faith informs presidential campaigns, or how religion shapes global conflicts. (Graham, 2017, 285–286)

It is clear that increasing religious literacy cannot mean mere learning simple facts about religion. Rather, it means creating understanding for the religious way of thinking. In the European cultural environment dominated by postmodern secularity, such a task of public theology may seem very useful and necessary. It can help both to understand refugees and temporary migrant workers (*gastarbeiters*) newly coming from cultures strongly influenced by religions in countries outside EU, and also it can help to create understanding between the cultures of individual EU countries which may, on the one hand, have centuries-old tradition of strict secularity (for example, France) or, on the other hand, their culture may still be very strongly influenced by religion (for example, Poland). This does not mean, however, that it is quite clear and obvious how the fulfilment of this task of public theology is to be achieved. Rather, we seem to be at a time when the ways to fulfil it are being sought; this book partakes in this search, aiming at making the Good Samaritan story understandable and comprehensible also to non-Bible readers in helping professions.

This is, of course, connected with the question of how to preserve the theological meaning in the face of public lack of understanding. As I have already stated, this primarily regards an internal problem of theology – the development of its thinking and the language in which it is expressed. However, it is also a problem that has accompanied public theology since its beginning. If the original theological meaning was lost, that is, for example, the theological meaning of the Good Samaritan story, theology would become a diffuse field on the border between social sciences and humanities imitating religion science, psychology, sociology of religion, literary science, and philosophy, or possibly social work and its discourse on spirituality with its influence on the client's life situation and the work of a social worker. This problem is certainly 'solved' by some theologians by enclosing theology in a mental ghetto where the existing theological language is defended against the reduction of theological ideas through newer forms of expression; this is also accompanied by the decline of students of theological faculties, the reduction of the number of their research-pedagogical workplaces, and finally, the end of the existence of individual faculties by their merging into a central one. While it is undoubtedly possible to insist that some theological ideas are irreducible and any attempt to translate them is also a denial of their fundamental identity, it cannot be overlooked at the same time that Christianity has always been a religion of translation: 'It has repeatedly translated and re-translated its message and its practices across time and place' (Cartledge, 2016, p. 163). In other words, public theology cannot abandon its passive translation task precisely because it is theology. The historical development of theological thought and the language in which it was expressed cannot be denied in Catholic theology, for example, by referencing dogmas proclaimed by general councils (Schillebeeckx, 1996). After all, this problem was discussed in Catholic theology at its last council, the Second Vatican Council (1962–1965), which decided not to proclaim any new dogma but to clearly formulate existing teachings. The term clarity meant both the intelligibility of the language in which the council expressed itself towards Catholics without theological education (for example, in the dogmatic constitution on the Church *Lumen Gentium*) and to all people regardless of their religion (especially in the constitution on the Church in the modern world *Gaudium et Spes*). Therefore, theological thinking is not threatened as much by our attempts to express it in a new – publicly understandable – language as by the resignation to its translational function and task. Without it, theology would be no longer Christian. That is why theology must not resign putting in the effort to focus on how to use a new – publicly understandable – language without reducing and denying the original identity and meaning of the newly formulated theological ideas. In this book, too, significant space will be devoted to the detailed exegetical analysis of the Good Samaritan story and its theological interpretations in order to present its innovated – publicly comprehensible – interpretation.

A note must be added, the need for which naturally follows from the chapter regarding the public of the theologies of Christian caritas and diakonia (▸ Chapter 1.3.2). If Christian caritas and diakonia, as well as their theological reflection, is *sui generis* public theology, this then enables the critical reflection upon the public activity of Christianity (Körtner, 2017, p. 55) and a dialogue leading towards the aforementioned post-secular reconciliation (▸ Chapter 1.3.4) and improving public affairs (Graham, 2017, pp. 287–289). Both interpreting tasks of public theology are fulfilled by Christian caritas and diakonia involved in broader assistance systems such as social security and social services systems in various countries, and their theological reflection (*caritas theory* and *the diakonics*), which interacts with social work and other fields focusing on helping professions. That is why the diaconia theme, that is, the theme of the Good Samaritan story, is manifested as the typical theme of public theology – a theme suitable for approaching from the point of view of public theology and a theme that public theology cannot, actually, avoid.

1.4 Who is my neighbour – a question for public theology

If the Good Samaritan theme proves to be typical for public theology, it is not merely due to its pertaining to the concept of public theology, its 'fitting' in. In a way, it can be said that the Good Samaritan story as such, as captured by the *Gospel of Luke*, is public theology.

As will be shown in Chapter 3, the literary adaptation of the story was also fuelled by the interest to clearly introduce the Christian view on the relationship between religious faith and practical action, between the teachings and ethics. The eternal and, in a way, sacred question around which the story revolves, namely, 'Who is my neighbour?', expresses the a priori orientation to the other person (Graham, 2017, p. 289).

> The issue for Jesus is not 'who is my neighbour', but 'what does it mean to be neighbour' in this and any situation of impoverishment. Jesus makes the answer to that abundantly clear; it is to show mercy, bind wounds, supply shelter, provide food and support those in need without distinction. (Schaab, 2008, p. 185)

The story thus clarifies that one cannot misuse the question of who my neighbour is as an excuse. At the same time, it also shows that this is a question that leads to interest in the other, in his distress and needs, in whether he understands me, and also in whether I have understood him. Moreover, the Good Samaritan story is not a mere pedagogical tool for Jesus but reflects his existential experience of himself being sent to the marginalised – that he himself was marginalised because of them. In the parable, therefore, experience shows the significance of being a neighbour. It is the experience of the importance of unconditional approach and action that favours openness and hospitality: 'No cultural, political or religious restriction, supposedly well-established or apparently well-justified, obstructs the stance of Jesus toward any marginalized person, for he too was marginalized' (Schaab, 2008, p. 191).

All of this makes the Good Samaritan story public theology *par excellence*. For public theology, it is a story to work with, while at the same time this story synergistically leads towards public theology and in a way becomes its biblical foundation.

2. Modern Allegorical Interpretations

As the parable of the Good Samaritan has always enjoyed the attention of Christians who have devoted themselves to caritas and diaconal activities, or simply to benefaction, its interpretations have arisen which not only focus on charity but also are based on it. This means that engagement in caritas and diaconal activity and, even more, their intellectual reflection, were a pre-understanding and a starting point for the interpretation of its kind. As early as at the beginning of the 20th century, disciplines such as *theory of charity* (in German Caritaswissenschaft) in the Catholic environment and *diakonics* (in German Diakonik) in the Protestant one began to emerge in the German-language area; within these, the interpretations of the parable began to appear, focusing on the ways of the parable's interpretation in such a way as to have significance and contribution for the current benefaction of Christians. Rather than utilising the findings of biblical exegesis and theology, such interpretations focused on current problems that caritas and diakonias had to face as well as issues arising in pastoral practice. We can identify at least four fundamental areas of such interpretations:

- The first three are essentially similar in their approach to the parable, differing in the emphasis within the content. These are *economic*, *methodological*, and *pastoral* interpretations, which can be described as *modern* allegories of the parable. We can call them such as they seek the current (modern) meaning of the parable hidden behind ancient realities and forms of expression. Just as the ancient allegories of the parable sought a hidden spiritual meaning in its secular impression, modern allegories seek in its historical form as specific impulses and meanings for contemporary charity as possible.
- In addition to modern allegories, we have to refer to the fourth area of current interpretations, which can be described as *diaconal exegesis*. Besides the work of the exegetes who aimed at actualising the parable for the needs of contemporary Christian charity, this also includes interpretations by theologians in the fields of caritas theory and diakonics who interpret the parable for the utilisation by (not only) Christian benefaction with strict regard to the findings of biblical exegesis.

The following chapter will be devoted to these four areas of interpretation (economic, methodological, pastoral, and diaconal exegesis). The primary purpose of this book is to assess these interpretations; this means, to carry out their deconstruction to the extent as they are compatible with the findings of modern exegesis in order to determine which of their parts are applicable also to the secular environment of helping professions, especially social work.

It should be noted, however, that modern allegories are not condemned beforehand as being confusing. As already explained in the previous chapter, understanding and interpreting parables is always also a cultural-interaction process thus virtually any interpretation – including the strictly exegetic ones – reflects its time. For example, in Germany during World War I, the parable of the Good Samaritan was interpreted in sermons with the meaning that the victim was the homeland; the robbers were German enemies and murderers (i. e. France, Russia, and England); and the priest and the Levite were traitors (pacifists calling for a ceasefire), the Samaritan was German front-line soldiers who – how else – are saving their homeland (Jens, 1973, pp. 16–17). As it is evident at first sight, the interpretation is not only completely reflecting its time but also in stark contrast to the message of parable. The message of solidarity and overcoming boundaries – even among the enemies – was considered to be the core of the parable. This is evident not only from the artistic expressions of the parable discussed in the previous chapter but also from its interpretations from antiquity to the present, which will be reflected upon in the next chapter. Thus, the example of the war's interpretation is far beyond the parable's message. Similarly, populist politicians in current Europe exploit the matter of the story and its wide popularity. This is despite the fact of the wide formal and factual secularity of particular people and nations in Europe (Spencer, 2017). In their reframing, the neighbour is the fellow man different from a neighbour in the sense of the man living in the next house or door, whereas the migrants and refugees coming to Europe are strangers. Thus, helping your neighbour means protecting men living in your neighbourhood and averting migrants and refugees from coming to the soil of the European Union or Europe in general. Moreover, helping them means supporting them in *their* neighbourhood, i. e., in their countries of origin. The politicians from these populistic parties, like *Alternative für Deutschland* (AfD) in Germany, overlook absolutely the Good Samaritan story's core statement that the stranger is the same neighbour (fellow man) as that neighbour living in their own neighbourhood. The German language, however, has two different words for neighbour – *Nächste* (encountered person) and neighbour – *Nachbar* (next door), which the politicians of AfD mix together (Neutel, Kartzow, 2020). In other languages, this word is often unmistakable, like in Czech: neighbour – *bližní* and neighbour – *soused*.

Therefore, in the case of allegorical interpretations of the parable focusing on caritas and diakonia, this book primarily aims at identifying which aspects are or are not legitimate with regards to exegetical findings – that is, they are within the exegetically identified framework of the parable's message.

After introducing the parable in the previous chapter, this chapter offers an overview of such interpretations which are intended to formulate the identity and mission of Christian caritas and diakonia as well as to theologically inspire helping professions. This overview will be followed by the exegetic chapter focusing on the interpretation of parable which arose from historiographic findings, hermeneutic methods for the analysis of ancient texts, and from archaeological findings. In this way, the frame of the parable's message will be identified, thanks to which it will be possible to determine in subsequent chapters which parts of modern allegories are applicable to the secular environment of helping professions, especially social work.

2.1 Economic interpretations

The first group of interpretations is based on the brief mention that the Samaritan entrusted the ambushed to the innkeeper whom he paid, promising to pay potential further costs for care on his return. In the health care and social care economy consideration, scholars consider the parable as an example of how to use wisely not only the money of donors or from church collections but also public funding (Duckett, 2022). In addition, the Samaritan's Dilemma is a thought experiment, a game in which the person of the donor is called a 'Samaritan'. This marking declares that this person is preparing to help the other in every case. The other person is a recipient of aid, who can consider if he will work or wait for help. When he does not receive the help, he will work; when he receives the help, he will not. Thus, when the recipient knows the Samaritan will help him in every case, he has no motivation to work (Goodman, Herzberg, 2020). The Samaritan's Dilemma lies in the decision either to help the other and contribute to his passivity or not to help the other but suffer from the cost of not helping (Marciano, 2022). This thought experiment is common in the economy and can be applied to the problem of donation, sponsoring, social benefits, etc. Another example of financial eisegesis of the parable is emphasising the payment at the inn as a provocation, that the care for the man in need should be free. This interpretation seems to be led by the current discussion about free care in the healthcare systems of particular states. However, unfortunately, it overlooks the exegetical fact that the Samaritan's payment is the minimum wage per day of a worker (Peng-Keller, 2021).

Founded on considerations, how wisely use money of donors, deliberations are developed that caritas and diakonia or social and health care are not free. More precisely, that it is relevant to consider how these would be financially secured because 'Luke's narrative of the Good Samaritan illustrates in an exemplary way the practice of living Jesus' mercy in the context of economic conduct' (Batz, 2017, p. 42). An important prerequisite for this is the identification of caritas and diaconal institutions with the innkeeper and his inn. In fact, this idea is not modern in its origins; its roots are found at the latest in the Middle Ages, when monarchs, who were patrons of particular artists, were in the fine arts identified with the innkeeper thereby showing that their social politics is important to them (▸ Chapter 1).

Entrepreneurial and ethical significance is also attributed to the fact that in v. 10:36[1] the innkeeper is not considered a potential helping person but only the three passers-by who passed the ambushed laying by the road (König, Hofmann, 2017, p. 17). Economic interpretations further note that the Samaritan helped because he was stirred by compassion but had not established any closer relationship with the ambushed. According to them, the story also includes the right balance between emotional closeness and factual distance of the helping person towards the client. Also, by paying the innkeeper, the Samaritan has made it clear that his life continues – he continues with his duties even though his concern for the ambushed remains (Batz,

---

1   Which of these three, do you think, proved neighbour to the man who fell among the robbers?

2017, p. 44). Thus, purely economic thinking is not the only leitmotif of these reflections because they are based on a certain ethos of help – ethics of thinking and ethics of action. Such ethos is usually guided by the current understanding of helping professions. It is then possible to say, for example, that in the parable we can identify the following specific elements of the Samaritan's actions:

- compassion – when he saw him, he felt sorry for him;
- action – he approached the ambushed, treated and bandaged him;
- he used his own resources for the ambushed (oil, wine, bandages, mule);
- delegation of care to the professional innkeeper, including the payment in advance;
- sustainability – the promise to reimburse the costs of deficit care.

These specifics of the Samaritan's actions also show that he left to the innkeeper that which he was not able to do by himself on the road, using the innkeeper's facilities and paying him in advance for further care (König, Hofmann, 2017, pp. 23–24).

The Samaritan's story also served as an inspiration for the development of a specific model of financial management for caritas and diaconal organisations that use public funding because they constitute a part in the system of providing social services. By its very nature, this system, in its various forms in different countries, leads to the fact that caritas and diaconal institutions are in deficit or still at risk of deficit and must seek additional funding for their services and projects. The Samaritan's promise to reimburse the innkeeper on the return journey, which is conditioned by the innkeeper's higher costs, entails in this model implications for ethics and management of helping organisations and their facilities (König, Hofmann, 2017, p. 14): 'There is a need for a kind of cost-centre of mercy in social services, which is refinanced through (church) tax or donations from the church community' (König, Hofmann, 2017, p. 34). This means that where there is no public funding for further costs, since this regards a diaconal or caritas institution, the Church as its founder should take on the responsibility. Institutionally, this would take place by transferring part of her income to charity organisations. In Germany, for example, this may regard the income from church tax and in the Czech Republic the income from, for example, the financial settlement with the state. While on the community level, this would take place by the parish or congregation as a community of believers deciding to fund a project or facility of (their) caritas or diaconal organisation, respectively, a helping organisation with which some form of partnership has been contracted. Here, on both levels, the Church acts as the Samaritan who pays the innkeeper and guarantees him to cover potential further costs.

At the same time, charity organisations in this model must observe and adhere to certain principles such as *sustainability, organisation,* and *economical nature.* That is, for the Church to be able to refinance the deficits generated by the way of financing within the system of social services, adequate general and financial management of caritas or diakonias are necessary. With regards to the donations from the church community or church tax income, such management must demonstrate that it has the necessary competencies and a plan for further care for its clients, together with the sustainability plan (König, Hofmann, 2017, pp. 38–153). It is clear that while this model might be beneficial to caritas and diakonias with regards to economy and management, its inspiration in the parable of the Good Samaritan is only indirect. There is nothing in the parable suggesting that the innkeeper would run his inn as a charity institution that would thus be permanently in financial deficit.

Economy interpretations, noting in particular the Samaritan's payment to the innkeeper and the promise to reimburse his extra costs, lead to several different statements for caritas and diaconal institutions:

1. The parable is in general used to justify the funding for Christian caritas and diakonias as a necessary part of its functioning and development.
2. Thanks to this, it is possible to differentiate professional and organised caritas and diaconal assistance (caritas' and diakonias' services and projects) from spontaneous and voluntary charity (ad hoc involvement of Christians, community activities in parishes and congregations). This makes it possible to separate positions and actions as well as various forms of helping practice – on the levels of a professional, volunteer, donor.
3. On such a foundation, it is also possible to build more sophisticated models for the managerial and economic running of Christian Caritas and Diakonia (i. e. professional organisations), in which the management of the resources provided by the church, or by its part as the founder, plays a crucial role.

2.2   Methodological Interpretations

The title of this chapter could easily lead to the assumption that only the interpretations given here are related to helping practice. In fact, virtually all modern allegories in the interpretation of the Good Samaritan parable are related to it. Therefore, if this chapter wants to address methodological interpretations, it will be those that take note of the course of the Samaritan's actions. While the previous chapter focused on what happened after the Samaritan had transported the ambushed to the inn, this chapter will focus on his actions right on the path between Jerusalem and Jericho that had preceded this.

The basic starting point for the methodological interpretations of the parable was explicitly articulated in the historically first document of the teaching office within the Catholic Church focusing on caritas – Pope Benedict XVI's inaugural encyclical:

> Following the example given in the parable of the Good Samaritan, Christian charity is first of all the simple response to immediate needs and specific situations: feeding the hungry, clothing the naked, caring for and healing the sick, visiting those in prison, etc. The Church's charitable organisations, beginning with those of Caritas (at diocesan, national and international levels), ought to do everything in their power to provide the resources and above all the personnel needed for this work. (Benedict XVI, 2006, 31.a)

Compassion, which is explicitly mentioned in the parable, is understood here in the sense that it is manifested not by exalted emotions but by practical action. This view is also held by older documents of the Catholic Church, such as John Paul II's letter *Salvifici doloris* devoted to the issue of suffering. The Samaritan

...does not stop at sympathy and compassion alone. They become for him an incentive to actions aimed at bringing help to the injured man. In a word, then, a Good Samaritan is one who brings help in suffering, whatever its nature may be. Help which is, as far as possible, effective. He puts his whole heart into it, nor does he spare material means. We can say that he gives himself, his very 'I', opening this 'I' to the other person. Here we touch upon one of the key-points of all Christian anthropology. (...) A Good Samaritan is the person capable of exactly such a gift of self. (John Paul II., 1984, 28)

The same elements of the parable are also noticed by recent Protestant diakonics. If the point of the parable lies in reversing the question at the end of it – instead of asking who my neighbour is, the question stands who has acted as a neighbour – then the question is whether one is touched by the other's need as much as to be provoked to help, thus becoming a neighbour. However, this also means, in principle, that nobody is excluded from helping, that there is no predetermined circle of neighbours (Rüegger, Sigrist, 2011, p. 67). The parable thus actually depicts and emphasises a radical disparity – a stranger vs. anonymous other, the helping person vs. the helpless victim. It crosses over all political orders and refers to the interdependence of people in a world where one's need concerns each of us (Benedict XVI, 2007a, pp. 142–143).

Similarly, Jesus using a parable where a Samaritan plays the key role is an example of how diverse Christian charity should be (Ebertz, 2016, p. 254). Thus, caritas and diaconal institutions established by churches do not have to show the same degree of homogeneity as the church communities that set them up. The parable here actually prefers the so-called orthopraxis over orthodoxy – right or correct practice over right or correct content of faith because God's will can be fulfilled by the action itself, not only by confessing the content of faith. The same does not mean, however, that caritas or diakonia may or should be indifferent regarding ideology and values, respectively, that their connection with Christianity is not essential. Without the connection to the values, there would be neither caritas nor diakonia as these two terms of Christian charity per se express the values. They make clear that they are related to God's service to man and to God's love. Therefore, they are like God's service and love without borders – they apply to both 'those inside' and 'those outside' and also to enemies and traitors such as Roman soldiers and tax collectors, etc. God becomes a slave because of them all (Phil 2:6–11). Such an understanding of love and service also includes the 'variegated' Samaritan, considered by many a heretic and schismatic, who slipped into the middle of Jesus' narrative in the biblical story: he is also a believer in God but a kind of a different believer, non-orthodox, suspected of paganism. The Samaritan thus refers to the fact that there is no harm for Caritas and Diakonia organisations to be 'variegated', both for helping professionals and volunteers. Moreover, it is clear from the parable that diversity is not abnormal, either on the part of donors and supporters, or amongst the recipients of help (Ebertz, 2016, pp. 251–252).

Having departed from the purely practical message of the story that compassion is manifested by action, and continued through the ideological roots of caritas and diakonia in God's service and love which can withstand a high degree of diversity, we now arrive at the issue of spirituality of diaconia, that is, to the spiritual foundation of the helping people and the spiritual meaning of their caritas and diaconal activities. This foundation is included in the parable by its connection with the dialogues between Jesus and the Law expert regarding the greatest commandment. Thus, the parable narration is essentially linked to the dispute over what needs to be done in order to obtain salvation – eternal life (Feiter, 2008, p. 87), which is mostly a spiritual issue. When it is said in modern translations of the Samaritan parable that he was moved by compassion (v. 33), the original meaning of the Greek text is weakened, which in fact refers to the womb and maternal love – the Samaritan is moved, is affected by the situation of the ambushed even in his 'loins'; we can also say that was tearing his heart (Benedict XVI, 2007a, p. 142) (more on that in the chapter 3.3). This expresses that he did not act with the intention of fulfilling the duty of solidarity under the Law of Moses or the ancient social ethos, and even – paradoxically – with the intention of gaining eternal life. If we can rephrase the Greek text in such a way that he has been moved within, in the 'maternal lap', it expresses the important idea that one can judge good and evil and be moved by compassion for suffering only when he is good 'inside'. But in the sense of theological anthropology, man cannot do this by himself, he needs God's help – so-called grace – to act correctly and as a good person (Feiter, 2008, pp. 87–88). Benedict XVI therefore writes in his encyclical *Deus caritas est* that love can be commanded as it was given first (para. 14). He thus interprets in his original way the connection of the dispute over the greatest commandment and narration of the parable of the Good Samaritan: the Samaritan was able to help only because he was loved by God. Here, however, concepts of the practical implications of this parable's spiritual meaning significantly diverge.

According to Feiter, Benedict XVI (2006) understands the parable in the encyclical *Deus caritas est* in the sense that the helping person needs to be a 'thoroughbred Christian' when he mentions in connection with caritas work that practical activity is not enough unless it is founded on meeting Christ. Thus, the ancient allegories that identified the Samaritan with Jesus Christ are not irrelevant (for more details, see ▸ Chapter 3) because in this way the love of man gains the true depth as a manifestation of God's saving love. In this sense, it is also necessary to read the encyclical *Deus caritas est* paragraph 33 that caritas is to be realised by people who have been touched by the love of Christ (Feiter, 2008, pp. 88–89).[2]

The stirring up of the Samaritan as a manifestation of God's empowerment to solidarity can also be interpreted in the logic of the variegated caritas and diakonia as mentioned above, i.e., that in principle all people are capable of carrying out caritas and diakonia – regardless of their relationship to Christianity. An important starting point for such an interpretation is the fact that the parable might have had a Christological meaning in the original oral tradition,[3] but this was clearly changed when

---

2   Given what Joseph Ratzinger wrote about ancient allegories (see ▸ Chapter 3) in his book Jesus of Nazareth (Benedict XVI, 2007a), the question is whether Feiter's interpretation really regards Benedict XVI's postulates or rather the editions of the encyclical text carried out by the Pontifical Council *Cor Unum*, whose representatives publicly stated that their views on the subject of the encyclical differed from that of the pope's (Cordes, 2008).

3   Christological meaning: this is an allegory in which the Samaritan saves the ambushed just as Christ saves the sinner.

recorded by the evangelist in favour of ethical, practical, and caritas-diaconal meanings. Then we can also agree with the constant meaning of ancient allegories that only when we see in the Samaritan Jesus Christ and his saving and liberating action towards man damaged by sin, the parable's message is grasped in all its greatness (Haslinger, 2009, pp. 248–249). However, practical implications might be different:

> 'Love for one's neighbour' (...) is no longer an 'internal Jewish affair' (respectively, a Christian affair [note Michal Opatrný]), it is an expression of every single person in his humanity. It is with this purpose in mind that Jesus tells the follow-up story (to the dialogue with the Scribe [note Michal Opatrný]) of the Good Samaritan. (Drewermann, 2009, p. 771)

For caritas and diaconal spirituality its formal (resp. ecclesiastical or motivational) legitimacy is not decisive but its interactive and functional legitimacy is. This means that caritas spirituality is not determined by formal affiliation to a church or by explicitly Christian motivation of the helping person but only by practical action. Biblically speaking, caritas or diaconal spirituality can only be recognised by the fruits. Jesus' parable says nothing regarding the spiritual motives of the Samaritan. It is only the pure interaction between him and the ambushed which expresses the priority of love for one's neighbour over everything else (Ebertz, 2016, p. 29). Therefore, the necessary outcome of the parable is the message that every man is empowered by God for caritas and diaconal activity and that the importance is not in the relationship of man to God – his Christian faith – but in the relationship of God to man. More precisely, it depends on God's grace, by which the parable – understood allegorically – expresses by the aforementioned God's service and love of man.

Thus, the spiritual message of the parable is not limited to the problem of the Christian motivation of the helper but is much broader. Its breadth is given in particular by the introductory and final dialogue between the Scribe and Jesus about the greatest commandment for man to fulfil to attain eternal life. With the question of who my neighbour is, the Law expert wants to limit the circle of people to whom he is to be related as one's neighbour – that is, to lighten up the commandment for himself. However, the fundamental message of all the Gospels says that God is wherever anyone suffers and where people respond in their humanity. Their ethnic and religious background is not decisive in this. True worship is therefore humanity, and this is possible for everyone – because he is human (Drewermann, 2009, pp. 776–777). With these conclusions about the spiritual message of the parable – perhaps surprisingly for some – the Church documents convene also. According to them, the parable of the Good Samaritan belongs to the Gospel of suffering as it shows the relationship each of us should have towards a suffering neighbour.

> We are not allowed to 'pass by on the other side' indifferently; we must 'stop' beside him. *Everyone who stops beside the suffering of another person,* whatever form it may take, *is a Good Samaritan* [note: emphasis M.O.]. This stopping does not mean curiosity but availability. It is like the opening of a certain interior disposition of the heart, which also has an emotional expression of its own. The name 'Good Samaritan' fits every individual who is sensitive to the sufferings of others, who 'is moved' by the misfortune of another. If Christ, who knows the interior of man, emphasises this compassion, this means that it is important for our whole attitude to others' suffering. Therefore one must cultivate this sensitivity of heart, which bears witness to compassion towards a suffering person. Sometimes this compassion

remains the only or principal expression of our love for and solidarity with the sufferer. (John Paul II, 1984, 28)

Taking interpretations of the parable in a way in which Jesus' narrative is an expression of God's support for each person to act as the Good Samaritan, they may eventually lead to the search for specific implications for caritas and diaconal practice, together with other helping professions. To fulfil the task of mercy, justice, and faithfulness (*Mt* 23:23) '… people, like the Good Samaritan, must see, be moved by compassion, and act – immediately helping them in acute need, indirectly committed to justice in relations and structures' (Baumann, 2013b, p. 82). Therefore, the parable also prescribes the manner of conduct of professionally organised Caritas because Jesus exactly described how help should take place:

- Recognise the need;
- Let ourselves be moved by it;
- The person in need has priority;
- Help always contains the best possible (oil, wine, bandages);
- Sustainable help (involvement of the innkeeper);
- Employing one's own means (2 denarii for the stay)
- Meeting on the level of eyes – the relationship is the foundation for the help actually being received (Küberl, 2013, p. 17).

The assumption of God's help and love that empowers man to charity ultimately leads to the search for methodological procedures for how to proceed in caritas and diaconal practice and how to arrange their organised form:[4] 'Although professional diaconia of ecclesial institutions does not rely on its own "constitutional story" in the New Testament, it can nevertheless be related to this parable. Diaconia takes place in areas and practices of various interpersonal and professional dimensions, as well as on similarly varied local and structural levels' (Fuchs, 1990, p. 112).

Therefore, according to modern allegories we can find a *methodological triple-step* for Christian caritas and diakonia in the parable (Lehner, 1999–2000, pp. 410–411); it is a sufficiently specific process, consisting of three clearly identifiable steps by which Christian caritas and diakonia should proceed. At the same time, these three steps are formulated in a sufficiently general way that they can be followed in different situations of human need:

1. The Samaritan, when looking at the ambushed, was moved by compassion (*Lk* 10: 33), which means that the *first step* of caritas work is authenticity or empathy, most precisely, neighbourly love. At the end of his narrative, Jesus turns the original Scribe's question of who his neighbour was (*Lk* 10:29) to the question of who has acted as a neighbour (*Lk* 10:36). When the Samaritan did not remain indifferent to the ambushed, he showed him the neighbourly love because the word neighbour

---

4   Here, it is possible to say that seeking specific processes in the Scriptures means resignation regarding human responsibility and on seeking historically conditioned – that is, most suitable – approaches through the reason; this nowadays applies, for example, to social work.

determines the one who has fulfilled the commandment of love for another person.
2. The *second step* is to help here and now with what is currently available – an alternative approach to help that is otherwise provided by the system however is failing currently or is not available at all. In the situation where, besides the Samaritan, everyone else who was supposed to have the good of others on their hearts bypassed the ambushed, hidden emphasis is laid on helping those overlooked by others. Moreover, such help must be provided even at one's own expense – selflessly (*Lk* 10: 34–35).
3. The last, *third, step* of caritas work method is integration, that is, handing over the ambushed to someone who is more fit to help; who is equipped to help. The Samaritan drove the ambushed to the inn (*Lk* 10:34–35), which was the 'facility' to help the pilgrims on the path between Jerusalem and Jericho. For caritas and diakonia this means that handing over a client to professional care and integrating those in need into the social welfare system frees them to be able to continue focusing on those who are in need while others overlook and circumvent them.

A similar interpretation to Lehner on the border between the economic and methodological can also be found in English written literature (Duckett, 2022). These modern allegories, however, do not only work with the motif of caritas and diakonia as a spontaneous and charismatic help which, after doing the most necessary, hands over its clients to professionals working in the field of modern social service systems. As in the case of economic interpretations, we can find the motif of identifying the innkeeper with caritas and diakonias as social services providers and the motif of identifying the inn with a caritas or diaconal social services facility. This means that not only the Samaritan but also the innkeeper in the story was helping, thus the innkeeper becoming an allegory of professional Caritas and Diakonias providing social services with the participation of the client. The outcome of this is the postulate that Caritas and Diakonia organisations should therefore help spontaneously, charismatically, and at their own expense to those who are lacking other help – i. e. such as the Samaritan; however, at the same time they can be social service providers that receive public funding and the possible participation of clients within the system of social services – i. e. as the innkeeper (Lehner, 1997, p. 396).

However, this modern allegorical interpretation is not widely shared. For example, Haslinger rejects the perception of the inn and the innkeeper as an example of contemporary diaconal institutions, explicitly and critically referring to Lehner from whom this allegory originated. He articulates the suspicion that this is 'eisegesis', that is, something is being read in the ancient story that can only be read through today's eyes. Furthermore, it may be somewhat paradoxical in such interpretations that Caritas and Diakonia will not be sufficiently critical about their theological foundations and standards for their practice. Haslinger contrasts this with the words used in the parable (taking care) and the payment of two denarii.

1. *Take care*: The Samaritan took care for the ambushed and also called the innkeeper 'to care' and paid him for it. The down-to-earth way he acts here may seem to completely suppress the emotional aspect mentioned initially. But this, according

to Haslinger, is the main point – to rid the help, respectively diaconia, of romantic notions of long-term successful help: caritas and diakonia are not a matter of sentimentality.

2. *Two denarii*: This was a labourer's wage for two days. For the Samaritan, it's part of his help. This means that help and diaconia have costs, and therefore Haslinger criticises pastoral interpretations discussed in the next chapter adding self-critically regarding his earlier works that financial support for those helping is also a part of caritas and diakonia. According to him, donating cannot be simply denigrated as redeeming one's self from direct help. In this way, he refers to a number of theological works, especially of German origin, which emphasise the need for all Christians to be directly involved in caritas and diaconal activities, otherwise it would not possible to speak of the Church and its components such as a parish.[5] The idea that as many people as possible are involved in practical help is naïve because, for example, in doing so, millions of people who financially support Caritas and Diakonia organisations in Germany would be offering to volunteer there (Haslinger, 2009, pp. 261–262).[6]

In this sense, Haslinger modifies Lehner's triple-step to a *methodological quintuple-step*, which follows from the parable of the Good Samaritan for the practice of caritas and diakonia:

1. *Compassion:* While the priest and the Levite avoided the ambushed, the Samaritan 'moved with compassion' came to him. 'Moved by compassion' means in the Greek original to be, literally, stirred within. That is why the term merciful is apt for the Samaritan because it indicates that the helping person is affected inside – in his heart. Moreover, all this is intensified by the context of the ambush taking place in the wilderness between the centres of religious and secular power, in the excluded area of social death.[7]
2. *Rescue:* Wounds treatment is what needs to be done at that moment to save the ambushed.

---

[5] That is, in a parish, congregation, or community, everyone should not only attend Sunday services but should also engage in caritas and diaconal activities of a professional Charitas or Diakonia or another organisation, eventually should realise one's own projects.

[6] However, it should be at least noted that pastoral interpretations criticised by Haslinger do not usually say that all Christians should become volunteers in Caritas and Diakonias. Pastoral interpretations are interested in another matter, as will be shown in the next chapter.

[7] Haslinger deduces the social dimension of the problem from the fact that the robbers are mentioned in a plural, and from the fact that the robbery has clearly not been an isolated event – all of Jesus' listeners knew it was a dangerous place. According to him, this indicates a 'hole in the system'. He then concludes that the story implicitly requires a change of situation and refers to, in the German-language area, a well-known quotation of Bishop Kamphaus from 1987 that robbers must also be caught (Haslinger, 2009). Obviously, it is a pure construct that does not follow from the text or the context of the parable in Luke's Gospel.

3. *Transport to safety:* Putting him on a mule and taking him away is not a minor part of the help but one of its essential elements because he saved him from the situation and did not leave him in the situation.
4. *To take care*: When care in the inn is articulated by the expression to take care, it means that both emotional and interpersonal nuances of help as well as professional nuances are included.
5. *To leave:* The Samaritan went on his way, not making the ambushed dependent on him. This does not mean, however, that he has remained unchanged since both have become neighbours to each other – without mixing their identities and without one being at the disposal of the other (Haslinger, 2009).

At the same time, both the methodological triple-step and the quintuple-step diverge from the view that it is possible to contrast spontaneous and voluntary caritas and diakonia on the one hand and professional and organised ones on the other. This takes place when pastoral practice underestimates the activities of charity and diaconal organisations, while their practice relies only on professional forms of social work and other helping professions (Fuchs, 1990, pp. 112–114). However, professional help alone will not help in the sense that it is also necessary to change the environment in which it takes place. This should be a matter of parishes, respectively, pastoral practice, as will be shown in the next chapter.

Moreover, the allegorical interpretation in which the Samaritan and the innkeeper are symbols of spontaneous neighbourly help and institutionalised carrying-out of social care in market conditions are not necessarily to be understood only negatively. Within this, it can also be concluded that caritas and diakonias must, in the first place, be better than others in performing the tasks of the innkeeper – that is, to be true professionals in the social services system so that they can pursue activities similar to those of the Samaritan when they can help those who are outside the social services system. Although this concept of caritas and diakonia (their dual identity) may seem important at the time of the economisation of social services (Rüegger, Sigrist, 2011, pp. 254–255), the opposite practice is also known where help is provided to those whom the system cannot help, taking place at the caritas' or diakonia's own cost (Janebová, Celá, 2016). There are therefore two different models of practice that follow from the interpretation of the parable:

- While organised and professional help is to be a matter for charity and diaconal organisations, spontaneous and voluntary help is to be a matter for parishes, congregations, and communities,

or:

- spontaneous and voluntary help, as well as organised and professional help, should be a matter for caritas and diaconal organisations.

Thus, the testimonies of methodological interpretations of the parable of the Good Samaritan prove to be very broad and varied. They are characterised primarily by the range of themes they see in the Samaritan's action on the path between Jerusalem and Jericho. At the same time, it is also typical for them to differ in their applications

2.2 Methodological Interpretations

for practice. Thus, methodological interpretations are a kind of core of the parable's modern allegories, which give the most impetus to current caritas and diaconal practice:

1. They fully correspond in understanding the parable as an expression of the emphasis on the interconnection of compassion and action – as if they were two sides of one coin. Compassion – being stirred up over the situation of a person in need of help – is manifested only by factual and effective action, not by the exalted manifestation of emotions, verbally, etc. That is, in the case of such a compassion, emotions are not what leads the conduct of the helping person. This is much more led by the rational reflection of that movement that one experiences because otherwise it would hardly result in factual and effective action.
2. The story of the Good Samaritan does not directly say anything about his motives but by connecting the story with the dialogues between Jesus and the Law expert, the Gospel writer tells us that this regards a religious and a spiritual problem. If the story at the same time talks about the Samaritan's action to be a manifestation of his compassion, this means that his motives could not have been religious in the sense which the Scribe initially considered the whole matter. The Samaritan acted because he was not indifferent to the fate of the ambushed; in this tension between dialogues on explicitly religious topics and the Samaritan's actions, the message is 'encoded' in the text about the spirituality of the helping person. Methodological interpretations agree with each other that the Samaritan was able to act effectively and as a matter-of-fact because he was made able to do this by God; this is also the broad context of the story as the *Gospel according to Luke* considers man and God (see next chapter). We might understand this in the following way:
   a) The helping person must therefore be a full-fledged Christian who finds nourishment from God to help others.
   b) God makes every person capable of helping others, as is manifested by one's being stirred up over the distress of the other. But he himself must decide that he will also respond to his stirring with factual and effective action.
3. Therefore, if the parable wants to convey that compassion – being stirred up regarding a need – is a manifestation of God's making man able to help others in factual and effective action, then it is possible to deduce practical implications – specific methodological steps for caritas and diaconal practice and tasks for caritas and diaconal organisations. Here, two key themes arise. One is the Samaritan's approach to helping the ambushed – he felt compassion for him, he treated and bandaged the wounds of the ambushed, took him to the inn, took care of him and paid extra care, and last but not least went on his way. The other theme is the roles of the Samaritan and the innkeeper as the representatives of spontaneous and voluntary help on the one hand and professional and organised assistance on the other. In addition to criticising the image of the innkeeper as a social or health service provider, practical applications lead to the two following statements:
   a) Spontaneous and voluntary help is a matter of ecclesial communities (parishes, congregations, and specific communities) while the professional and organised one is a matter of caritas and diaconal organisations as social service providers.

b) Both spontaneous and voluntary help, and professional and organised help are matters of caritas and diaconal organisations as providers of social and health services; however, in order to be truly committed to spontaneous and voluntary help they must first manage professional and organised help at a high level.

2.3 Pastoral Interpretations

In the parable of the Good Samaritan, theoretical and abstract theological statements are connected to specific and practical ethical imperatives. The parable strongly emphasises that the two 'loves', of which the dual greatest commandment speaks,[8] are indivisible. There is no '… love for God at the expense of love for man. He who puts love for God above love for man does not understand God, damages religion and hurts himself' (Drewermann, 2009-, p. 776). This connection of two 'loves' is the focal point of pastoral interpretations that, based on the parable, consider especially the practice of Christian communities – parishes, congregations, and communities, perhaps even religious communities.

As the allegorical spiritual motif was appearing for centuries in the parable interpretations – that the Samaritan, as Jesus Christ, helps the ambushed (as a man affected and beaten by sin) and entrusts it to the inn (that is, to the Church) to look after him – the importance of the caritas and diaconal, i.e., the ethical, interpretation of the parable has been increasingly disappearing:

> The limitation to Christological interpretation overlooks that the parable of Luke (…) shows Jesus' answer to the ethical question of the Law expert 'who is my neighbour' (*Lk* 10:29) which arises from the dual commandment of love for God and neighbour. (Clement, 2015, pp. 112–113)

In this sense, the parable works with the theme of need and help as a part of the core of Jesus' teaching on man which was in the Catholic theological tradition expressed by Benedict XVI in his postulate that '… the imperative of love was written by the Creator into the very nature of man' (Benedict XVI, 2006, 31). Love for neighbour is understood as a part of humanity, not being its addition – love for one's neighbour is not something that Christianity adds to humanity.

Therefore, this is also a part of the most fundamental commandment in terms of the expectation God has of man as his creator. But if the binding nature of this commandment is part of humanity regardless of one (not) affiliating himself with Christianity, it becomes even more binding for Christians – their faith in God and knowing God's will, that is, their relationship with God – obliges them with doing so. Thus, among the interpretations of the parable we can identify those that focus on it in terms of its specific or greater obligation for Christians. While the priest and the Levite have seen and passed by the ambushed, the Samaritan was stirred up when

---

[8] You shall love the Lord your God with all your heart, and with all your soul, and with all your strength, and with all your mind; and your neighbor as yourself (*Lk* 10:27).

seeing him – the Greek original uses an expression that is etymologically related to maternal womb (for more details, see Chapter 3). Also, the Hebrew term for compassion *rechem*, which is used in the Old Testament in connection with God, is also etymologically related to the maternal lap. The fundamental characteristic of God is therefore mercy, being in the 'maternal sense' of these words. If such terms are used to characterise God or the conduct God desires, those who believe in him should act in the same way: 'If we mystically immerse ourselves in such God, we must emerge in a diaconal way alongside the poor' (Zulehner, 2006a, p. 131). Thus, the higher degree of obligation of the commandment of love for Christians does not follow from it being a commandment but from the very characteristics of God: one cannot believe in a merciful God without being merciful himself. That is why such interpretations can be described as pastoral.

What does this actually mean for a particular pastoral practice in ecclesial communities? 'The Good Samaritan expected no reward, not even a "reward from heaven". He didn't feel particularly good either. He recognized the need and carried out what was necessary. That was enough. The true "Samaritan service" is self-explanatory and does not need any "Why?". This is how human compassion corresponds to the gratuitous mercy of God' (Moltmann, 2018, p. 75). The expression that the Samaritan was stirred with compassion is linguistically related to the expression that his compassion came from within, which can also be translated as from the guts. Therefore, we can say that he did not feel well – that he was disgusted, etc. Therefore, he did not need to expect any factual or spiritual reward for his help, or psychological reward – he did not necessarily have to feel good about it all. Therefore, the greater commitment of the commandment of love has for Christians nothing to do with the fact that they might expect an earthly reward or a reward in the eternal life, not even a reward in the form of a good feeling. It is pure selflessness, gratuitous help – just as God is in his mercy selfless and gratuitously merciful. There is no other reason why a person who believes in such God should help another person, simply, that the other – another – needs help.

The area of ecclesial communities (parishes, congregations, and specific communities) should therefore be not only a space of belief in selflessly and gratuitously merciful God but also the space of selfless, gratuitous help. This postulate (Congar, 2014) reappears in Catholic theology before the reform of the Second Vatican Council (1962–1965), continuing to grow subsequently. It is also manifested in the methodological interpretations of the parable of the Good Samaritan, which interpret the role of the innkeeper as today's professional and organised provider of social and health services and – hence – the role of the Samaritan as charismatic and spontaneous help that should take place in ecclesial communities (see Chapter 2.2). And this should take place not only among their members but especially towards their surroundings – the social environment (local body, town districts) in which the ecclesial community meets for worship and where its members live. In this sense, the parable is also understood pastorally because its interpretation answers one double-question: What should the pastoral practice of professionals (priests, preachers, deacons, pastoral officers and assistants, catechists and religious education teachers) focus on in the ecclesial communities to constitute a community and at the same time engage it in relations to its social environment? It is the practical benefaction carried out in a group, in this case the ecclesial community, that has the characteristics of both building the ties to the social environment of the community, and shaping the community itself – by engaging in the benefaction, the fellowship of faith and solidarity is being constituted.

In addition, organised professional caritas or diakonia, i. e., their institutional organised form (formerly, for example, monasteries and city hospitals, nowadays helping non-profit organisations), can be similarly related to the parable of the Good Samaritan in the pastoral sense despite of no Scriptural story existing regarding its establishment. Thus, on the basis of the parable of the Good Samaritan, this can be understood in a way other than as understood by methodological interpretations in the previous chapter. When the Samaritan tells the innkeeper that he would pay any additional costs of help when he returns, interaction between various forms of caritas or diakonia takes place which is difficult even in their current form. A classic example is the communication between an informal caritas or diakonia of the ecclesial community and a professional caritas and diakonia of a Christian helping organisation. Methodological interpretations say that these two forms of help are supposed to complement each other, respectively, are supposed to cooperate. In essence, the question is what an informal voluntary caritas or diakonia can do to support their professional organised fashion in the form of ecclesial helping organisations. The subsequent practice is then logically limited to collections – financial and material.[9] This, of course, is not wrong or erroneous in itself (see Chapter 2.2); however, it is also necessary to ask, above all, whether in caritas or diakonia of Christian communities professional helpers are involved in relevant ways. That is, for example, whether a streetworker working in Caritas with drug addicts can meet with parishioners. During a discussion, they would talk about the image the parishioners hold about his clients when they collect money to support the work with them. However, this is often not the case, but rather thanks to professional Caritas and Diakonia organisations, the ecclesial communities hold their task of loving one's neighbour to be 'done' – often without the material support referred to by the methodological interpretations. Thus, Christian communities remain merely places producing Christian worldview. They would become trustworthy and healing places that testify to God, who is selflessly and graciously merciful, only if they turn also into a social environment for helping organisations and help centres. These then would gain a greater influence in the social environment of their clients. Although the ambition of helping professions and especially social work is to help the clients directly together with working with their social environment (family, community), this does not mean that such interventions are always successful. Working with clients' social environments may not even occur for various reasons, which often include systems for financing

---

9   For example, in Germany, it has been considered for many years how to support and develop the mutual interconnection of caritas carried out in ecclesial communities and ecclesiastical helping organisations. However, successful and sustainable models have not been found.

various forms of care and help. This should therefore also be the interest of ecclesial communities – parishes, congregations, and communities – to strive to change the social environment they share with the clients of 'their' caritas or diaconal organisation. Doing so, the ecclesial community fulfils what the parable expresses by saying that the Samaritan has paid for the innkeeper's care and promised him to even up the lacking on his way back (Fuchs, 2004, pp. 280–281). Thus, methodological interpretations of the parable must be supplemented in the described pastoral sense so that the interaction between spontaneous and voluntary caritas or diakonia and their professionally organised forms is reciprocal. Although it is pointless for all members of ecclesial communities to engage in professional and organised caritas or diakonia as volunteers due to the greater binding nature of the commandments of neighbourly love (Haslinger, 2009, pp. 261–262), their material and financial support alone is not enough. Professional organised caritas or diakonia must influence the ecclesial communities in the sense to be understood by them and therefore also be provided with moral support – including understanding the working targets and procedures of helping organisations and having sympathy for the clients in their life situations. As a result, the ecclesial community may undergo a certain change of mindset which will be reflected in further relationships towards their social environment; in turn, the environment will eventually become a moral support for the activities, practices, and targets of caritas and diaconal organisations set up by churches.

Some other modern allegories of the parable, which we can also call pastoral in the previously described sense, proceed even further in applying the parable for the practice of contemporary ecclesial communities. According to them, the parable itself is not so much a continuation of the dialogue on the greatest commandments as the answer to the Scribe's first question: *How to obtain eternal life*? It is therefore a religious question – a question about God, regarding the search for God. And such a question, moreover, is contrasted by the parable with the exercise of power by religious castes – clergy, theologians, priestly families and tribes, etc. (Drewermann, 2009, pp. 771–772). Besides the *caritas-diaconal tradition*, which lives off the motif of the Samaritan story and contains impulses for 'carrying out help', we can say that this is another tradition in the interpretation of the parable which speaks of a *spiritual-pastoral interpretation*[10] that challenges certain predominant 'plausibilities' (Steinkamp, 30 Jan. 2019):

- In the parable, the theological definitions of eternal life (salvation), regarding which the Scribe asks in the opening dialogue, are replaced in the parable with a story of simple interpersonal help. This expresses that '... the unwitting affection for the poor and the inferior has a meaning in itself, without mentioning salvation and God' (Steinkamp, 1991, p. 130).
- The Samaritan is considered to be a logo of Christian charity that expresses its specificity; but at the same time he is a member of a religiously inferior tribe.

---

10 So, this regards a different interpretation than the ancient allegories offered; these spoke of a spiritual interpretation of the parable when, in the Samaritan, they saw Christ who was helping the ambushed as a man beaten by sin and was entrusting him to the inn, that is, the Church.

That is, Christians can and should learn *compassio* – in Latin meaning compassion as co-passivity in suffering – even from those who are different. *Compassio* is not a Christian specialty but a gift from heaven to all people of good will (Steinkamp, 30 Jan. 2019).
- In all of this, the criticism of priestly castes is included. The Old Testament priests tried to 'imprison' God in the Temple, thus strengthening their power. When the priest avoids the ambushed, he only does what is typical of him. Moreover, when nothing more is said about his motives, it simply confirms that it regards a clerical motive: his humanity has been completely absorbed by his priesthood, so he does not seem to be alive and he cannot help the one whose life has been endangered.[11]
- In the audience of Jesus, respectively, with the readers and listeners of the Gospel of Luke, then an expectation had to arise that the third on the way after the priest and the Levite would be a Jewish layman. When a Samaritan appears, being of a religiously inferior tribe, a scandal breaks out. Josephus Flavius mentioned Samaritans in the *Antiquities of the Jews*, that between AD 6 and 9, they profaned the Temple mountain in Jerusalem with human remains. The scandal, therefore, takes on a colossal dimension when the Samaritan comes to the half-dead, being considered someone who does not treat the dead appropriately and who profaned the abode of God with corpses. But it is the Samaritan who does not hold in his sight only the ritual God of the Jerusalem Temple thus nothing prevents him from having compassion and helping (Drewermann, 2009, pp. 775–776).

Thus, by challenging the expected plausibilities, the parable says that one who seeks God will not find Him in religious authorities but in His heart. God cannot be found where he is made a prisoner but where there is compassion with those suffering (Drewermann, 2009, p. 776). The storyline takes place between two people, both of whom are at the margins of society, so from the Christian point of view, help is not necessarily an expression of a premeditated attitude. Much more, it is compassion that is a decisive manifestation of human (and thus also of Christian) action (Clement, 2015, p. 113). Therefore, in turning from love of neighbour to neighbourly love, the parable also expresses that the helping person is also the one who receives. A situation where a person can help someone is the moment when the helping person is experiencing salvation (Steinkamp, 1991, p. 144). This means that he has received from God in order to then act the same as God: *He turned his compassion into action without compromising his relationship to himself, other people, and God himself.* For the helping person, compassion can be destructive to his own self as well as to his surroundings, including whom he is helping; also, it can also lead the helping person away from his relationship with God to pure activism. Compassion as *compassio*, that makes the helping person the neighbour who receives, is a situation where these relationships – to

---

11 Drewermann (2009, pp. 774–775) explains that even the Levite avoids the ambushed by saying that although the same rules of ritual purity did not apply to him, he applied the rule of ritual purity also to himself because the priest was a model of pious life. In this way he contrasts the law of helping his neighbour and the law of loving God, thus revealing the degeneration of these forms of piety.

one's own self, to other people, and to God – are in a healthy balance. However, one cannot achieve such a situation by himself; it is God's gift and therefore it is also an experience of salvation.

Such a *spiritual-pastoral interpretation* of the parable is therefore rather reserved with regards to organised forms of help of professional Caritas and Diakonia organisations, and ecclesial group projects such as in parishes, congregations, or church communities. In this case, caritas and diakonia overlap with pastoral care – in both meanings of the word pastoral: this regards the relationship of the Church (all Christians) to the world, and the work of professionals and volunteers[12] for the ecclesial community and providing care within it. In the spiritual-pastoral interpretation of the parable, pastoral care is replaced by activities that at first glance may seem primarily of a caritas or diakonial nature:

- Pastoral care as the Church's relationship to the world takes place in the openness of the ecclesial community towards all who are marginalised both in the Church and society: it may be the poor and excluded (for example, refugees or homeless) or new minorities (for example, homosexuals). The ecclesial community should be their home (Zulehner, 1997) and solidarity should be its characteristic.
- In this way, the care of the community is realised, developing through mutual *compassional* relations and through *compassional* relations to its surroundings and the environment to which it is open.

Then, the community does not need religious professionals for spiritual guidance but to take responsibility for maintaining and opening up relations to its surroundings (Steinkamp, 1999). Therefore, in the true sense of the word, this then does not regard so much caritas and diaconal activities as compassion in the sense of *compassio*. This then opens the possibility of being given by God and experience salvation in solidarity with the poor and the excluded. And since an encounter with God is thus experienced, this is after all Christian spirituality and such an approach to the practice of the Christian community is therefore pastoral.

Thus, the spiritual-pastoral interpretation of the parable proceeds further than its pastoral interpretation discussed above:

1. While pastoral interpretations in the line of caritas-diakonal tradition assume a significant role of interaction between Christians and helping professionals – which reflects the interaction of the Samaritan and the innkeeper – the spiritual-pastoral interpretation does not actually expect the helping professionals.
2. At the same time, however, one resigns from the autonomy of the world which, as created by God, is competent to seek effective solutions on its own even without the influence of Christians acting according to their faith (*Gaudium et spes*, 1965, 36). Here, we can perceive the thinking that the assisting profession regards cri-

---

12 That is, priests, preachers, pastors, deacons, pastoral workers, officers and assistants, catechists and teachers of religion, etc.

tically as the so-called *soft cops* – that is, as a part of the repressive tools of society designed to pacify its inadaptable members (Janebová, 2018).
3. Unlike the spiritual-pastoral interpretation, the interaction of the Christian community and helping professionals in the classical pastoral interpretation preserve the essential element of their own professional competence in helping professions that can benefit the environment of Christian communities (*Gaudium et spes*, 1965, 44) and inspire them (Opatrný, 2013). The realisation of the work of helping professions as *soft cops* does not consist in them being helping professions but in them being actually thus understood by social structures and within these social structures also by those who carry them out.

2.4 Diaconal exegesis

The previous three ways of interpretation perceived the parable of the Good Samaritan primarily through the prism of the context on which they themselves are founded (economics of caritas and diaconal organisations operation, work practices in caritas and diaconal institutions, and pastoral practice). Therefore, they must be necessarily understood as modern allegorical interpretations. The fourth way of current interpretations, addressed in this chapter, differs in its starting point. It follows the anthropological-ethical or caritas-diaconal message of the parable which it examines by means of biblical exegesis and theological hermeneutics. In this sense, it is no longer a modern allegory in the true sense of the word. However, the exegetic and hermeneutic work with the story is concentrated only on its importance for the diaconal task of the Church and Christians which is realised both through caritas and diaconal organisations and in private lives of individual Christians, as well as in pastoral practice.

Diaconal exegesis does not overlook ancient and medieval allegories but reads them in a different way: if in oral tradition the parable was originally of Christological significance which was clearly altered by Luke's editorial work in writing the Gospel in favour of ethical, practical, and diaconal meanings, then it is also true that only when we also see Jesus Christ and his saving and liberating action in the Samaritan that its message is grasped in all its fullness (Haslinger, 2009, pp. 248–249). That is, the identification of the Samaritan with Jesus Christ adds to the ethical-anthropological or diaconal-caritas message of the story in its significance by radicalising it in the Christ-like sense.

The prophetic message of Jesus is that God is merciful and that this mercy is not subjected to the principle of justice. The key point is found in *Lk* 10:33, where it is said that the Samaritan was stirred by compassion – in Greek *splagchnízomai* (Söding, 2016a, pp. 23–24). This word is etymologically originally related to the designation of the guts of a sacrificial animal, later related to a lap – especially maternal lap. This then led to the metaphorical sense of the heart being the seat of human emotions and feelings. In late Judaism and in the New Testament, the general meaning was transferred to its being the seat of mercy coming from the heart. In the synoptic Gospels, it is often used to express the strong feelings of *acting* people to whom Jesus in parables expresses the totality of mercy or anger with which God turns to men. The term is also used to characterise Jesus as the Messiah, which also suggests that the parable of the Good Samaritan may truly have soteriological origin in the story of Jesus saving man beaten by sin. In addition to the synoptic Gospels, related expressions can be also found in other New Testament texts (*Phil* 2:1 and *1 John* 3:17). In *Lk* 10:33, it expresses the emotional reaction to seeing a person in a great need, this being the decisive fundamental attitude of human and Christian *action* before God (Bopp, 1998, pp. 118–119): as God is not indifferent to the need of man, the Samaritan is not indifferent to the need of the ambushed either; similarly, other people, especially Christians, should not be indifferent either. In this sense, the Samaritan's stirring – mercy – shows two matters:

1. The Samaritan not only saved the life of the ambushed but also took care of him as best he could, paying for him to stay at the inn. Mercy is therefore presented here as an action that does not finish with one immediate response to a need but only when the need for help ceases.
2. In fact, the Samaritan was an enemy to Jesus, the Scribe, and the listener of their dialogue. By acting as a neighbour, it means that mercy inspires ethics that surpasses cultural and religious boundaries (Söding, 2016a, pp. 23–24).

Using a term based on the Greek concept *splanchnon* (in *Lk* 10:33f: the merciful Samaritan and *Lk* 15:20f: The Merciful father[13]) makes it clear that in the Bible there is a two-fold structure associated with mercy, that is, *to see* and *to have compassion*. It is a way of thinking that leads to concrete conduct and therefore also represents the saving action of Jesus himself. In contrast to 'acknowledgment', this regards a holistic perception of the human person and his problems that leads to spontaneous compassion, which in turn leads to spontaneous action (Bopp, 1998, pp. 228–230). This is based on the somewhat strict logic of Jesus' theology, which in the story of the Good Samaritan provides the connection with the dialogue of the greatest commandment. This means that it becomes apparent only through the parable how Jesus interprets the Law; it is not evident from the dialogue itself. But the parable itself has nothing about the Law in its content (Haslinger, 1996, p. 663):

> Through the context, that is, through the connection with the two commandments of love for God and neighbour, is guaranteed that the parable can in no way be read non-theologically, that is, as a relativization or negation of God's love. But it is its inner logic according to which it is closely interwoven with the question regarding his neighbour; it is even being evoked by it, thus it cannot, above all, be understood non-ethically. When Jesus uses the Samaritan's parable to interpret the dual commandment of love, he does not relate to the non-problematic acceptance of the commandment of love for God but to its other half, to neighbourly love, which proves to be problematic and requires clarification. (Haslinger, 2009, p. 249)

---

13 The parable is more known as the Prodigal Son; for more details, see Chapter 3.

This exegesis draws an important double-conclusion for Christian caritas and diakonia:

Firstly, the emphasis on action in the whole story and in the dialogue between Jesus and the Law expert is related to the question of salvation. When it comes to answering the question of how to fulfil the Law of Moses, one's own salvation is not at the core but that of another person. The question, then, is what I can do for the salvation of the other in order to fulfil the Law. One's own action should not serve one's own salvation but the salvation of the other – the other, who is in a bad situation so that he should be healed and freed (Haslinger, 1996, p. 664). Moreover, when 'the neighbourly love of the Good Samaritan, which is expected by God and exemplified by Jesus' is described in a secular way so much that we hear nothing of the Samaritan's religious motivation, or of the spiritual comfort for the ambushed, or any prayer is said or blessing given, so the ambushed only receives some sympathy and first aid, this then paradoxically means that the classic narrative of Christian motivation to help contains nothing specifically Christian. 'On the contrary, the whole narrative and literary approach of the story of the Good Samaritan can be seen as a challenge that motivation to help is possible for everyone, regardless of his religious beliefs' (Rüegger, Sigrist, 2011, p. 66). To fulfil the Mosaic Law in the sense of helping the other, as the parable refers to, is possible even for the person does not know it at all: 'In essence, there is nothing else said here than the renowned saying that "The Sabbath is for man, not man for the Sabbath" (*Mk* 2,27). For Jesus, the fulfilment of the commandment as such has no purpose in itself; affection for people is not a factor in fulfilling the Law, but the Law is a factor of healing and liberating affection to people; and where this does not take place, it loses its authority' (Haslinger, 1996, p. 665).

Second, the dual Biblical structure of perception of need prevents one from being overwhelmed by emotions in connection with compassion. To see is to be looking at the situation accurately and critically. Thus, compassion in German-language diaconal exegesis is interpreted by the word *Betroffenheit* (Bopp, 1998, p. 234), which can mean both being affected and in horror. Action is necessarily associated with this accurate and critical vision. Seeing the half-dead along the road, the priest and the Levite represent the usual behaviour and approach to those in need when avoiding him. Thus, the story prevents the rapid identification of listeners and readers with the Samaritan because everyone knows that he could act in the same way as the priest and the Levite (Haslinger, 2009, p. 258). By contrast, 'the Samaritan first of all helps out of his spontaneous compassion for the assault victim. His heartfelt help' is the action following up the seeing but taking place

> in specific points and has boundaries: as quickly as possible, he delivers the wounded to the nearest inn and there organises further 'stationary' care for this man. The next day he sets on the journey again. Helping conduct often needs to combine both forms of spontaneous personal commitment and institutional-professional service to be effective. (Rüegger, Sigrist, 2011, p. 68)

Therefore, it is also true that seeing and acting are only possible under very specific social conditions. The helping person and the one receiving help must meet in the life situation of the recipient, while keeping him in his own living space in order for the helping person to be able to encounter the recipient and thus be able to be solidary with him (Bopp, 1998, p. 241). Changing the question of who my neighbour is to who became a neighbour shows that the measure of diaconia is man and nobody else – only when the help is practical (so that someone receives it) does the helping person become a neighbour (Haslinger, 2009, pp. 254–255).

The dual structure of the perception of human need and suffering represented by the parable – that is, to have compassion and to act – thus clarifies the concept of mercy. In some languages, the parable is called the Good Samaritan, in others the Merciful (in German *Barmherzig*, in Czech *milosrdný*) Samaritan. The word mercy is used throughout the text only once by the Law expert when in the last sentence of the second dialogue he responds to Jesus with a periphrasis of the Samaritan: 'He who has shown mercy to him' (*Lk* 10:37a). Because of, or perhaps despite of, how subtly the word mercy is employed in the story, the parable of the Good Samaritan is for the diaconal exegesis a significant Biblical place explaining mercy. The convergence between theological and humanistic motifs appearing in the story shows that mercy is not an exclusively religious or Judaeo-Christian concept but elementary and universal human conduct surpassing cultural and religious boundaries. Although there is no mention about God throughout the story, the Samaritan's spontaneous and clearly purely caring behaviour without religious interests and motives corresponds to God's will. The Samaritan is involved in the situation of the ambushed only in a limited way, when he does not allow his compassion to push him to self-destructive forms of help but helps according to his means and pays for the care given by someone else. Thus, human mercy is not without boundaries but has finite greatness which is determined by love for one's own self.

Mercy also needs the social environment the story refers to when the priest and the Levite fail. Their characters thus show that an environment that emphasises religious-cultural norms and ways of perception can paralyse mercy. Mercy is, on the other hand, explained as symmetrically understood neighbourly love. This results from the reversal of the initial question at the end of the narrative, when the Samaritan became the one to be helped, that is, one's neighbour. But it also follows from the fact that the Samaritan came from a socially excluded stratum – in the story, the one who is socially, culturally and religiously marginalised is the one who is helping the other who is marginalised by his unfortunate destiny. Although the story describes the situation of seemingly unsymmetrical help, its point is that neighbourly love is not interpreted as an asymmetric relationship but, conversely, mercy is interpreted as a symmetrically understood love for neighbour. Therefore, one becomes a neighbour, it is not a predetermined status. While the priest and the Levite did not become neighbours, the Samaritan became one because he acted mercifully. Being merciful, therefore, is a process of interaction that, regardless of cultural, social, religious, or other boundaries establishes new relationships between people that are based on neighbourly love and prove to be life-saving. Carrying out acts of mercy that enable people to be neighbours is, according to the parable, conduct required by the Law of God, and through which one can stand before God's judgment (Bopp, 1998, pp. 118–124).

The consequences of such a revised understanding of mercy have very practical implications for the actions of caritas and diaconal institutions as well as for the pastoral conduct of churches, which should follow these principles:

1. *Humanity of action.* The Samaritan's story shows that the two parts of the greatest commandment are not opposed to each other, nor are they interchangeable or substitutable. It is saying that love for God takes place in love for man. There is no loop in the story for some 'added value', something more than simple help. This humanity is therefore at the core of the conduct desired by God. Helping is not concerned with race or nationality, etc., or with religion, or correct cult. At the same time, man is God's child not because of belonging to a nation or religion but because of being a human. Thus, humanity is not a reduction but a radicalisation of Christian faith.
2. *Neighbour's priority.* The change in the question at the end of the story means that one who encounters the need of the other has yet to become a neighbour. Given that the Samaritan was on the way and yet helped the ambushed and transported him to the inn, this means that it is not possible to be a neighbour when I adapt the other to my ideas and my own life ideal or model (in German *Lebensmuster*). Being a neighbour means focusing on the other and his needs, changing one's own position, and giving one's life another direction.
3. *Removing social boundaries.* The priest and the Levite are attached to the cult and therefore avoid the ambushed not giving priority to the second part of the greatest commandment. The Samaritan's helping is therefore not a criticism of the cult but an emphasis placed on the fact that religious and ethnic affiliation is not necessary for acting according to God's will. Any boundaries (religious, social) do not affect the infinite God and His will as to who should be a neighbour. So, in the story, Jesus places man before God without any boundary, that means infinitely, and therefore the requirement for love of neighbour is in this sense also infinite (Haslinger, 1996, pp. 671–673).

3. Exegesis of the Samaritan story and criteria for evaluating the allegorical interpretations

For the first generations of Christians, Jesus was the narrator of the parable. In the Gospels according to Mark, Matthew and Luke, we might find a total of 41 different parables, which could have been recorded no earlier than 40 years after Jesus' death. For him, the parable was a medium conveying his message. But we can also say that the narrator of the parable was himself a 'parable of God' – Jesus' life, his words and actions, life, death, and resurrection are one great parable of God. Therefore, it can also be assumed that the parables relatively accurately encapsulate the image of historical Jesus. Jesus was of the same likeness as depicted in the parables. In fact, the suspicion that the early Christians might have modified them during the time when these were being passed on merely orally is, as a matter of fact, a suspicion that they wanted to change or falsify them. This means that, as theology is no longer trying to reconstruct what in the parable had come from Jesus and what had not, as it used to in preceding decades, the parable ought to be read as a part of the tradition that sought to convey its authentic message of Jesus Christ (Zimmermann, 2007b, pp. 3–5).

In this sense, this chapter focuses on the exegesis of *Lk* 10:25–37, that is, on the present state of understanding of the Good Samaritan parable interpretation. Unlike in previous chapters, theological exegetic literature is predominantly utilised here, which focuses on the critical analysis of biblical texts from the literary and historical points of view, while taking into account the findings in archaeology and in analysis of other ancient sources. Thanks to this approach, also known as the historical-critical method, it is possible to create a certain profile of the text author – how he employed the language, the then current characteristics and environment, the Old Testament, other ancient literature, etc. Similarly, it is possible to determine roughly whom the author addressed, what pre-understanding and knowledge he assumed of his listeners and readers, thus what he had to explain regarding context. Based on this, together with the chronological and geographical data in the text, it is then possible to determine also the approximate time and place of writing the biblical text.

First, however, the literary genre of parables will be specified here. This is a matter that would be worth an extensive work in itself, thus only a few essential remarks will be made here, especially on the issue of parables and their interpretation in the *Gospel according to Luke*. Subsequently, attention will be paid to the characteristics of the third Gospel per se. Thus, the reader should gain some insight in the necessary context significant for understanding the parable of the Good Samaritan. This will be discussed in the following two parts of this chapter. The first one will focus on the general analysis of the parable and the second on the commentary of its individual verses. All of this will create a foundation to formulate criteria at the end of chapter that cannot not be missed out in interpreting the text with regards to the practice, not only of Christian caritas and diakonia but especially of helping professions in general.

3.1 Notes on parables as a literary genre

Jesus' parables have long been considered a genre of its own kind, unlike any other. Their resemblance to rabbinic literature is only partial while the resemblance with the rhetoric of antiquity has not been considered for a long time at all. Actually, the parables arch between the Hebrew *maschal* and an ancient literary form:

- *Maschal* is not a literary type per se, rather being a term for a number of literary forms within the Old Testament and rabbinic literature such as proverbs, popular sayings, or parables. They can also be understood as a comparison or even a riddle. The Septuagint[1] translates Old Testament *Maschal* into Greek as *parabolé*, that is, a parable.
- In ancient rhetoric, the parable belongs to several genres: *parabolé, paroimia* (proverb), and *paradeigma* (example). Ancient fable is also sometimes considered a specific form of parable.

While the shorter parables in the New Testament are more like the *maschal*, the longer ones show elements of ancient rhetoric. This 'arch' appears to be theologically important: Jesus uses old wisdom forms in a new way. He combines and modifies them in the way that traditional forms are dynamically used to express something new (Zimmermann, 2007b, pp. 5–8). Such an approach also seems to be consistent with the way the author of Luke's Gospel approaches the content of this work (see Chapter 3.2).

However, the oldest interpretations of the parable were so-called allegorical. Parables were considered a genre containing some veiled meaning that is hidden behind their literal – textual – sense (Erlemann, Nickel-Bacon, 2014, p. 17). Coincidentally, it is the allegory of the Good Samaritan that perhaps best explains the allegorical approach. The God of Christians is foreign, i.e., incomprehensible to man. For this reason, the Son of God became a man, Jesus from Nazareth, so God comes close to humankind. Therefore, according to this interpretation, the Samaritan is a revelation of Jesus' closeness to all men, which refers to both of the parable's allegorical and exegetical interpretations (Bonilla, Mora, 2022). There even exist detailed overviews of its allegorical interpretations that identify the Samaritan with Christ (Fitzmyer, 1970–1985, p. 885); here, however, it suffices to present several major examples and significant comments. As will be shown below, the case of allegorical interpretations is not a dead-end branch in the history of biblical texts exegesis. On the one hand, they were definitively abandoned only recently, that is, only with the adoption of the historical-critical method of interpretation of the Scriptures (Bovon, 1989, pp.

---

[1] *Septuagint* (abbrev. LXX) denotes the first translation of the Old Testament from Hebrew to Greek (3th – 2nd century BC).

93–98) – in the Catholic environment this being in connection with the Second Vatican Council (1962–1965) – while on the other hand, it is possible (and also necessary) to continue working with some of their important aspects.

Scholastic allegories saw in the story the ambushed man who was robbed of the glitter of supernatural grace given to him by God and who is wounded in his nature. According to Ratzinger, such an allegory reaches far beyond literal sense. However, according to him, it is also an attempt to precisely define the two types of injuries weighting down humanity. The road from Jerusalem to Jericho thus appears as the image of the world history; the half-dead man, living on the road's edge, is the image of humanity. The priest and the Levite pass by him: salvation will not come merely out of the power of history, merely from their culture, or their religion. If the ambushed is the image of humanity per se, then the Samaritan may be the image of Jesus Christ. God himself, who is a stranger to us, and distant, has opened himself up to adopt his beaten creature. God, distant, has become a neighbour in Jesus. The image of healing Sacraments was seen in the oil and wine poured by the Samaritan into the wounds of the ambushed. The Samaritan, and thus Christ, entrusts the man to the inn and makes a deposit for this care; that is, he entrusts him to the Church, where he is taken care of (Benedict XVI, 2007a, p. 144). Martin Luther (Luther, 35–36) interpreted the parable in a similar way. Thus, these allegories interpreted the parable in the Christological-soteriological sense as a story communicating something about Jesus Christ and the salvation he brings to man.

At the same time, however, it cannot be said that allegorical interpretations were the sole ones in the history. Among others, the Franciscan theologian Bonaventure (1221–1274) already distinguished at his time between textual and allegorical senses. He summarised the textual sense that the Samaritan had helped in weakness and had relieved from the misery (in Latin *supportatio infirmitatis et relevatio mendicitatis*), literally, he *supported weakness* and *relieved the distress*. As true mercy is manifested by deeds, the Samaritan acted – he treated the assaulted and transported him to the inn; Bonaventure referred here to the Old Testament, specifically the books of Ecclesiastes, Proverbs, and the prophet Isaiah (Chapter 58). So, according to him, the transport to the inn symbolises the journey to the Lord's house, being not only the Church but also man's life journey culminating in the encounter with God. At the end he emphasises that which appears important also in our current interpretations (see Chapter 3.3ff): 'And so it is clear that neighbourliness (*proximitas*) is more inclined towards natural love and compassion than to family affiliation' (Bonaventure, 1990, 499–501). Only then does Bonaventure pursue the allegorical interpretation, which he himself describes as the spiritual sense of the text:

- The ambushed man is Adam, passing from Eden (Jerusalem) to the world (Jericho);
- The robbers are demons;
- The priest and the Levite represent the idea that man is saved neither by the Mosaic Law (priest) nor by the admonishments of the prophets (Levite);
- Only Jesus Christ, represented by the Samaritan, will help. His oil and wine poured into the wounds signify the grace of the Sacraments. He transports him to the inn,

that is, to the Church promising his return, that is, Christ's second coming at the end of history (Bonaventure, 1990, pp. 503–507).

Similarly, Erasmus of Rotterdam (1466–1536) distinguishes between textual and allegorical interpretation, although not as explicitly as Bonaventure. According to him, Jesus tells the story to show that God applies the commandment of love of neighbour to the whole of mankind. And this is despite the fact that sometimes the person who is a neighbour is, according to our relationship to him, above all a foreigner and enemy. According to Erasmus, while the priest and the Levite, as they have no compassion, do not help the assaulted even when it is clear that he will die, the Samaritan helps him even when being an enemy. Erasmus automatically considers the ambushed person to be a Jew. Not only does the Samaritan sympathise with him but he also acts practically: he treats his wounds there and, in addition, takes him to the inn (Erasmus, 2003–2016, pp. 272–274). At the end of his paraphrase on this part of the Gospel of Luke, Erasmus adds his interpretation, which is again allegorical; the key point is the identification of Christ with the Samaritan. Christ was despised by the Jews just as the Jews and Samaritans despised each other. The ambushed is a lost sinful human soul that the Christ-Samaritan saves. The innkeeper and inn are the Church to which the rescued soul is entrusted (Erasmus, 2003–2016, pp. 275–276). Even Erasmus, who clearly emphasises the harmony of words in the paraphrases of both dialogues of Jesus and the Scribe (respectively of faith and works), did not avoid allegorical interpretation as the Middle Ages ended and the Modern Age began. In his case this is somewhat paradoxical because the allegorical interpretations of the parable were significantly assisted by the fact that while in the first part – i.e., the dialogue between the Scribe and Jesus – it is clearly a theological problem, the story itself gives a fully secular impression.

That is why ancient and medieval theologians tried to give it a more religious character. But they could accomplish this only by the allegorical explanation that the Samaritan is Jesus who is saving the soul lost – attacked and beaten by sin or demons. Such exegetical attempts reveal the tentativeness of their authors regarding the religious text that does not speak about God at all. As far as the theological themes are present, they are negative because both 'theologians' – the priest and the Levite – fail in the story. That is why the Samaritan's story is not only secular but in a certain way we can also perceive in it an 'anti-theological' emphasis (Theißen, 2008, p. 95) in favour of love for the neighbour.

In 1886 and 1898, the German Protestant theologian Adolf Jülicher published his two-volume work *Die Gleichnisereden Jesu* in Tübingen, where he firmly broke away from the allegorical interpretation of the parable. According to him, Jesus was a brilliant educator and rhetorician and thus there is nothing to be 'explained' regarding the parables in the sense of the need to understand some hidden allegory (Erlemann, Nickel-Bacon, 2014, p. 17). Jülicher's work still influences biblical exegesis as it described several different kinds of parables. It distinguished between a parable (per se), a narrated parable (a parable in a wider sense) and an exemplary narrative:

- *Parable*: Generally, there is only one actor in a common everyday situation telling us something about the kingdom of God.

- *Narrated parable*: Usually, there are multiple actors with a certain tension between them; the story and its stylisation are also important, containing the introduction and conclusion.

The first two types of parables share the aspect that the issue discussed is parenthesised – not being expressed in the story at all. In order to understand what is being discussed, the listener or reader must know the context – the situation that Jesus is commenting on or some preliminary or additional explanation by Jesus.

- *Exemplary narrative*: According to Jülicher, in the case of Luke, this regards the Good Samaritan (10:30–37), as well as the stories of the great harvest and the demolished barns (12:16–21), the rich man and Lazarus (16:19–31), and the Pharisee and the tax collector (18:9–14). The common aspect of these is that the matter in question is not withheld. Thus they are a kind of case studies – examples (*exemplum*) in the form of casuistrics in order to provoke a change in behaviour when erroneous conduct is demasked and corrected by the narration (Erlemann, Nickel-Bacon, 2014, pp. 32–33).

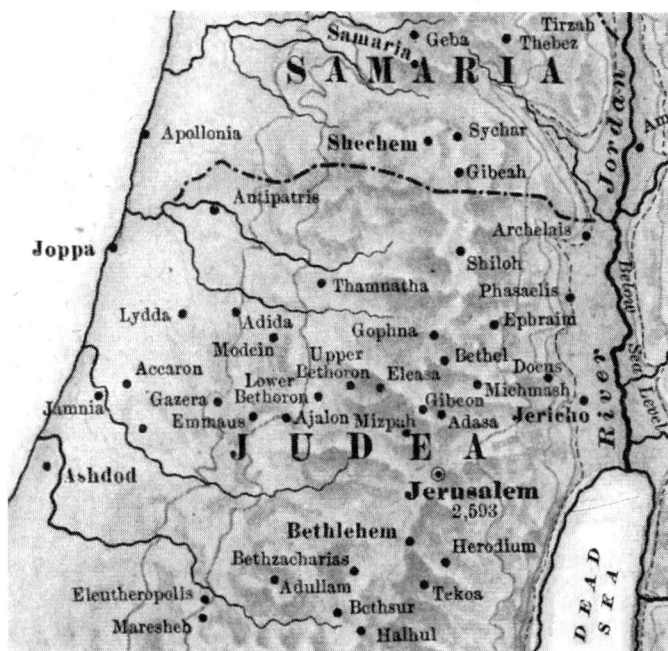

Fig. 14: Palestine in the Time of Jesus: Jerusalem, Jericho, Samaria (Mount Garazim is located near Sychar/Shechem)

This typology of parables has been either adopted or criticised by biblical scholars up to this day. The parable of the Good Samaritan is, according to each author's approach, understood either simply as a parable or as an exemplary narrative. Paradoxically, according to some authors, it is this parable that simply shows that Jülicher's typology is not relevant. Mentioning historical and geographical facts, such as the journey from Jerusalem to Jericho (▸ Fig. 14), does not affect the fact that readers and listeners have to deduce the meaning of the whole narration themselves – the same as in other parables. Moreover, in the story itself, there is no mention about the commandment to love one's neighbour. It becomes clear only from the context – from both dialogues between Jesus and the Scribe that is, from the interaction between the context and the story itself – that the story regards the interpretation of the Mosaic Law. Without this context, even a Jewish listener would have never thought of identifying one's own self with the Samaritan. That is why even here a metaphorical identification of a listener or reader with key figures of the parable takes place (Zimmermann, 2007b, p. 18). In 1947, Joachim Jeremias stood in his work from *Die Gleichnisse Jesu* against Jülicher's concept of parable which tells the 'eternally valid truth'. At the same time, however, he preserved Jülicher's anti-allegorical approach to parables. In this way, Jeremias understood parables as proclaiming the coming of the kingdom of God, including its soteriological and ethical consequences: the aim of the parable is to bring about a change in behaviour and decision-making. Therefore, it is necessary to reconstruct the situations in which the parables arose. Thus, Jeremias was seeking to find *ipsissima vox Christi* – the original words of Jesus Christ hidden under literary ballast piled up by the evangelists (Erlemann, Nickel-Bacon, 2014, pp. 18–19). In the Catholic environment, Pope Benedict XVI adopted the stance of abandoning the allegorical interpretations. According to him, in the case of the Good Samaritan, the individual features of ancient and medieval allegories may simply be dismissed. However, the great vision, that an alienated and helpless man lies along the path of history and that God himself in Jesus Christ becomes his neighbour, should be preserved among historical allegories as a profound dimension of the parable that affects us. For the powerful imperative of the textual meaning of the parable as to what it means to be a neighbour is not diminished by this but is only beginning to reach its full scope (Benedict XVI, 2007a, p. 144). However, the rift between these and allegorical interpretations of the parable began, on the Catholic side, as early as during the Reformation. It was Luther's Catholic opponent Cardinal Cajetan (Tommaso de Vio, 1469–1534) who in interpreting the parables coined the assertion of *omnis homo est proximus* – every man is a neighbour. Cajetan did not rule out the allegorical interpretation in this statement (Vio Caietani, 1639, p. 219) and laid at the time the foundation for ethical-anthropological interpretations of parables that emphasise man's practical conduct. Yet even in Protestant exegesis the position appeared that the original substance of the parable, which Luke had adopted and linked to the theme of the commandment of love of one's neighbour, truly had Christological content. There might have been a story about Christ who takes care for man beaten by sin. If, however, in the Gospel the story of helping the ambushed was linked to the dialogue about the greatest commandment, the content and message of the story itself has also changed. Therefore, it is possible even today to prefer the ethical-anthropological and thus the caritas or diakonic meaning of the whole text (the dialogue plus the parables) without excluding the Christological-theological meaning at the same time (Bovon, 1989, p. 82) which the allegorical interpretations have utilised since antiquity. For *Fratelli tutti* (Francis, 2020) e. g., the parable is not only an example of social friendship. The story before the parable of the Good Samaritan about the Samaritan's village where the residents refuse to provide accommodation for Jesus and his disciples and the disciples would have burned the village by fire (*Lk* 9: 51–56) can be read as the prelude to the parable. Jesus refuses the offer of the disciples to destroy the village and later shows in the parable the Samaritan as an example of social friendship. Therefore, also in this sense according to *Fratelli tutti*, Jesus is the Good Samaritan who set in practice social friendship among enemies (Phan, 2023).

Similarly to allegorical interpretations, the approach focusing on identifying the *ipsissima vox* of Jesus Christ was eventually abandoned because it is not at all decisive for understanding the parables. The decisive factor is Jesus' intention, being the purpose with which he tells the parable. But merely due to this, the historical and linguistic aspects of the parable cannot be considered self-serving. This would only lead to other cases of missing the parable's point, which would ultimately not differ from the older allegories. Historical and linguistic facts presented in parables can therefore always help to deepen the understanding:

> Historical background and linguistic form give the direction for the understanding which cannot be, with regards to the text, interpreted at will. At the same time, they should lead to a deeper understanding, which is pre-set by the impulses for interpretation but ultimately must be carried out by each reader always in a new way. (Zimmermann, 2007b, p. 16)

Thus, the parable is a genre open to interpretation by its listener or reader. He can identify himself with various figures appearing in the parable, and thus always draw a different conclusion for himself. Thus, while European Christians generally identify themselves with the priest and the Levite as being their bad conscience and with the Samaritan as the projected hero whom they would like to be, Christians in the poor neighbourhoods of South American cities see themselves as the assaulted stranger who has nothing left, is laying half dead on the road, and who remains forgotten even for those listeners and readers who would like to be identified with the Samaritan. At the same time, however, parables also contain the above described limits of their interpretation which are intended to decelerate the expansion of possible interpretations by readers and listeners. These regard factual data with which parables work seemingly only in passing. And it is these that must be followed and taken into account when assessing modern allegories, respectively, in attempts to create new modern allegories.

That is also why historical allegorical interpretations cannot be regarded as mistakes or a lack of expertise – the extent to which they respect the limits of the interpretation given by factual data in parables is how much they can be considered legitimate even today. For, while respecting the limits, they actualise the interpretation of the parable which is founded on their openness to various interpretations by readers and listeners. If such limits of interpretation are not exceeded, modern allegories arising within theology of caritas and diakonia are legitimate for the same reason.

3.2 The Gospel according to Luke

The Gospel according to Luke contains some of the most popular and well-known Bible passages – parables acting as miniatures of the Kingdom of God. These include the stories of the prodigal son, the friend who comes to ask for help at midnight, or the persistent widow whose wishes are met by a ruthless judge. Of course, these also include the story of the Good Samaritan as well as other popular biblical passages that are not parables, such as the most dramatic and beautiful narrative of the encounter between the disciples and risen Jesus on their way to Emmaus (Moessner, 2016, p. 13). The so-called third gospel, along with those of Mark and Matthew, is classified as one of the three synoptic (written in the same way) Gospels; at the same time, however, it has its own specifics, just as the other synoptic Gospels have. The most significant one is the emphasis on the so-called greatest commandment – to love God and to love neighbour. Thus, while Luke does not challenge the everlasting validity of the Old Testament he concentrates and unites the entire Mosaic Law in the greatest commandments which may be fulfilled even by some Samaritans (10:26ff) and God-fearing pagans (*Acts* 15) (Pokorný, 1997, p. 47). Therefore, the parable of *Lk* 15:11–32, which tends to be called the Parable of the Merciful Father or of the Lost Son and which is known primarily as the Parable of the Prodigal Son,[2] is regarded as the centrepiece of the Gospel (Pokorný, 2004, p. 14). Thus, in the *Gospel according to Luke*, the

---

[2] Jesus continued: 'There was a man who had two sons. The younger one said to his father, "Father, give me my share of the estate." So he divided his property between them. Not long after that, the younger son got together all he had, set off for a distant country and there squandered his wealth in wild living. After he had spent everything, there was a severe famine in that whole country, and he began to be in need. So he went and hired himself out to a citizen of that country, who sent him to his fields to feed pigs. He longed to fill his stomach with the pods that the pigs were eating, but no one gave him anything. When he came to his senses, he said, "How many of my father's hired servants have food to spare, and here I am starving to death! I will set out and go back to my father and say to him: Father, I have sinned against heaven and against you. I am no longer worthy to be called your son; make me like one of your hired servants." So he got up and went to his father. But while he was still a long way off, his father saw him and was filled with compassion for him; he ran to his son, threw his arms around him and kissed him. The son said to him, "Father, I have sinned against heaven and against you. I am no longer worthy to be called your son." But the father said to his servants, "Quick! Bring the best robe and put it on him. Put a ring on his finger and sandals on his feet. Bring the fattened calf and kill it. Let's have a feast and celebrate. For this son of mine was dead and is alive again; he was lost and is found." So they began to celebrate. Meanwhile, the older son was in the field. When he came near the house, he heard music and dancing. So he called one of the servants and asked him what was going on. "Your brother has come," he replied, "and your father has killed the fattened calf because he has him back safe and sound." The older brother became angry and refused to go in. So his father went out and pleaded with him. But he answered his father, "Look! All these years I've been slaving for you and never disobeyed your orders. Yet you never gave me even a young goat so I could celebrate with my friends. But when this son of yours who has squandered your property with prostitutes comes home, you kill the fattened calf for him!" "My son," the father said, "you are always with me, and everything I have is yours. But we had to

love of neighbour is the ethos of Jesus' redemptive mission which is expressed, in particular, in his 'policy statement' in *Lk* 4:17–21 (see also *Isa* 61:1f):

> and the scroll of the prophet Isaiah was handed to him. Unrolling it, he found the place where it is written: 'The Spirit of the Lord is on me, because he has anointed me to proclaim good news to the poor. He has sent me to proclaim freedom for the prisoners and recovery of sight for the blind, to set the oppressed free, to proclaim the year of the Lord's favor.' Then he rolled up the scroll, gave it back to the attendant and sat down. The eyes of everyone in the synagogue were fastened on him. He began by saying to them, 'Today this scripture is fulfilled in your hearing.'

It is precisely due to this identification of love of neighbour with Jesus' mission that allegorical interpretations in history perceived the Samaritan as an image of Jesus (Söding, 2015, p. 140). The Gospel as a whole is designed in the way that listeners and readers can identify the story of their faith with the story of Jesus and the story of his disciples in the *Acts* (Wolter, 2008, p. 26). That is why historical allegorical interpretations, which lead to the identification of the main character of the parable with Jesus, touch upon one of the essential intentions of the Gospel, despite sometimes overlooking the essential messages of the text that witness to man and his mission in the world.

The origins of the *Gospel according to Luke* is related to the origins of the Gospels according to Mark and Matthew. All three of them are written in a very similar way – being, as already mentioned, *synoptic*; in key places such as the Passion Story, they are virtually identical. On the other hand, they significantly vary, for example, whether they contain any passages about Jesus' childhood and, possibly, upon what topics they focus later. While Matthew and Luke speak of Jesus' childhood, and each of them in a completely different way, Mark does not mention it at all. Similarly, there are specific themes, including the story of the Good Samaritan, which can be found only in one of the synoptic Gospels. The so-called two-source hypothesis might be generally accepted as the explanation of the correspondence and difference between the synoptic Gospels; although it is not excluded that this hypothesis might undergo certain changes, these, however, will most likely be only partial. Theories that work with the older hypothesis (Krämer, 2016), that the original Gospel was the one according to Matthew, etc., while both Luke and Mark were inspired by it, can be considered to be overcome.

The two-source hypothesis in the essence says that both Matthew and Luke had two other sources for writing the Gospels in addition to their own exclusive content. One of them was the *Gospel according to Mark*, or some of its unpreserved version, the other being a hard to specify source containing Jesus' statements, referred to as Q (from German *Quelle*). This theory is known as the so-called necessary hypothesis (Kern, 2007, p. 50), and it entails for the *Gospel according to Luke* that it originated on the foundation of the following sources:

---

celebrate and be glad, because this brother of yours was dead and is alive again; he was lost and is found.'"

a) SG-Lk (*Sondergut Lukas*): Luke's own source not shared with the authors of Mark's and Matthew's Gospels. It also includes the parable of the Good Samaritan although Luke adopts the opening dialogue of the greatest commandment from Mark. In the whole of Luke's Gospel, approximately one-third of the parables is original (Merz, 2007, p. 513).
b) Dt-Mk (*Deuteromarkus*): Mark's Gospel in a certain editorial arrangement that is unknown to us. It is assumed that the presently known text (the oldest preserved copy) is older than the copy used by the author of Luke's Gospel.
c) Q-Lk (*the source containing the statements of Jesus*): The author of Luke's Gospel had this source identical with the author of Matthew's Gospel, however each of them utilised it in a different way and used different parts.

For a long time, the references to Paul of Tarsus in the *Acts of the Apostles* served to determine the period of the Gospel's origin. Paul is the author of other New Testament writings – letters to the first Christian Church communities, that on the foundation of historical facts in the text allow a more accurate dating of its origin. The book of *Acts* is actually the second part of Luke's Gospel (see below). It was therefore deemed that when the *Acts of the Apostles* mentioned Paul without saying anything about his death, these had to be created before his death. Thus, thanks to the facts mentioned in Paul's writings, it was possible to deduce when approximately the *Acts of the Apostles* together with the *Gospel according to Luke* were created. However, Acts, let alone the Gospel, are not Paul's biography; thus the absence of reference to his death used as the evidence for the Acts's origin is a pure speculation. The only truly historical reference to the Gospel of Luke is its first preserved quotation from the mid-second century by Justin Martyr; thus, the Gospel had to originate earlier. This, of course, does not exclude its traditional dating to AD 80s derived from Paul's writings.

From the textual criticism of the *Gospel according to Luke* it is clear that its author possessed encyclopaedic knowledge of the Old Testament, respectively, of its current translation into Greek – the Septuagint – as well as social and cultural realities of that time. Therefore, it must be assumed that he underwent the first Jewish socialisation in his family and his secondary socialisation was also Jewish. It can be said about him that in the Gospel he even attempted to imitate the Septuagint by describing the stories from the life of Jesus Christ as a continuation of Israel's history[3] (Wolter, 2008, pp. 9–10). In other words, he was a Jew who converted to Christianity and was thus well

---

3   The term 'history' in the context of biblical writings should be used with significant caution; it is certainly not possible to understand the then conception of history in today's positivist sense as a description as accurate as possible which is based on preserved sources and archaeological findings. For biblical man, history means above all its interpretation, that is, a theological interpretation of historical events which is significantly more important than reporting of exactly what happened, where, and to whom. In this sense, Luke's Gospel is a history of Jesus Christ because it seeks to show and clarify the events from his life as a continuation of the history of Israel which Septuagint had introduced by its Old Testament structure as the theological explanation of events in Israel-God relationship.

acquainted with Judaism of the time while being perhaps even better orientated in the Hellenic pagan culture in which he, as an urban man, lived and was active.

The scheme of the Gospel of Luke is characterised by its scope and breadth where in the stories of Jesus and his parables, the whole world of that time is reflected, being the 'world' around the Mediterranean Sea. Only in Luke do political and military figures appear in the parables. Also, we can find hatred among ethnicities, as in the case of the Samaritan's story. Typically, everything takes place in a town, which can also be an important context for some of the parables narrated by Jesus at someone's house in a particular town. Sometimes the description of rural reality is not entirely accurate, which corresponds to the fact that the Gospel author is an educated townsman thus knowing only town-life. It may seem, therefore, that the Samaritan story is not particularly typical matter for Luke. On the other hand, it regards a journey between two important towns; this certainly posed a great challenge for the town dwellers at that time, as is evident from the parable working with the theme of an ambush. Another characteristic change in Luke as opposed to Mark and Matthew consists in who represents whom or what – thus in Luke, God can be represented even by a woman (15:8–10).[4] Some parables also contain immoral heroes such as the dishonest steward (16:1–8)[5] or the Samaritan. Here, both the despised Samaritan and the greedy innkeeper with a dubious reputation act correctly (or at least not incorrectly). All of this corresponds to the broad intertextual network of Luke's parables as a spectrum of Old Testament and Hellenistic-Jewish tradition together with the Greek-Roman literary tradition (Merz, 2007, pp. 515–516).

It has already been said that the *Gospel according to Luke* and the *Acts of the Apostles* arose as a two-part literary opus. They are interconnected by both the literary addressee – noble Theophilos (in Czech Bohumil, being a God-loving reader) – as well as the theme of journeys, together with the image of life and faith as journeys. Thus, while in the Gospel Jesus travels to Jerusalem, where he would die and be resurrected while passing on his message to the disciples, in Acts Jesus' message travels through his disciples from Jerusalem to the centre of the world at that time – to Rome. We

---

4   Or suppose a woman has ten silver coins and loses one. Doesn't she light a lamp, sweep the house and search carefully until she finds it? And when she finds it, she calls her friends and neighbors together and says, 'Rejoice with me; I have found my lost coin.' In the same way, I tell you, there is rejoicing in the presence of the angels of God over one sinner who repents.
5   Jesus told his disciples: 'There was a rich man whose manager was accused of wasting his possessions. So he called him in and asked him, "What is this I hear about you? Give an account of your management, because you cannot be manager any longer." The manager said to himself, "What shall I do now? My master is taking away my job. I'm not strong enough to dig, and I'm ashamed to beg – I know what I'll do so that, when I lose my job here, people will welcome me into their houses." So he called in each one of his master's debtors. He asked the first, "How much do you owe my master?" "Nine hundred gallons of olive oil," he replied. The manager told him, "Take your bill, sit down quickly, and make it four hundred and fifty." Then he asked the second, "And how much do you owe?" "A thousand bushels of wheat," he replied. He told him, "Take your bill and make it eight hundred." The master commended the dishonest manager because he had acted shrewdly. For the people of this world are more shrewd in dealing with their own kind than are the people of the light.'

can therefore perceive the structure of the Gospel as episodic narratives about Jesus' journeys to Jerusalem:

1. 2:22–40: Joseph and Mary bring the child Jesus to Jerusalem Temple.
2. 2:41–52: Joseph and Mary travel with twelve-year-old Jesus to Jerusalem Temple.
3. 4:9–14: The Devil takes Jesus to the top of the Temple to tempt him before the beginning of his public ministry.
4. 9:51–19:44: The great journey of Jesus from Galilee to Jerusalem. In the Gospel, this narrative takes place of approximately 40% of the text and includes the story of the Good Samaritan.
5. 22:54–24:51: The Passion Story in which Jesus goes – though later being led handcuffed – to the Father, starting from the Last Supper, through the Mount of Olives, to various courts in Jerusalem, Golgotha, the tomb, and Galilee, where resurrected he meets his disciples.

Importantly, both the fourth and fifth journeys are journeys of Jesus' free decision. The execution is therefore not presented as something that Jesus would obey but as what he accepted voluntarily and out of love (Moessner, 2016, p. 22–28). This reflects the main thematic intention of the Gospel, that is, to convey God's love for man which goes to the extreme – Jesus dies rather than intervenes with divine power against the people doing him wrong and hurting him. However, it is also necessary to add that in his narrative of stories about Jesus and his teaching, the author does not separate the individual episodes by any headings or at least spaces, etc. He divided the Gospel text only by the way of writing it, thus separating the episodes as a part of the text. That is why we can find in exegetic literature quite a lot of alternative approaches and explanations of the structure of the third Gospel (Wolter, 2008, p. 16).

As the whole Gospel is based on the theme of God's love for man, which goes even beyond the death of the Son of God, the fundamental elements of the theology of Luke's parables might be characterised as follows:

- Forgiveness of sins and God's search for those lost (7:42–43; 15:1–32; 18:9–14);
- Change of status and abandonment of status – abandonment of the attributed socio-cultural status in favour of the status obtained by right conduct (14:7–24; 18:9–14);
- Criticism of property ownership and property *paraenesis* – encouragement of suitable property management (12:16–21,22–34; 16:1–13,19–31);
- Prayer (11:5–8,11–13; 18:1–8,9–14).

On the other hand, in comparison with the Gospel of Matthew, he does not pay much attention to the Last Judgment, except in situations of criticism of greedy property ownership (16:23–26,28). The emphasis on active conduct is important also, which appears also in the story of the Good Samaritan (Merz, 2007, pp. 516–517). The scheme of the whole Gospel seems nowadays much more important than the issue of its sources. Thus, the preference is given to the synchronous interpretation of the Gospels (rather than the diachronic interpretation) where each author had his image of the story of Jesus Christ thus it is necessary to consider how he presented this story (Wolter, 2008, p. 11).

3.3 The Good Samaritan in contemporary exegetic literature

The well-known quote from Mark's Gospel (4:9) is true for this parable: Whoever has ears to hear, let them hear.

> The ambiguity of each parable thus corresponds to the structure of its call. Since it is not always possible to determine precisely the meaning of the figurative language in text, it must be sought and found by the reader. Since the parables are open to interpretation, they are also active in interpretation, i.e., they evoke interpretation. In other words, parables invite readers and listeners to engage in the process of understanding. (Zimmermann, 2007b, pp. 13–14)

Such a characteristic is true for the Good Samaritan story more than anywhere else. The whole parable, including the opening and closing dialogues between Jesus and the Scribe, has almost a Socratic nature and structure (Söding, 2015, p. 130) as questions quickly follow one another thus provoking the listener or reader to answer them before the answers appear in the following verse:

- The Scribe asks Jesus about the meaning of life (v. 25);
- Jesus asks back by referring to the Law (v. 26);
- The Scribe quotes the dual commandment of love (v. 27);
- Jesus confirms this and calls us regarding conduct (v. 28);
- The Scribe asks Jesus about the identity of one's neighbour (v. 29);
- Jesus asks back by telling the parable (vv. 30–36);
- The Scribe gives the right answer (v. 37a);
- Jesus calls us regarding conduct (v. 37b).

When interpreting the parable of the Good Samaritan, it thus must not be forgotten that the dialogues between Jesus and the Scribe are integral parts preceding and concluding the parable itself, respectively, framing it. According to some opinions, the dialogues and the parable itself belong together right from the beginning; they are a part of the tradition upon which the Gospel author drew. This is indicated by their linguistic similarities (Bovon, 1989, p. 88), however, according to other opinions, the author connected the story of the Good Samaritan from his own source to the dialogue of the greatest commandments he had adopted from Mark's Gospel. In fact, the commandment of love required from the Israelites the same attitude toward the Lord and the neighbour (Fitzmyer, 1970–1985, p. 878). In the *Gospel according to Luke*, these two commandments are indeed connected joined into one – they are more equal than in both other synoptics; it is all the more logical to link the dialogue of the greatest commandments to the story of the Good Samaritan (Johnson, 2005, p. 195). If the Scribe was asking from the beginning the question of who the neighbour is in order to push Jesus into a corner, he probably was asking about what Jesus had talked about repeatedly. Therefore, he then also wanted to justify himself. It follows that, according to the tradition of Luke, Jesus principally emphasised the interconnection of the two commandments, respectively, the practical way of life according to the commandments (Jeremias, 1984, p. 134). When Jesus in the dialogue first refers to the

Law of Moses and to one's conscience by letting the Scribe find the answer himself, the passage also aims at showing Jesus' convincingness and humanity. As a result, the persuasiveness of the commandments of love is also shown (Söding, 2015, p. 130). At the same time, it is evident that the author of the text deliberately uses elements of dialogue in the style of Wisdom literature that are known from rabbinic wisdom when he says 'you think' instead of 'is' and uses the term 'was neighbour to' rather than 'my neighbour' (Bovon, 1989, pp. 82–83). In fact, he is trying put the listener or reader to the position to identify himself with the Scribe and to let himself be drawn into the search for answers to the questions asked.

The exceptions to the love of neighbour, that is, to the question of who to consider as a neighbour, were probably a subject of discussions among Jewish scholars of that time. In fact, the series the Scribe's questions regards how far his duties go (Jeremias, 1984, pp. 134–135). Thus, the parable refers to the practice of that time when, contrary to *Lev* 19:34,[6] foreigners were 'crossed out' from the law of love, respectively, outside of Israel the law of love was restricted only to the proselytes.[7] The Pharisees then 'crossed out' even those Israelites who did not abide by the Mosaic Law (prostitutes, tax collectors, etc.), and directly forbade the love to Israel's opponents (Stöger, 1964, p. 300). However, as with the other two synoptics, Jesus does not criticise such a question but answers it (Söding, 2015, p. 131). Only in Luke's gospel, however, does he respond with the story of the Samaritan who helped the half-dead assaulted by the road. Although it may seem obvious today, it is not at all certain that neither the listeners of Jesus at that time nor the listeners and readers of Luke's Gospel associated the commandment of love for one's neighbour with universal human solidarity. The Samaritan's course of action corresponded to the ancient ethos of the time that it is right and necessary to help a person in need; this does not therefore formulate any new, specifically Christian, ethics. In comparison with Mark and Matthew, however, there is another significant difference in Luke's Gospel, regarding how the dialogue about the greatest commandment is presented. For, the Scribe does not ask directly about the greatest commandment but about what to do to gain eternal life.[8] For

---

6   The foreigner residing among you must be treated as your native-born. Love them as yourself, for you were foreigners in Egypt. I am the Lord your God.

7   Converts to Judaism.

8   *The Gospel according to Mark* 12:28–34: One of the teachers of the law came and heard them debating. Noticing that Jesus had given them a good answer, he asked him, 'Of all the commandments, which is the most important?' 'The most important one,' answered Jesus, 'is this: "Hear, O Israel: The Lord our God, the Lord is one. Love the Lord your God with all your heart and with all your soul and with all your mind and with all your strength." The second is this: "Love your neighbor as yourself." There is no commandment greater than these.' 'Well said, teacher,' the man replied. 'You are right in saying that God is one and there is no other but him. To love him with all your heart, with all your understanding and with all your strength, and to love your neighbor as yourself is more important than all burnt offerings and sacrifices.' When Jesus saw that he had answered wisely, he said to him, 'You are not far from the kingdom of God.' And from then on no one dared ask him any more questions. *The Gospel according to Matthew* 22:34–40: Hearing that Jesus had silenced the Sadducees, the Pharisees got together. One of them, an expert in the law, tested him with this

some authors, this is the reason to believe that Luke's dialogue is not at all related to those of Mark and Matthew (Schürmann, 1994, pp. 129–140).

The author of the *Gospel according to Luke* gives the story his own specific meaning through connection with the dialogue about the greatest commandment. He expresses the idea that the Law given by God must be interpreted with love being its meaning. An interpretation of the Law that would be against love or would be preventing it would be wrong. Knowledge of this Law must therefore lead to concrete actions (Stöger, 1964, p. 300). The interconnection of the two parts of the text – the dialogue and the parable – is very close or even intimate, despite Jesus not actually answering the Scribe's question (Fitzmyer, 1970–1985, pp. 882–883). Instead of answering, he tells him a parable that is

> ...the opposite of the parable of the merciful father. The commandment of love, summarising the Law, knows no boundaries. In the *Gospel according to Luke*, parables act as responses to the attempts of Jesus' disciples who wanted to punish the Samarian village (*Lk* 9:51–56), as Elijah had done to the scoffers in the Old Testament (*2 Kings* 2:23–25, cf. 1:10,12). Luke certainly knows the stories of miraculous punishment (see *Acts* 5) but the first and decisive movement that accompanies faith is in his interpretation the movement of concrete, creative love. (Pokorný, 1997, p. 194)

This is clear also from the story following that of the Good Samaritan, namely from the story of Mary and Martha (*Lk* 10:38–42).[9] Both stories regard the tension between love for God and love for neighbour. The author of the Gospel thus follows his basic intention that theology (and especially Christology as the teaching about Christ) and service to one's neighbour (diaconia) are one – to be listening and acting (Hoppe, 2006, p. 33). This is the author's obvious literary concept, which links parables throughout the whole Gospel into thematic groups that are intended to illuminate the subject through several different narrations (Merz, 2007, pp. 513–514). Thus, such a conception of Luke's Gospel, where the author connects secular and theological themes – love for neighbour and love for God – can be understood that love for neighbour as expected by God can be exemplarily carried out even by those who do not have apparent religious motives for helping others (Theißen, 2008, p. 95).[10]

---

question: 'Teacher, which is the greatest commandment in the Law?' Jesus replied: '"Love the Lord your God with all your heart and with all your soul and with all your mind." This is the first and greatest commandment. And the second is like it: "Love your neighbor as yourself." All the Law and the Prophets hang on these two commandments.'

9   As Jesus and his disciples were on their way, he came to a village where a woman named Martha opened her home to him. She had a sister called Mary, who sat at the Lord's feet listening to what he said. But Martha was distracted by all the preparations that had to be made. She came to him and asked, 'Lord, don't you care that my sister has left me to do the work by myself? Tell her to help me!' 'Martha, Martha,' the Lord answered, 'you are worried and upset about many things, but few things are needed – or indeed only one. Mary has chosen what is better, and it will not be taken away from her.'

10 This motif also appears in Matthew's Gospel in the well-known discourse on the Last Judgment (*Mt* 25:31–46) which is sometimes preferred as a theory of Christian, and especially Catholic, charity. If read superficially, it would be easy to confuse the person who needs

However, love for neighbour is exclusive neither to the *Gospel according to Luke* nor to the New Testament; it is shared with the Old Testament. The boundaries between the Old and New Testaments are not so much in the neighbourly love as in the love of the enemies (Gollwitzer, 1962, p. 40) which is, in a certain way, emphasised and explained by the story of the Good Samaritan. In the Old Testament, love for one's neighbour was understood as mutual loyalty, respectively, reciprocity, and therefore it was applied primarily to members of their own nation. Nevertheless, from the understanding of love for the enemies both in the Old and New Testaments, it is evident that in some parts of the Old Testament it is also understood in the sense of reciprocity as known in antiquity: through solidarity, enemies must be 'pulled' back into the ties of reciprocal solidarity. From this point of view, the parable of the Good Samaritan does not bring any specific ethos, except that the love of neighbour is applied also to situations of general interpersonal help to those in need (Stegemann, 2010, pp. 290–295). In the pagan environment, which together with the Old Testament had a considerable influence on Luke's Gospel – at least in literally aspects (see Chapter 3.2) – at the time of the Gospel, philanthropy was understood passively in the spirit of Stoic philosophy, that is, not as an activity but rather an attitude. It consisted in avoiding conflicts and recognising humanity. For Luke, philanthropy and neighbourly love are, on the contrary, a mission, missionary work, and active rescue of the one who is lost in some way. His Gospel, including the Good Samaritan story, might therefore be read also as an active protest against those who have drawn the boundaries in the Hellenic world other than of passive philanthropy. For Luke, active conduct of man is a manifestation of assumed responsibility, connected with the renewal of the whole God's creation. Such conduct is forthcoming to fulfilling Jesus' message of salvation from God for man (Pokorný, 1997, p. 195). Jesus will not, in this sense, universalise *Lev* 19:18 (a commandment of neighbourly love); however, he shows who is a member of God's covenant people. Thus, it is one who is able to fulfil the commandment of neighbourly love from *Lev* 19:18, i. e., a Samaritan from the geographical and religious periphery (Brown, Yamazaki-Ransom, 2021). Therefore, the primary intention of the text is the question of man's salvation, not the ethical consideration of acting in a particular situation. Indeed, it was also the opening question of the expert in the Law at the beginning of the dialogue.

The story of the Good Samaritan thus connects the different 'worlds' in the same way as their borders are to be overcome in God's kingdom in the vision brought by Jesus Christ of the future relationships between man and God, men to each other and to the whole creation. The story thus transcends the boundaries of hostility between the Israelites and the Samaritans in favour of love for the enemies. It crosses the boundaries between religious legalism and active solidarity in favour of love for one's neighbour (Hoppe, 2006, p. 31) because of which it also emphasises the crossing of

---

help with Jesus Christ and thus ascribe noble religious motives to one's own helping actions. In fact, in its own text, the passage explicitly excludes this by repeatedly saying that those helping are not aware of helping those in need because Jesus Christ has identified himself with those in need.

the boundary between the passivity of declared attitudes and the activity of practical conduct. The theme of love for one's neighbour is therefore one of the key themes of the whole of Luke's Gospel which thus thematically moves closer to the fourth Gospel, that according to John, despite no textual link between them. At the time when both Gospels emerged there seemed to be the need to better explain the question of Christ's death on the cross, which was interpreted as a sacrifice for sins in the Mark's and Matthew's Gospels and in Paul's letters. This is why John substitutes the story of the Last Supper with the story where Jesus washes his disciples' feet before the Last Supper as if he were the last slave in the house – this being the story of Jesus' service which should be a model for other people. Luke's interpretation of Jesus' death also seeks to revive an older profession of faith than that of Paul's teaching regarding justification or Mark's substitutive sacrifice of Christ for man's sins. Paul and Mark deepened the teaching on the substitutive sacrifice drawing new consequences for Christian faith and practice. Subsequently, Luke came up with an even newer interpretation which, however, is connected with much older concepts of Jesus' significance among the early Christians. In Luke's story, Jesus is, in his whole 'history', the fulfilment of true humanity from which one can learn the true character of God. In this sense, Jesus is the Son of God – it is the whole of his life story (later described as the Incarnation, that is, God becoming man), not merely his death on the cross, that is the matter of salvation (Pokorný, 2004, pp. 10–12). Therefore, it is not at all surprising that before Jesus begins to tell the story of the Samaritan, the Scribe asks what to do to gain eternal life. In parallel places in Mark and Matthew, the question regards 'merely' which commandment is the greatest in the Mosaic Law. The Scribe's question of eternal life in Luke shows that he belongs among the Pharisees[11] who believe in the resurrection and the decisive role of earthly life for the afterlife. And this is the theme of interest in the *Gospel according to Luke*.

The question of what a man must do to inherit eternal life (10:25) does not have a clear answer in the Torah. It does not have the particular quotation which could be assigned to this question as the proper answer. Therefore, this question is open to different answers with different hermeneutics of Moses' law in the background (Keddie, 2020). In the story that Jesus tells instead of answering the question of who one's neighbour is, the most surprising character is that of the Samaritan. When the ambushed is not helped by the priest or the Levite, the then listener or reader expects an ordinary Israelite to help – due to the triad of priests, Levites, and the whole of Israel, which the Jewish nation understood through periphrasis at that time. Therefore, the story was surely provoking disillusionment and disappointment in Jesus' listeners when suddenly a Samaritan appeared (Zimmermann, 2007a, pp. 547–548). The Israelites and the Samaritans could be to each other a so-called 'proximate other'. In their faith and self-understanding, they were too similar and, therefore, too close to each other. That could be a solid reason to set up and develop different forms of demar-

---

11 Pharisees was the religious party of Judaism in Jesus time. They focused their lives on very precise keeping the precepts of the Mosaic Law (Torah) and oral tradition of its interpretation.

cation to each other (Keddie, 2020). Thus, if the helping person is a Samaritan, this reveals the then extravagant intent of the Gospel author to create a paradigm impression of the text in the sense that *the love of one's neighbour also includes helping a person in need – and this includes also enemies* (Stegemann, 2010, pp. 295–296). It can therefore be said that the parable of the Good Samaritan clearly expresses Jesus' innermost purpose (Schürmann, 1994, p. 150): if the parable of the merciful father is a kind of an opposite to the parable of the merciful Samaritan, this is so that the former presents the image of God as should be seen by man, while the latter is the image of man as is seen by God — that is, how God *wants* to see him. It was as early as Luther who argued that the parable presents love for one's neighbour as a 'test question' regarding love of God: God does not need anything, therefore he wants Christians to help those in need in order to show their love to God (Luther, 29).

When the Samaritan sees the ambushed, he is, according to Czech translations, 'moved by compassion' (Czech Ecumenical Translation) or 'felt sorry for him' (Czech Liturgical Translation); 'er sah ihn und hatte Mitleid' (German Einheitsübersetzung); in English 'took pity on him' (NIV) or 'when he saw him, he had compassion on him' (KJV) or 'was moved with compassion when he saw him' (RNJB). However I am using primary the NIV translation in this book, is necessary take regard to the original text and its purpose, which is with "took pity" in NIV slightly obscured. The other translations emphasise the original Greek meening, the Samaritan is moved by compassion from within (this can also be translated as from the bowels, entrails, or from maternal lap) and not from the heart as we would say nowadays. In the ancient culture of that time, the heart was the seat of reason, mind, rational thinking. While on the other hand, within-ness was the seat of emotions, that is, including compassion and pity (Stegemann, 2010, p. 296). Here, the Gospel author uses the expression based on the Greek *splángchnon* to express the Samaritan's feelings. This is a word that denotes the within as a place of such stirrings as compassion, eventually, generosity and kindness. So, if we wanted to somehow describe this expression, we could say that when the Samaritan came to that place and saw the ambushed, everything stirred within him. Likewise, the Gospel author speaks a few chapters further on about the father who from a distance watches his prodigal son return. His father was stirred (*esplagchnízomai*) when he saw him coming even in the distance. This is not meant as empty sentimentality. The father's stirring has its context, being his righteousness: although the younger son has squandered away his whole inheritance, the mercy of his father allowed his joy to be the same as that of the older son but without the father depriving the older one of anything (Söding, 2016b, pp. 22–23). Similarly, the story of the Samaritan has its context in the practical help that the ambushed received from the Samaritan. The true humanity, as is seen by God, consists in the love for neighbour, which then reveals God's true character. This is seen in the combination of the two stories and their interconnection through the stirring moment: the Samaritan, as a human, was completely stirred when he saw the ambushed laying nearby the road similarly to everything stirring in the father, as did in God, when he saw his returning son.

The author of Luke's Gospel is characterised by telling a story using a triad – alternatively a pair – of characters. This can regard opposites, gradual escalation, as well as complementation. This enables the listeners and readers to identify themselves in various degrees with different characters thus through the parable it strengthens and evokes new behaviour and conduct as well as the parables' interpretations (Merz, 2007, p. 514). Thus, in the parable we can see the escalation in the triad of the priest, the Levite, and the Samaritan, with the failing pair of the priest and the Levite, the assisting pair of the Samaritan and the innkeeper, as well as the self-help pair of the Samaritan and the ambushed.

According to the concept of his Gospel, Luke divides parables into several units. The largest part is in 9:50–19:27 – in the so-called report on the great journey from Galilee to Jerusalem (Merz, 2007, p. 513). So, Jesus tells the parable of the Good Samaritan as his first parable after setting out on a journey to Jerusalem. He talks about this journey between Jerusalem and Jericho exactly when he is setting out on it. He shows that God's way is not a way of confrontation – with the Samaritans, Romans, and various pagans. It therefore regards an invitation to God's path of peace (Wright, 2016, p. 162). Jesus tells many parables and many times comes into dispute over the interpretation of the Law of Moses but only in the case of the Good Samaritan is the interpretation of the Law illustrated so clearly by a parable (Hendrickx, 1997, p. 54). From the textual point of view, the dialogue about the greatest commandments and the story of the Good Samaritan are two independent segments that may exist separately but here they were organically combined into one unit (Theißen, 2008, p. 94). As a result, the author's foundational intention becomes clear, that is, that the love of neighbour is not required as much as a condition of salvation but coincides with Jesus' ethos per se. This is underpinned by the fact that Jesus expresses this requirement at the beginning of the journey which ends with his condemnation and crucifixion. He expresses the requirement for love for one's neighbour in the view of his death and resurrection, and as something that man has inscribed in his heart (Söding, 2015, p. 143). However, this also means that the only aspect that matters is action, due to the death and resurrection of Jesus Christ. It is therefore possible to paraphrase the Letter of James (*James* 2:15–17)[12] which warns against the combination of faith and compassion without the consequences of concrete actions: 'faith by itself, if it is not accompanied by action, is dead' (Gollwitzer, 1962, p. 54).

---

12 Suppose a brother or a sister is without clothes and daily food. If one of you says to them, 'Go in peace; keep warm and well fed,' but does nothing about their physical needs, what good is it? In the same way, faith by itself, if it is not accompanied by action, is dead.

3.4   Commentary on individual verses in *Lk* 10:25–37

Although it is clear from the Old Testament books that the law of love for neighbours regarded all Israelites[13] as well as the aliens living among them,[14] the story of the Good Samaritan shows that its fulfilment has not been without difficulty. Yet the initial dialogue between Jesus and the Scribe helps the listeners and readers of the Samaritan story to focus on essentials aspects. In this chapter, therefore, attention will be paid to the individual Bible verses the story is comprised of in order to provide sufficient understanding of particular themes that make up the whole parable. Regardless of the importance of the initial dialogue between Jesus and the Scribe for the proper understanding of the parable, attention will be paid here above all to the Samaritan story itself. The dialogue and its matters (the greatest commandment) were discussed in the previous sections of this chapter and it is also the context of the key theme within this book.

The following section will be divided according to individual verses.

> 10:25 On one occasion an expert in the law stood up to test Jesus. 'Teacher,' he asked, 'what must I do to inherit eternal life?'
> 10:26 'What is written in the Law?' he replied. 'How do you read it?'
> 10:27 He answered, '"Love the Lord your God with all your heart and with all your soul and with all your strength and with all your mind"; and, "Love your neighbor as yourself."'
> 10:28 'You have answered correctly,' Jesus replied. 'Do this and you will live.'
> 10:29 But he wanted to justify himself, so he asked Jesus, 'And who is my neighbor?'
> 10:30 In reply Jesus said: 'A man was going down from Jerusalem to Jericho, when he was attacked by robbers. They stripped him of his clothes, beat him and went away, leaving him half dead.
> 10:31 A priest happened to be going down the same road, and when he saw the man, he passed by on the other side.
> 10:32 So too, a Levite, when he came to the place and saw him, passed by on the other side.
> 10:33 But a Samaritan, as he traveled, came where the man was; and when he saw him, he took pity on him.
> 10:34 He went to him and bandaged his wounds, pouring on oil and wine. Then he put the man on his own donkey, brought him to an inn and took care of him.
> 10:35 The next day he took out two denarii and gave them to the innkeeper. "Look after him," he said, "and when I return, I will reimburse you for any extra expense you may have."
> 10:36 Which of these three do you think was a neighbor to the man who fell into the hands of robbers?'
> 10:37 The expert in the law replied, 'The one who had mercy on him.' Jesus told him, 'Go and do likewise.'

10:25 On one occasion an expert in the law stood up to test Jesus. 'Teacher,' he asked, 'what must I do to inherit eternal life?'

---

13   'Do not seek revenge or bear a grudge against anyone among your people, but love your neighbor as yourself. I am the Lord.' (Lev 19:18)
14   'The foreigner residing among you must be treated as your native-born. Love them as yourself, for you were foreigners in Egypt. I am the LORD your God.' (Lev 19:34)

Both Luke's Gospel and the Pharisees, who act there as opponents of Jesus, use the meaning of earthly life as their constitutive foundation for the life after death – earthly life for eternal life. As already explained, the parable of the Good Samaritan is therefore one of the neuralgic places of the third Gospel. In essence, the dispute between Jesus and Pharisees regards nothing less than how to live earthly life so that after death it might continue with eternal life, that is, with life with God. On the one hand, it is a purely religious and highly complicated theological question, on the other hand it is a reality of everyday life – as individual parables show. That is why the parable of the Good Samaritan is also introduced by the question expressing the core of the dispute, what must be done to obtain eternal life. While Jesus sees the answer thanks to the Law of Moses as quite clear, the Scribe, as was shown immediately afterwards, follows from the onset his own strategy of the Pharisaic side; this is indicated by the remark that he intends to push Jesus into a corner.

> Thus, by his question, the Scribe revealed both the entire attitude of the Pharisaic side as well as a man subjected to strict divine demands: he revealed the secret egoism which this situation is forced him into and which falsifies worship to be self-service. But at first, he does not mind this at all. He is certain of his cause, he is certain of the correctness of such piety. (Gollwitzer, 1962, p. 31)

10:26 'What is written in the Law?' he replied. 'How do you read it?'

Jesus knows the answer to the opening question very well, nevertheless he lets the Law expert answer it by himself. There are several good reasons for this. The first one is the aforementioned literary intention of the Gospel author when he draws his readers and listeners into the situation to identify themselves with the Scribe and to answer for themselves before hearing or reading the answer. With this question Jesus affiliates himself with the Mosaic Law, submits to it, and rules out denying it. At the same time, however, he submits also the Scribe to the Law, who raised himself above the Law through the combination of his competencies and manipulative questioning (Gollwitzer, 1962, pp. 32–33). Jesus disarms the Scribe escaping from his rhetorical trap immediately after it was set up. He thus takes control over the situation – from now on, only he asks questions, respectively, the Scribe no longer asks them to push Jesus into a corner but merely in self-defence. Thus, Jesus is not being dragged by the development of the situation but is in control of it; in his hands it becomes a means to convey one of the most important parts of his message about God and man.

10:27 He answered, '"Love the Lord your God with all your heart and with all your soul and with all your strength and with all your mind"; and, "Love your neighbor as yourself."'

Unlike in Mark and Matthew, in Luke's Gospel it is the Scribe, not Jesus, who pronounces the dual commandment of love. As referred to in the previous verse, the dual commandment is thus presented as a 'reading of the Mosaic Law' – thus the foundational orientation for Christian life is given already by the Mosaic Law. By affirming the answer to the Scribe with the words 'Do this and you will live,' Jesus takes the Old Testament prescription making it a Christian position (Fitzmyer, 1970–1985, pp. 878–879). Here, Luke builds on his intention to present the life and work of Jesus Christ as a continuation of the Old Testament thus the Scribe with his correct and specific answer actually confirms the continuity between Judaism and Christianity (Wolter, 2008, p. 394). Because he is a layman, his authority does not stem from the priesthood but only from his Scriptural knowledge (Gollwitzer, 1962, p. 27). Thus, when he, and not Jesus, cites the Law of Moses and its dual commandment of love for God and neighbour, it is more than apparent that the commandment of love for neighbour did not appear with Christianity. Therefore, the story of love for neighbour and help to neighbour which is considered to be a classic Christian example, that is, the Samaritan story, actually does not bring anything new *in the matter of justification of specifically Christian motivation to help*. On the contrary, it makes it possible for all people to recognise, understand and appreciate the motivation to help. More specifically, it makes it possible to recognise, understand and appreciate also other motivations to help which may not be explicitly only Christian or Judeo-Christian (Theißen, 2008, pp. 95–96). The story of the Good Samaritan is thus a Judeo-Christian view of the problem of interpersonal solidarity as a phenomenon that is not exclusive to either Jews or Christians.

10:28 'You have answered correctly,' Jesus replied. 'Do this and you will live.'

Almost unprecedented emphasis on the practical conduct, which is the climax of the first dialogue, is related to man, not to God, thus this does not regard self-justification (Bovon, 1989, p. 87). So, the parable is not intending to say that man could deserve eternal life by practical solidarity, that is, to force God to reward him after death. Both Old and New Testaments oppose in many places this concept of religion as a 'something for something' exchange between man and God. God is a sovereign who acts out of love and affection for his creation and for man in it, not because man gained him to his side or somehow brought him under control. Such an approach would be magic, not a religion of a Judeo-Christian concept. Therefore, God reveals the demands required of man in the way as is shown in the dialogue of Jesus and the Scribe, respectively, in the story of the Good Samaritan. The connection between eternal life as a reward from God and the practice of everyday life is therefore in this story far from the system of rewards for merits.

> The connection is not that the ethics of love is made a precondition of salvation; it much more consists in the fact that the possibility of eternal life lays requirements on earthly life to seek love for one's neighbour. The deep reason lies in the fact that love for one's neighbour – within the limits of human abilities – serves life where its fulfilment can come only from God in his love. (Söding, 2015, p. 132)

Salvation as the eternal life with God, about which the Scribe asks at the beginning, is not a reward for solidarity. Rather, it is an offer freely given and always available which commits those interested to act in accordance with it: if one wants to accept it, he should in ordinary situations of life act towards other people as selflessly and willingly as God does when he gives his offer to him.

3.4 Commentary on individual verses in Lk 10:25–37

> **10:29** But he wanted to justify himself, so he asked Jesus, 'And who is my neighbor?'

In the context of the Old Testament, respectively *Lev* 19:17f and 19:34, this is not a bad question. On the contrary, the commandment of love in the Old Testament raised other questions, especially to whom the commandments of love apply *here and now*. Therefore, for example, according to Söding it is a mistake to speculate about the Scribe's dubious motives, even when the whole pericope is introduced by the comment that he wanted to push Jesus into a corner (Söding, 2015, p. 133). In Judaism at that time, however, it was the Pharisees who were inclined to the interpretation that not all the contemporaries should have been considered neighbours. The way the Scribe asked therefore points to him being one of the Pharisees. Such questions are always asked where competition takes place between loyalty towards different social environments. It is therefore clear that this problem soon became a controversial point among Christians as well when it was applied to their relationship to the Jews or Gentiles. In the end, it became one of the factors separating Christianity from Judaism (Pokorný, 1997, p. 193), (Wolter, 2008, p. 395). Therefore, in the interpretation of the text, it is often emphasised that it is a manifestation of the Scribe's self-love. He loved himself and therefore he wanted to justify himself – he wanted to rid himself of the sentence pronounced over him by the commandment to love his neighbour, being a self-loving and thus, in fact, not-loving person (Gollwitzer, 1962, p. 47). With such a question he attempts to save his own eternal life because if he casts doubt upon the notion of his neighbour he also casts doubt upon the commandment to love the neighbour (Bovon, 1989, p. 87). The core of the matter is clarified at this point when the Scribe asks who his neighbour is. Only now the Scribe does not ask about a banality that every little boy must have known then, that is, which the greatest commandment is. Now he starts dealing with Jesus openly. Verses 29 and 36 are therefore crucial for the story:

- v. 29: And who is my neighbor?
- v. 36: Which of these three do you think was a neighbor to the man who fell into the hands of robbers?

Both verses seem to contradict each other linguistically when in verse 36 Jesus reverses the original question of v. 29; in fact, it is the author's obvious intention to make the listener or reader connect the two verses (Meisinger, 1996, p. 53). Thus, with his question of who his neighbour was, Jesus now took full charge of the dialogue with the Scribe.

> **10:30** In reply Jesus said: 'A man was going down from Jerusalem to Jericho, when he was attacked by robbers. They stripped him of his clothes, beat him and went away, leaving him half dead.

In the dialogue with the Scribe, Jesus has the Scribe answer what he reads in the Law. This confirms the commandment of love for one's neighbour in the Old Testament from which Luke wants to continue. However, Jesus' narrative per se is a new interpretation of the Law of Moses which distinguished Christianity from Judaism itself and Jewish sects of that time (Bovon, 1989, p. 83). It is also worth noting that Jesus does not attack the Scribe in any way, that is, he does not doubt his question nor argue with his approach to the Law. Jesus does not attack his certainty (Gollwitzer, 1962, p. 49) but gives him space – as is typical of the genre of parables – to see for himself that he is mistaken. This is then manifested in the final dialogue when the Scribe recognises that the commandment of love for neighbour had been fulfilled by the Samaritan.

The road from Jerusalem to Jericho was infamous for ambushes (Bovon, 1989, p. 89). The towns are only about 27 km apart as the crow flies, however, they lie at very different altitudes. From 750 m above the sea level where Jerusalem lies one descends to Jericho to a lowland lying 400 m below the sea level. The elevation of 1150m must be overcome, accompanied by a significant climate change. Although the Romans later built a road here, at the time when the parable was written this was not the case. For the climb and descent, a path through a rocky desert and wadi to the Dead Sea was probably used. Jesus probably had in mind the route through the wadi *Qelt*. It was therefore a difficult path to pass in such terrain which allowed an easy possibility of ambush and eliminated military intervention against robbers (Zimmermann, 2007a, p. 543). In his 1984 publication on Jesus' parables (first ed. 1947), Jeremias even uses the present tense claiming that the road from Jerusalem to Jericho *is* known for ambushes (Jeremias, 1984, p. 135). The Czech Catholic liturgical translation is the only translation that uses the verb 'descended', thus quite accurately showing what the road from Jerusalem to Jericho probably looked like and how the travellers journeyed there.

The narrative text allows the listener a double identification – with the ambushed and with the Samaritan. Until the Samaritan appears in the story, the ambushed is the only positive or rather non-negative character to which the listener or reader can relate (Meisinger, 1996, p. 53). The parable says nothing about the victim of the robbery. He is neither characterised as Jude nor Gentile (Schottroff, 2005). It is characterised with the phrase 'a man' – that is to say, 'a person' – which is a typical trait in the *Gospel according to Luke*, being a typical 'figure' in the stories of Luke's Gospel (Pokorný, 1997, p. 194). After the ambush, 'a person' is lying half-dead near the road which creates a situation where nothing but love for one's neighbour helps. This then also creates the narrative figure when anyone who comes to the place is the only one who might change the situation; when he is the only one, he must change it (Söding, 2015, pp. 135–136).

In modern allegorical interpretations of parables and sometimes also in exegesis, robbers are often referred to as an overlooked group of characters in a story, leading to speculations about who they might be. Given that the robbers are not mentioned in the text in any detail, except that they had taken everything from the ambushed and left him half dead, it can be concluded that the Gospel writer does not mean any radicals, guerrillas, or partisans fighting against the Romans, etc., but merely common robbers and thieves (Zimmermann, 2007a, p. 544). When it is said that they robbed the ambushed of everything, it means in the Greek original that they took even his clothes. This shows the utter helplessness of the ambushed, which most artistic expressions of the parable tried to emphasise.

> **10:31** A priest happened to be going down the same road, and when he saw the man, he passed by on the other side. **10:32** So too, a Levite, when he came to the place and saw him, passed by on the other side.

The priest and the Levite do not appear on the way from Jerusalem to Jericho by accident. In fact, Jericho was a priestly town (Hoppe, 2006, p. 28) with the members of the Israeli tribe of Levi living in it and around it, who served as priests and Levites in Jerusalem Temple. Their travels on this road were therefore not as much surprising as expectable. The priests together with the Levites were a significant group during the so-called Second Temple period, when the story takes place; probably, there were several thousands of them. Therefore, a system of approximately weekly services was introduced in Jerusalem Temple, to where a number of priests commuted. They were divided into 24 groups (in Hebrew *mischmarot*) alternating in service, which consisted of priests from four to nine families. In addition to offering sacrifices and other religious duties, the ministry of priests consisted of teaching and executing judiciary authority. Probably they also held a role in assessing the so-called cleansing of the sick, i. e., they held medical competencies corresponding to the current Hygiene Services. Thus, priests were subjected to a number of religious measures, such as a purificatory bath before commencing the Temple service, a proscription of any contact with pagans, menstruating women, and the dead during their Temple service – they were not even allowed to touch them. Other measures applied to them for life. Levites, however, were not under the same rules of ritual purity as priests. Although they had a similar system of alternation in the Temple service, they carried out different activities. In particular, they guarded the Temple, sang Psalms, and also taught (Zimmermann, 2007a, p. 544).

An overview of the possible reasons why the priest and Levite avoided the ambushed and did not help him is offered in many commentaries. In the middle of the 20th century, Gollwitzer summarised these (Gollwitzer, 1962, p. 51), and, as they cannot be overlooked, such interpretations are incorporated – very speculatively – later in modern allegorical interpretations of the parable in caritas theory and practical theology:

- The priest would become ritually unclean. He would not be able to exercise his office for a longer period of time. This, however, was not the case of the Levite, who was under softer ritual prescriptions.
- If they stopped and delayed, they also would risk being attacked in this dangerous region.
- Thus, they have interpreted the prescription to take care of a neighbour in need as their duty to their own families who must not be put to the risk of finding themselves without a father and breadwinner. That is, they placed the commandment of love for neighbour regarding the ambushed against the commandment of love for neighbour regarding their families.

In fact, these are the typical clerical excuses we know from Christianity when spiritual need (they will not be able to exercise their office) is placed on the same level against obvious material-healthcare need, or when the hypothetical need (it could endanger my own family) is placed against the real need.

Commentaries that emphasise that the priest and the Levite avoided the ambushed to preserve their ritual purity overlook that if they went in the same direction as the ambushed – as the text implicitly suggests – they would be returning home from Temple service thus having enough time to ritually purify themselves before they continue their Temple service. Furthermore, even in Judaism at that time there was a dispute as to whether ritual purity could be violated in the event of danger to life – its inviolability was therefore not absolute. If the story truly regarded ritual purity, then the Samaritan would not have to appear in its climax but a Jewish layman would suffice. Involving the priest and Levite in the story therefore suggests that their duty to help others was without doubts – nobody would doubt them in connection with helping others. They are therefore referred to in the story in order to create moral scandal which then creates a contrast (Söding, 2015, p. 136), or more precisely a contrasting background, which makes the Samaritan's actions even more evident (Johnson, 2005, p. 195). Nowadays, it would perhaps be similar if we were to say that a doctor and a fireman accidentally following the same path avoided the ambushed. The remaining two reasons (self-safety, regard for one's family) then appear as the usual excuses for which there is no indication to justify them in the text. Thus, they become pure speculation.

Above all, however, in these interpretations, which speculate on the motives to refrain from help due to the preference of ritual purity, it remains completely overlooked what a Jewish listener would have been able to perceive compared to that of a Hellenistic listener originating from pagan culture without a better knowledge of Judaism. The Jewish listener or reader knew that the priest might be wary that the assaulted was dead as the law of ritual purity proscribed him from touching the dead. He also knew that he would become ritually unclean even if the ambushed died during the help being provided. He also knew that the Levites were subjected to significantly different and milder cultic stipulations. However, for the Hellenistic addressee of *Luke's Gospel* all of this remained not only completely unintelligible but he probably couldn't even guess this was the case. It is even questionable whether the Gospel author himself knew this well. That is why it is highly probable that all of this is merely the author's strategy to create a sufficient contrast for what comes when Samaritan enters the scene (Hoppe, 2006, p. 29). Working with such contrasts is not alien to Luke and he actively uses with it in several places of the Gospel text. For example, the parable of the Pharisee and the tax collector (18:9–14)[15] works in a similar way to that

---

15 To some who were confident of their own righteousness and looked down on everyone else, Jesus told this parable: 'Two men went up to the temple to pray, one a Pharisee and the other a tax collector. The Pharisee stood by himself and prayed: "God, I thank you that I am not like other people – robbers, evildoers, adulterers – or even like this tax collector. I fast twice a week and give a tenth of all I get." But the tax collector stood at a distance. He would

of the Good Samaritan: both regard the religious establishment of Israel which fails, while the 'main protagonist' is a controversial figure – a Samaritan or a tax collector[16] (Parsons, 2007, p. 119). However, they do not necessarily have to follow the specific obsessive adherence to cultic and other religious stipulations; rather, they focus on the general tension between orthodoxy and cult on the one hand and life practice on the other. Thus, for example, as early as in Luther's interpretation (Luther, 14) it was indicated that the Gospel writer wants to question the purely cultic form of reverence of God when the priest and Levite appear as the negative characters in the story because the service God desires is the service to one's neighbour – he desires to be worshiped through the help for those who are in need because only in this way can the love of God be shown.

The note that the robbers also stole the assaulted man's clothes suggests that his identification according to the social class, tribe and group was impossible. Notwithstanding, without clothing it was easy to identify whether the assailant was circumcised (i. e., Jew or Samaritan) or uncircumcised (i. e., Gentile) and thus one to whom the majority Old Testament understanding of the commandment to help one's neighbour does not apply (Keddie, 2020). However, as nothing at all is said about the motives of the priest and the Levite, it is not worth speculating about them (ritual purity, expecially), thus other explanations need to be sought as to why they are mentioned explicitly. In addition to the explanation regarding the need to create a narrative figure – scandal and contradiction – it is also likely to be an allusion to a periphrasis of the entire chosen nation where the priestly strata played important religious and sociocultural roles. This was the periphrasis: the priests, the Levites, and all Israel. In this sense, the scandal and contradiction further intensify when it is the Samaritan who appears on the scene fulfilling the commandment of love of neighbour (Hendrickx, 1997, pp. 67–68), (Wolter, 2008, p. 396).

> **10:33** But a Samaritan, as he traveled, came where the man was; and when he saw him, he took pity on him.

'The story explains that a Samaritan approached the victim and "seeing," just as the priest and the Levite did, he has compassion (10:33). It appears clear contrast between the Samaritan and the identical actions of the two temple authorities' (Keddie, 2020, p. 267). Moreover, Samaritan took pity and acts upon it. The Samaritan, however, is a hereditary enemy for Jesus' listeners, who – although having the same roots of faith – has no connection to Jewish faith and cult. As is explained to the Hellenistic

---

not even look up to heaven, but beat his breast and said, "God, have mercy on me, a sinner." I tell you that this man, rather than the other, went home justified before God. For all those who exalt themselves will be humbled, and those who humble themselves will be exalted.'

16 Tax collector (publican) collect taxes on behalf of the Roman Empire. Therfore, he was geneRaly judged as collaborator with Romns and traitor of his own nation. Moreover, he participated therfore also on the then coruption system used by Romans for better control of occupied teritories.

listeners and readers several verses previously, the Samaritans themselves expelled Jesus when he wanted to rest in their village as he was travelling to Jerusalem (*Lk* 9:52–56). The relationship between the Israelites and the Samaritans at that time is therefore compared to the relationship between the Jews and the Palestinians today (Söding, 2015, pp. 136–138). However, despite the explicit hostility, the parable of the Good Samaritan proves to be rather an enmeshing of the communities of Jews and Samaritans in the first century CE (Pummer, 2016). In addition:

> Samaritans are not considered gentiles by Luke, but as belonging to the people of God, despite the tension they sometimes have with the Jewish people. Luke does not deny this tension (e. g., Luke 9:52–55), but he does show how Jesus and then the early church seek to bridge the gap and thereby restore the unity of the people of God. Since one of the obstacles to reconciliation between Jews and Samaritans was the issue of the proper place for worship, Luke shows how this problem is ameliorated by the decreasing centrality of the Jerusalem temple after Pentecost. (Brown, Yamazaki-Ransom, 2021, p. 244)

Nevertheless, the Jews never considered the Samaritans to be of their own kind – not even in need, as Josephus Flavius showed. In short, the Samaritan was simply regarded as someone who was not a neighbour (Zimmermann, 2007a, pp. 547–548). He represents marginalised groups that nothing is expected of or granted to them (Meisinger, 1996, pp. 55–56), while it is he who '…chooses action to express his compassion' (Bovon, 1989, p. 89). While Jesus' listeners expected an Israelite – a Jewish layman (an ordinary believer) – to come to the scene after the priest and the Levite, there comes someone from whom nothing good was to be expected, a despised Samaritan. Paradoxically, he does exactly what the listeners expect. The Gospel author thus creates a situation in which Jesus' listener have to desire to identify himself with the Samaritan (Hoppe, 2006, pp. 29–30). And it is this Samaritan who transcends all physical and other conceivable boundaries (Gollwitzer, 1962, pp. 54–55).

The biblical exegesis works rather extensively with the animosity between Jews and Samaritans because of the second half of *John* 4:9 where the Samaritan woman says to Jesus: '"You are a Jew and I am a Samaritan woman. How can you ask me for a drink?" For Jews do not associate with Samaritans,' and because of their subsequent dialogue (Pummer, 2016). According to the traditional understanding, this hostility between the Israelites and the Samaritans had its roots in the 8th century BC. At that time, the Assyrians conquered the so-called Northern Kingdom. The rest of the local Jewish population, who had not been taken captive, then mingled with the new pagan colonists. In the eyes of the Southern Kingdom Jews, they left their Israelite-Jewish identity. The division was then fixed, so to speak, by the Samaritans abandoning the Jerusalem cult and building a new sacrificial place on Mount Garazim. Later, differences were added in the understanding of the Biblical canon and the issues of the custom law – *halakha* (Hoppe, 2006, p. 28). A partially different course of historical events taking place is perceived by some new research to be the reason for why the Samaritans were considered by the Jews to be unbelievers and idol-worshippers. The Samaritans had been a specific group in Judaism even before the Assyrians conquered the Northern Kingdom. It was the population of the region which had changed several times with regards to ethnic and religious aspects. In one place there lived together groups that could be described as Jewish, syncretist, and pagan, each of them having very different relations both to the religious centre on Mount Garazim as well as to their southern neighbours. Also, extensive archaeological excavations from the late 20th century revealed the diversity of '...the Samaria settlement structures during different eras and great differences in the socio-cultural profile of the main sites in Samaria' (Böhm, 1999, p. 2). Since 1982, when the excavations at Mount Gerizim started, there has been raised for religious studies, exegesis and theology, history and archaeology, a couple of new questions regarding Samaritans (Dušek, 2014). The split between the Jews and the Samaritans referred to by the Gospels, however, occurred only after the construction of the so-called Second Temple (516 BC – 70 CE), when the Samaritans' religious place on Garazim Mountain near Sichem was established. In 128 BC, the Samaria worship place was destroyed and since then there had been open hostility between the Jews and the Samaritans. The Samaritans were accused of desecrating the Temple in Jerusalem with impure items (the bones of the dead), they were being expelled from synagogues and they were found to be excluded from eternal life. In view of this, it is no coincidence but an intention to supplement in Jesus' narrative the two clerical representatives from Jerusalem Temple, responsible for the cult, with a Samaritan who is excluded from the cult. This reflects a wider and deeper dispute over the interpretation of the Law of Moses, which both Jews and Samaritans claimed to be following the orthodox interpretation (Zimmermann, 2007a, p. 545), than merely a dispute over the greatest commandment. It is clear from archaeological excavations that there was a relatively significant cultic place on Mount Garazim, which had to have its own 'staff' – from the Jewish perspective these were false priests worshipping here and offering sacrifices. This also means that these priests considered themselves and their believers to be faithful to the Lord while in the eyes of Jerusalem priests, who considered their cult and Temple to be exclusive, the Samaritans were heretics (apostatising from the true teaching) and schismatics (creating their own hierarchy and cult). The situation therefore led to differing interpretations of the Law of Moses while both feuding sides considered their interpretation to be the authentic one. This context means that when a Samaritan appears on the road in the story following the priest and Levite from Jerusalem, the then listener or reader perceives this as a dispute as to whose interpretation of the Law of Moses is more authentic (Böhm, 1999, p. 100). Thus, the Samaritans, who appear several times in Luke, are probably understood by the Gospel writer as members of the people of God who are unjustly ostracised (Twelftree, 2009, pp. 189–190). Moreover, only in the Gospel according to Luke does Jesus travel to Jerusalem through Samaria. In Mark and Matthew, he avoids this territory (Brown, Yamazaki-Ransom, 2021). The parable of Good Samaritan, together with the story about the ten lepers, where only one returned to praise God for the healing, shows the intention of the author of the Gospel to overcome religio ethnic barriers because that is God's will (Pummer, 2016).

However, one of the characteristics of the Samaritans was solidarity. Samaritan myths and non-biblical Jewish writings show that solidarity was of high value to the Samaritans and that the ethos of help and altruism was characteristic for them. This is also referred to in the Old Testament in *2 Chron* 28:15,[17] from where Luke might have taken his inspiration (Keddie, 2020, pp. 267–268), (Hendrickx, 1997, p. 71) for the Good Samaritan story because here the Samaritans from the Israeli army take care of the prisoners – they tend their wounds, dress them, and transport them to safety. That is why the text seems to work with the fact that to Jesus' opponents a Samaritan is indisputable as a helping person – it cannot be objected that a Samaritan would never do this. If they do not want to host Jesus and his disciples in a Samaria village in the preceding chapter (*Lk* 9:51–56), this is evidence of failure with regards to their own ethos of solidarity and altruism. This is also apparent from Jesus' reaction to the rejection that he did not come to destroy but to save (Theißen, 2008, p. 102). This connection then raises questions as to what extent the author of Luke's Gospel considered the Samaritans to be his readers and listeners. In fact, as the theme of Samaritans appears in his work quite often, it may be in a certain way an offer of reconciliation towards the Samaritans from Christians to whom the Gospel author belonged and who were on the path of slowly but certainly abandoning their Jewish origin. In fact, the message for the Samaritans here is that Jesus came also for them and also that his followers considered them to be close because they had a similar understanding of the Mosaic Law to that presented by Jesus. Thus, 'Luke's Jesus presents the Samaritan as an ideal Israelite who is faithful to the law and so part of God's people, Israel' (Brown, Yamazaki-Ransom, 2021, p. 245). Nontheless, some authors have concerns about such a interpretation that Luke saw Samaritans as unquestionable members of Israel (Keddie, 2020). However, 'in Acts, the inclusion of Samaria within Israel's restoration is even more apparent' (Brown, Yamazaki-Ransom, 2021, p. 245).

The intention of the author of Luke to get the Samaritans on Jesus' side supports the story about healing the men with leprosy (*Lk* 17, 11–19). The only one who returned to thank Jesus was a Samaritan (*Lk* 17, 16). Because the Samaritans cannot worship God in Jerusalem's temple, so stresses the author of the Gospel with this story, they can worship him in Jesus' person. Jesus is the new and true temple, also for people like Samaritans and especially for them (Brown, Yamazaki-Ransom, 2021).

> **10:34** He went to him and bandaged his wounds, pouring on oil and wine. Then he put the man on his own donkey, brought him to an inn and took care of him.

The Samaritan's help is far from being limited to merely what is necessary but actually is on the level of medical knowledge at that time. The text clearly emphasises practical and thought-through action (Söding, 2015, pp. 136–138). 'At the same time, everything happening here is completely non-miraculous, even non-religious, and is sober and secular. Everything remains within everyday human abilities' (Gollwitzer, 1962, p. 55). If the characters of the priest and the Levite in the narrative bear their

---

[17] The men designated by name took the prisoners, and from the plunder they clothed all who were naked. They provided them with clothes and sandals, food and drink, and healing balm. All those who were weak they put on donkeys. So they took them back to their fellow Israelites at Jericho, the City of Palms, and returned to Samaria.

meaning to create a contrasting situation, such a contrast becomes more acute also due to the Samaritan replacing the last in the triad Priest-Levite-Israelite. The emphasis on overcoming religious and ethnic intolerance is also achieved by the Samaritan not being a victim but acting proactively as the helping person. And although the Gospel writer does not state it explicitly, he also wants to convey the message that even a non-orthodox Jew can be carrying out God's will and attain salvation by fulfilling the commandments of neighbourly love (Meisinger, 1996, p. 56). Being a Gospel text, it is clear that this idea is transferable to Christianity so even a non-Christian is able to be fulfilling God's will and attain salvation when he fulfils the commandment of the neighbourly love.

In the Greek original, the description of the Samaritan's helping action is expressed practically only by verbs – i. e., a deed after a deed (Hendrickx, 1997, p. 70). Therefore, according to the parable, love for one's neighbour is first of all *compassion*, that is, pity and sympathy with the sufferer causing everything within the person to stir in the face of the other's need and injustice. *However, it is only manifested in a practical action in favour of the sufferer* (Söding, 2015, p. 142).

> **10:35** The next day he took out two denarii and gave them to the innkeeper. "Look after him," he said, "and when I return, I will reimburse you for any extra expense you may have."

As the Samaritan was well equipped for traveling (with his animal, oil, wine) and carried money, it can be concluded that he was a merchant, which is, however, usually overlooked in interpreting the parable (Hendrickx, 1997, p. 69). As a merchant, he could also easily arrange with the innkeeper a somewhat surprising solution that he would pay for any extra costs on his way back. As a frequently travelling merchant, he also must have been well acquainted with the environment of the kind of inn to where he had brought the ambushed.

Antiquity, including Judaism, distinguished between two types of inns (hostels, dormitories). One was in a way non-profitable, managed through the ethos of oriental hospitality (in Greek *katalymata*). The other was profit-oriented and was therefore also considered somewhat disrespectful in asking the guest openly and bluntly for money (*pandocheion*). The etymology of the word suggests that it was an inn 'for anyone'; this is why it could have been identified with the Church in historical allegories. This kind of inn was therefore mainly used by clients to whom no one particularly wanted to provide hospitality which, of course, influenced the environment and the level of services. In addition, it was possible to expect sexual services from female staff. Therefore, the innkeepers managing such a *pandocheion* also had a poor reputation. In Palestine, such work was not carried out by Jews.[18] The text of the Samaritan story leaves no space for doubt that it was one of these poor reputation inns by using

---

18   The Christian type of inn – hospice (in Greek *xenodochium* and Latin *Hospitium*) – is to be found from the 4th century onwards. Besides caring for the travelling foreigners, these institutions soon assumed the role of caring for the sick and poor as well.

the word *pandocheion* in the Greek original. Therefore, it is also explicitly mentioned that the Samaritan paid the innkeeper. Two denarii are the cost of one-day meals (Zimmermann, 2007a, pp. 545–546), respectively, a two-day wage of a hired worker. It was therefore a rather small amount. All this implies that: 'What the Samaritan does is not particularly heroism but merely everything that is necessary to save the other' (Stöger, 1964, p. 303). This, of course, is of far-reaching importance for how the parable is interpreted. These historical and linguistic facts show that the narrative of the Good Samaritan cannot be used to justify endless helping (hyper-)activity. Similarly, it is not possible to simply *ad hominem* malign the lack of professionalism – replaced by the helping person with emotionally expressed altruism – by using the word 'Samaritan'.

> **10:36** Which of these three do you think was a neighbor to the man who fell into the hands of robbers?'

The connection between action and mercy with which the conversation began (v. 25) is now unexpectedly and deeply modified, similarly to the term 'neighbour'. In this, Jesus' final question reaches to the core of Pharisaic activism which sought that carrying out good deeds would entail the reward of salvation from God. However, the act of neighbourly love in this parable is not founded on man's moral initiative; it is not up to man to act as the first one and thus cause a rewarding response from God. Man's love has its prehistory in God's love for man (Gollwitzer, 1962, p. 61). As a heretic and schismatic, the Samaritan is actually an immoral figure, thus even the listeners or readers could not expect him to have his moral initiative only of himself – as if there were no God. Jesus' intention, with which he turns around the Law expert's original question, thus pursues a much more complex problem. He does not want to push him into a corner or make him out as a fool but to point out that anyone who asks regarding his neighbour always asks regarding himself – regarding his own responsibility, his own practice, and his own love. The answer of the Scribe shows that he changed his mind, that he understood Jesus (Söding, 2015, pp. 138–139). By reversing the logic of the term neighbour, Jesus reveals the question 'And who is my neighbor?' as an attempt for self-justification (Fitzmyer, 1970–1985, p. 883). Thus, he turns the audience's attention from the protagonists of the story – the priest, the Levite, and the Samaritan – to whom they should care for the most in the whole story, to the ambushed. Jesus thus shows that the ambushed was as dead to the audience as he was to the priest and the Levite (Gollwitzer, 1962, pp. 58–59). The Scribe enquires regarding the object of love, Jesus regarding its subject. The Scribe asked from his position where the boundaries of his duties are while Jesus shows him that he should ask from the position of the ambushed (Jeremias, 1984, p. 135). Therefore, both formally and content-wise, the listeners and readers of the parable find in the text the possibility of self-identification with the two main characters – the Samaritan and the ambushed.

> Thanks to them, it is clear that Luke regards the universal extension of the commandment of love. He is not limiting it to the people in need. It is the designation of the Samaritan as a neighbour (v. 36f) which reveals that Luke means foreigners in general, even hostile

groups, to whom he is relating. In addition, we find interest in marginalised groups as well. (Meisinger, 1996, pp. 57-58)

However, it should also be added that there are also opinions that the parable merely seemingly changes the meaning of the concept of neighbour from the object to the subject. Even in modern languages, the term neighbour expresses primarily the relational nature and is always determined by the external conditions of the relationship. Thus, the story might regard this meaning rather than changing the content of the term neighbour (Bovon, 1989, pp. 91-92). In any case, it would be more accurate to use the term '*neighbourly love*' instead of the phrase '*love for one's neighbour*' due to the parable of the Merciful Samaritan.

It is always easier to speak about fundamental attitudes, values, norms, and reasoning using stories rather than abstract ideas. Hence, here it is more than just a didactic tool (Theißen, 2008, p. 107). As a result, we can see clearly that the parable as a whole is an appellative question culminating in Jesus' question as to which of the three was a neighbour to the one who fell into the hands of robbers. It is typical for Jesus to answer the question in such a way that in the end he himself asks another question. Therefore, he has a specific approach which is more than mere simple rhetorical didactics. He wants to say that it is not enough to change only knowledge and attitudes but above all it is necessary to change behaviour – but he does not achieve this through pressure but through insight. Therefore, he first asks whether the Scribe understood the parable before saying that he should do the same (Söding, 2015, p. 135). When the Scribe then replies that it was the Samaritan who became a neighbour, the term 'neighbour' is both clarified and generalised at the same time: a neighbour is anyone who is in proximity to us, one whom we met or passed and who is in need of our help (Pokorný, 1997, p. 194). The parable thus depicts and emphasises a radical disparity: a stranger vs. an anonymous person, a helping person vs. a helpless victim. The parable goes across all political orders to refer to the interconnectedness of people in the world where the need of another person anywhere in the world affects each of us (Benedict XVI, 2007a, pp. 142-143). Neither the Scribe nor Jesus are particularly interested in theoretically defining the concept of neighbour but rather in its reach. The difference is that while the Scribe asked theoretically, Jesus posed his final question on the basis of a practical example (Jeremias, 1984, p. 136).

> **10:37** The expert in the law replied, 'The one who had mercy on him.' Jesus told him, 'Go and do likewise.'

Thus, the form of the Scribe's final answer shows that he underwent internal development and understood the importance of practical action (Bovon, 1989, p. 92). The man in need of help in the parable thus becomes the sole rule of action. This obvious aspect, however, was for the Scribe covered by misguided stereotypes, such as that the Samaritan was a heretic and schismatic; thus, even then in his last reply to Jesus, he does not speak directly about the Samaritan using the circumlocution 'He who showed him mercy' (Fitzmyer, 1970-1985, p. 883). The whole story thus takes place in a very concrete reality for which the character of the Samaritan seems to be not fitting as a neighbour. For the listeners of Jesus, the Samaritan was the last one they would determine as a neighbour (Zimmermann, 2007a, pp. 542–543). Nevertheless, it does not necessarily have to be a mere circumlocution by which a pious Jew avoids the word Samaritan.

With regards to the conception of the whole Gospel in which the author is intending to enable the listener or reader to move away in his life from the formal identification with social status and cultural-religious paradigms, it becomes clear that this is more than a mere circumlocution. It is the preference regarding content-identification for the Christian listener or reader to self-identify with the Samaritan's conduct (Meisinger, 1996, p. 55). In his question of who a neighbour is, the Scribe primarily pursues his own righteousness. And because he quoted *Lev* 19:18, his neighbour is exclusively a member of the chosen nation. So, he wanted to have his approach confirmed by Jesus. Not only did Jesus confirm nothing to him but he also told the story of the Samaritan, which breaks down the social boundaries that the Scribe envisaged, reversing the whole logic of the Scribe's inquiry: it moves from concentrating on how to justify one's own self through a neighbour to whether I myself act as a neighbour (Hoppe, 2006, p. 32). The compassion shown to the ambushed is an example of love which is an essential part of the journey to eternal life. The parable thus suggests that the way to eternal life has been found by the Samaritan, not by the priest or Levite, thus demonstrating Luke's concept of universalism of salvation (Fitzmyer, 1970–1985, pp. 884–885). The text here opens up the meaning of the context: Jesus is interested in the fact that the identity gained by acting in favour of the ambushed suppresses the identity ascribed. As the priest, the Levite, and the Samaritan represent different approaches to religion, this puts to the fore the third tradition,[19] that is, the priority of the ethical paradigm over the religious one (Wolter, 2008, pp. 397–398); this is, actually, characteristic for the tradition of understanding Jesus' mission and its continuation in the *Gospel according to Luke*.

However, it may seem that the assaulted was a neighbour in the sense of being the object of help while Samaritan was the subject – the active administer of help. However, if the Samaritan was described as a neighbour in the preceding verse, the situation also changes for the ambushed: the Samaritan became the addressee of neighbourly love while the ambushed its subject – that is, a neighbour (Meisinger, 1996, p. 54). Jesus' appeal to go and do likewise is then much more than an appeal to follow the Samaritan's example:

> The commanded love of neighbour is, according to the parable, the kind of action by which I help the other to neighbourly love. Thus, Jesus reverses the original logic with which the whole conversation began: If a neighbour was a means for the Scribe to attaint eternal life for himself, I myself should now be a means for the neighbour so that he too could share the hope of eternal life. The question of how to enable others to become neighbours in this

---

19 In this context, Wolter makes further references to other places in Old and New Testaments which mention the third tradition preferring the ethics of acting (*ortho-praxis*) over the purity of doctrine and cult (*orthodoxy*): *Hos* 6:6; *Mi* 6:6–8; *Pr* 16:7; *Pr* 21:3; *Sir* 35:1–4; *Mt* 9:13; *Rom* 12:1–2.

sense is answered by the whole New Testament and its message that love for God is actualised by love of neighbour. (Gollwitzer, 1962, p. 65)

While up to the verse 36 it was possible for listeners and readers to identify themselves with the ambushed as the main character of the story, from verse 37 it is necessary to identify oneself with the Samaritan – a requirement arises to act like him (Meisinger, 1996, p. 54): to actualise love of God by being attentive to other people. While in the writings of Luke and Paul, Christianity was in this sense open to all, that is, not only the Jews but also to the pagans converting to Christianity, on the ethical level the problem developed in a different way. Priority was given to mutual solidarity among Christians. However, it is the story of the Samaritan that clearly shows that the commandment of love for one's neighbour should not have any limits when a 'half-Jew' provides help to 'some man' (Pokorný, 1997, p. 194).

3.5 Unsurpassable criteria for caritas and diakonic interpretations of the text

Following the necessary systematisation of the various interpretations of the parable, the last part of this chapter will focus on the criteria that follow from what the story says about the individual characters and their actions. These will then be used to assess existing interpretations focusing on caritas and diakonia practice (see Chapter 2).

Given the attention paid so far to the parable's interpretation, it could not have been overlooked that even modern interpretations using the historical-critical method and utilising archaeological findings, etc., cannot completely avoid religious and dogmatic questions; this includes the question as to what the story of the Good Samaritan tells us about its narrator – Jesus Christ.

> The 'word' of Jesus has its power as the fulfilment of the promises of the Scriptures (Lk 4:21). This means that Jesus' parables are not teachings about the Kingdom of God but telling the parables acts like Jesus working with 'all authority' (Lk 4:6; 5:24; 20:2) as a part of the Kingdom of God and the way of his actualisation in the world. [...] And what is referred to as the victim is related to the way it is told. He gave his life for the image of God as the merciful father who is not keeping away from sinners. God affiliated himself to this image represented by Jesus at his resurrection (for example, Acts 13:30,37–38 within the context). (Pokorný, 2004, pp. 22–23)

This is clearly visible through the connection of the parable per se with the dialogue between the Scribe and Jesus which focuses on the fulfilment of God's Law, that is, on God's will. In fact, the Gospel author answers the question of what is ultimately new in Jesus' message. He brings neither new nor radicalised older ideas but he brings Jesus himself as an event in history. Jesus does not speak as a wise teacher but expresses his own self, his non-transferable reality thus reaching out to his listeners. This means that even the stories – the parables that Jesus tells – are inseparable from him: if Jesus' listeners see Jesus himself in his stories, the stories gain a new meaning otherwise the stories lose it (Gollwitzer, 1962, p. 44). Whether the story of the Good

Samaritan is understood in the spirit of ancient and medieval allegories as the image of Christ himself or in the spirit of contemporary exegesis as the image of the person Christ holds about him, there will always be a message of strong stirring over poverty and evil which is converted into active conduct that is no less than the fulfilment of God's law. According to Bovon, both approaches – historical allegories and modern historical-critical analyses – can be harmonised. If the purpose of the text is primarily to encourage *imitatio* – imitation – it regards the area of ethics and practical action while not excluding the Christological-soteriological aspect. It follows that the story can also be understood as a call to *imitatio Christi*: just as Christ cares for every person wounded by sin, people should care for each other when they are wounded by the consequences of sins (Bovon, 1989, 93 and 98–99). Such interpretations might therefore be described as of *Christological-soteriological* direction. They tell who Jesus Christ is (Christology) and explain his saving action (soteriology).

Related to this is that which is further evident from the broader context of the Gospel of Luke and what is not explicitly stated in the parable, that is, the parable encounters the belief in the openness of the message of Jesus Christ also to the Samaritans and pagans – expressed in Biblical terms – that the hour is coming when God will be worshiped in other places than in Jerusalem and on Mount Garazim in Samaria (*John* 4:21). The narrower context implies that while the Gospel as a genre in essence emphasises the openness and love of God, it contains the law to be fulfilled, being neighbourly love which in itself implies love for God (Schürmann, 1994, pp. 145–148). Since both the *Gospel according to Luke* and the *Acts of the Apostles* repeatedly refer to the Samaritans, it is clear that the author had some intention in mind, that he referred to some reality in the situation in which he was writing his two-part work. It might have been a missionary intention towards the Samaritans (Böhm, 1999, pp. 5–6), who, while standing on the margins, were notorious for their solidarity and hospitality. Therefore, the Gospel author might have been trying to address them saying that it is their solidarity and hospitality through which they fulfil the Law of Moses, respectively, that they live according to the Gospel which was brought by Jesus Christ. It would then actually be an educative narrative with missionary-gaining intentions or potential (Meisinger, 1996, p. 56).

However, the missionary interpretations of the story need to be accompanied by an important note on the way of the *sine qua non* condition. Given the tensions between the Samaritans and the Israelites contained in the story, this *excludes the missionary focus of Christian caritas or diakonia as such*: 'In the story about the Good Samaritan, Luke is not intending to defend or emphasise the care for outsiders but the necessity of the care amongst the legitimate members of God's people who do not live in peace with all others.' Therefore, the care for others is not a missionary work but a manifestation of humility and faith in God (Twelftree, 2009, pp. 190–191). The parable is striking for its non-religiousness, in what a secular way the problem is presented. This therefore excludes interpretations that would hold the approach to Christian caritas or diakonia as a means or instrument of missionary activities towards those receiving the help.[20]

The missionary message of the parable in the above-described sense can be held true due to interpretations that appeared in the second half of the 20th century and which abandon the exclusive meaning of the parable as a text intended solely for Christians. In fact, according to these, the parable is not meant only for Christians. If it follows from the parable that help is justified not merely by a family or religious affiliation but only by all people being neighbours, this then entails that each person has the same infinite value. This value is determined by all people being a part of God's creation (Theißen, 2008, p. 108). Subsequently, help is no longer justified in so much Christological or soteriological terms as it is through the theology of creation and human nature: the parable actually says here that everyone has God's law of help within them not by affiliating themselves with Jesus Christ (the Law of Moses, the cult in Samaria, etc.) but by being a human. Therefore, many interpretations also mention that the parable does not actually bring anything specifically Christian. The crucial mater is that the helping person is one whom God created with this law in his heart. Thus in Catholic theology[21] it can be said that '... the imperative of love was written by the Creator into the very nature of man' (Benedict XVI, 2006, 31). We can therefore speak in this sense of a line of interpretations based on the *theology of creation and human nature*.

Of course, none of the interpretations avoid the matters connected with the helping practice. The meaning conveyed by the parable in this aspect is so clear that it is not left out even by historical allegories. Given the legitimacy of the Scribe's question and the fact that it corresponded to the discourse of the time, it is important that Jesus shows neighbourly love to be the centre of the Law that the Jewish scholars then sought without abolishing the commandment to love God; nevertheless, the moral level is given priority over ritual obedience (Bovon, 1989, pp. 85–86): 'It offers a practical model for Christian conduct with radical requirements and acceptance/rejection of certain models of action' (Fitzmyer, 1970–1985, p. 883). The logic of the whole parable moves from the obligation to act according to the Law regarding the one who deserves my love, towards my giving: giving to the one I can manifest myself as a neighbour (Johnson, 2005, p. 194). Hence the line of interpretations that follows

---

20 It is possible to add here that Lk 10:25–37 does not essentially differ from (but on the contrary coincides with) another well-known biblical text which is interpreted in the way of caritas, that is, with the speech regarding the Last Judgment in Mt 25:31–46. Here, those determined as righteous, because they helped, do not realise that they helped the king – Jesus Christ. That is, they did not pursue other goals than to help the hungry and thirsty, the travellers and the naked (that is, those overburdened with debt), the imprisoned, and the sick.

21 The issue of human nature constitutes one of the differences between Catholic and Protestant theologies. Here, in simple terms, the question is whether a sinful person can be good in himself because he was thus created (the Catholic concept of human nature) or his nature was completely destroyed by sin so whatever is good in him comes exclusively from God as a re-gifted grace (the Protestant conception of human nature).

the subject of man and his conduct proves to be important. These regard what the parable tells about man (theological anthropology) and how one should do good and act as best as possible (ethics). We can therefore speak of the *anthropological-ethical* line of the parable interpretations.

For better orientation, we can divide the above interpretations of the parable according to two basic criteria:

a) Whether the parable tells something about man or Christ.
b) Whether the parable is aimed at the life practice of Christians or of all people.

This means that we can ask whether the interpretations focus on what the parable tells about Jesus Christ and his significance for man (Christological-soteriological meanings), and what they convey about man and his life tasks (anthropological-ethical interpretations). At the same time, we can also ask whether the parable as an appellative example calls the Church – as a community of Christians – to specific conduct (ecclesiocentric interpretations) or whether it addresses all people regardless of their Christian denomination, respectively, religion at all (interpretations based on theology of creation and human nature). Placing such distinctions of the parable interpretations in a table (Table 1) creates a matrix enabling us to see the three basic messages of the parable that follow from the interpretations:

- *Cultic message* is a Christological-soteriological interpretation focused ecclesiocentrically, that is, on the conduct of the Church as a community of Christians. The Samaritan and his actions are an allegory of Christ who saves man wounded by sin and the consequences of sin. As a result, purely religious reverence for God is challenged because in this way Jesus Christ says that God, who does not need anything from men, desires to be worshiped also by people helping those in need.
- *Missionary message* regards Christological-soteriological interpretation focused on human nature and the whole creation, that is, how all people should act. This message is not normative but descriptive; it aims at describing and showing the life practice of man in God's eyes – that is, as God expects it. Thus, the story is intended to capture and gain for Jesus Christ even those who are on the margins or outside Christianity (for example, Samaritans).
- *Praxeological message* is an anthropological-ethical interpretation focused ecclesiocentrically, that is, on the conduct of the Church as a community of Christians. Most of the interpretations in practice-oriented theological disciplines are directed towards this message, amongst these being caritas theory, diakonics, practical and pastoral theology, theological ethics, moral theology, and social theological ethic (see Chapter 2).

3.5 Unsurpassable criteria for caritas and diakonic interpretations of the text

Tab. 1: Diagram of interpretations of the Good Samaritan parable

	Ecclesiocentric interpretations (How should the Church / Christians / Caritas and Diakonia organisations act?)	Interpretations based on the theology of creation and human nature (How should people act?)
Christological-soteriological interpretations (Christ saves the sinner)	Cultic message	Missionary message
Anthropological-ethical interpretations (omnis homo est proximus)	Praxeological message	**Public message**

In the table, the fourth message of the Good Samaritan parable has not been discussed. It is a message based on the anthropological-ethical interpretation which focuses on what the parable tells about man and his calling by God – his life tasks – while asking, in the spirit of the interpretation based on theology of creation and human nature, how all people should act. Such a message could be described as *public* (German *öffentlich*, in the Czech original *veřejné*).

This interpretation is the main theme of this book. Theologically, it is justified by two important elements of the parable itself: the connection of the Samaritan's stirring with his actions, and the primacy of the acquired identity over the ascribed one which follows from the final dialogue between Jesus and the Scribe:

- *Regarding the connection between stirring (compassion) with action*: When the Samaritan appears in the story, it is immediately clear to the listeners and readers of the time that it will regard a problem of proper respect and religion with relationship to God, as there was a dispute between the Jews and Samaritans whether it was possible to worship God only in Jerusalem or also elsewhere, that is, on Mount Garazim. Surprisingly, however, Luke turns the story elsewhere saying that when the Samaritan saw the ambushed he felt compassion for him – everything stirred within him. In doing so, he builds the sentence so that the point of seeing and having compassion emerged at the very end (Wolter, 2008, pp. 396–398). Indeed, the compassion or stirring within of the Samaritan means the ability to understand the situation, stand on the side of the wounded, have empathy with him, and take steps that would bring him relief (Bovon, 1989, p. 90).
The whole 'world' of helping professions with its steady growth, the growth of voluntary engagement, and the engagement of people within their own families and on the community level, all of these are the clear proof that the point saw and was stirred is not exclusively Christian. On the contrary, it is open to a much wider audience of the parable, that is, to all people.
- *Regarding the primacy of the identity acquired before the attributed*: From the first help up to the payment to the innkeeper, the narrative of help is designed to make show the Samaritan's engagement. Verse 37 ('The expert in the Law replied, "The one

who had mercy on him." Jesus told him, "Go and do likewise."') thus implies the fundamental statement of the parable that it is the person of the Samaritan that justifies that every man is a neighbour (Vio Caietani, 1639, p. 219). This expresses and emphasises the precedence of the ethical paradigm over the religious one: although the priest along with the Levite and then the Samaritan have different cultural and social identities, the decisive identity is the one acquired – the identity of a neighbour, that is, the identity the Samaritan acquired through his engagement with the ambushed. So, this is the main point of the story, not the point to help those in need (Wolter, 2008, pp. 396–398).

The laconic statement of medieval theology *omnis homo est proximus* – every person is a neighbour – thus acquires a brand-new dimension. It is not merely a statement to help everyone and not to ask whether or not he belongs to my kind – whether or not he is my neighbour. When the identity of one's neighbour is acquired through the combination of *seeing-stirring-action*, any person who applies this in his life can become a neighbour.

Ortho-praxis, as presented by the parable, therefore connects Christians of various denominations. At the same time, however, it also connects all Christians with those who respect the rule of the priority of ortho-praxis over orthodoxy but who cannot be described as orthodox. As explained in the interpretation of the parable on the basis of the present exegetic discourse, this regards neither self-justification nor empty sympathy. Thus, the combination *seeing-stirring-action* does not have its origin merely in man but in God. That is why we can regard this as the public message of the parable, and, furthermore, as the public theological message.

The whole story emphasises the realisation of what the Scribe himself answered in the first part to the question with which he had intended to test Jesus: 'Jesus does not clarify an article of the Law but turns the Law into the Gospel' (Johnson, 2005, p. 196). This means that in the parable all boundaries of love are abolished. This does not mean, however, a declaration of universal love but a concrete conduct in favour of others (Pokorný, 1998, p. 149). Therefore, the following criteria cannot be ignored when interpreting the text for caritas and diakonia practice as well as for helping professions in general:

1. The parable says nothing specifically Christian; everything essential is already determined by the Old Testament or also in the ancient social ethos. Nevertheless, it entails a special commitment for Christians.

The parable's binding nature regarding Christians corresponds to the Mosaic Law but in a different way than as a prescription that must be unconditionally observed. The binding nature is given here through Jesus' ethos in the sense as it is introduced by the *Gospel according to Luke*, and which have already been paraphrased by historical allegories. So, if in allegorical interpretations Jesus, as the Samaritan, cared for the man wounded by sin, it still holds true that man should imitate this Jesus just as the Samaritan cared for the man ambushed and beaten by robbers. Thanks to modern exegetical knowledge, it is obvious that this is mainly due to the core of Luke's Gospel in the parable of the Merciful Father introducing the image of God. Anyone who encounters this God can either despise him or act as the merciful Samaritan analogous to the merciful father – within the conditions of his humanity. And he who acts as the merciful Samaritan analogous to the merciful father, however without knowing God, by his action implies such knowledge – he presupposes and anticipates it. That is why the parable has its witness value not only for Christians but also for non-Christians; but also due to this, it becomes binding for Christians.

2. Factual data in the parable are important in determining the basic direction of its understanding, from which far-reaching conclusions of doctrinal, moral, pastoral and charity nature cannot be drawn.

Besides the pair of its key figures (the ambushed and the Samaritan), the parable also includes other people – robbers, the priest, the Levite, and the innkeeper. It also refers to two sites – the road from Jerusalem to Jericho and the inn. These constitute, more or less, static backdrops for the story and are important in creating the situation which needs to be solved (the robbers), in creating a contrasting background to the Samaritan's conduct (the priest and Levite), and for the story to have some kind of outcome (the innkeeper). Similarly, it also serves to indicate that this is a trivial common emergency (a dangerous route from Jerusalem to Jericho) and the minimum necessary to be done (the inn). This is not, therefore, for theologians to build their own speculative constructs reflecting their time, culture, and specific current interests. It can be noted that historical allegories did not do this; they simply approached the parable through the spiritual interpretation as a whole. Thus, far-reaching conclusions from the statists and backdrops of the story primarily point to the authors' inconsistent work with the historical-critical method of Scripture interpretation. Some interpretations even discuss yet another – completely static – figure of the parable, the Samaritan's mule or horse or donkey – who passively carries the ambushed to the inn; by this, we are moving completely beyond rational and spiritual reflection upon the text.

In particular, this criterion means that no conclusions can be drawn about the robbers and similarly about the path from Jerusalem to Jericho. Both are important in the sense that they create very realistic environment for the story taking place. However, the figures of the priest and the Levite call for some interpretation, being obvious representatives of the establishment and the cult. In addition to their ignorance of the ambushed, which creates the contrasting background to the Samaritan's action, it is possible to consider other levels of contrast between them and the Samaritan, such as the opposites of the elites and the outcast they despise, or different interpretations of the Mosaic Law at the then spiritual centres in Jerusalem and Mount Garazim in Samaria. However, it is not possible to deduce what is not said anywhere or indicated between the lines that they were led to ignore the ambushed by giving preference to cultic purity over helping, etc. The innkeeper with his facility is in a similar situation. By using the word *pandocheion* and mentioning that the Samaritan paid the innkeeper, the Gospel author makes it quite clear that he did the minimum necessary and continued travelling on. Any further speculation about the inn, the innkeeper, and the payment for taking care of the ambushed means that the story is

3. The parable and the dialogues explain what the commandment of love for one's neighbour consists in when they identify the helping person as a neighbour. So, it is necessary to talk about neighbourly love rather than love for one's neighbour.

In the story, the term 'neighbour' refers to common situations of significant need. When confronted with such a situation, that is, when it is seen, everything stirs within man. This in itself is, however, only the first step towards a specific helping action. That is, the parable speaks here of the three steps in which the Samaritan *saw*, was *stirred*, and *acted*. In order for the Samaritan to become a neighbour to the one who had fallen into the hands of the robbers, he had to perceive these steps and act upon them as one unit, as an indivisible, integral conduct or action, being linguistically derived from the Latin *actio* – to act.

That is why it is not appropriate to refer to love for one's neighbour. In fact, this phrase only goes back to the question of the Scribe who his neighbour was. In the parable, however, the issue is not the definition of the neighbour but what neighbourly love is. It is precisely the fact that even a social outcast might act in the correct way aims at showing that no one can make excuses from the commandment of neighbourly love (Schürmann, 1994, p. 144). The parable thus says that neighbourly love consists in the triple-step *seeing-stirring-acting*, and that any person is capable of such neighbourly love.

4. The parable approaches the help to a man passed by others as part of the cult. In its spirit, therefore, it is not possible merely to criticise the rigid adherence to cultic rules or to appeal to the interconnection of faith and deeds.

Although the parable itself does not say anything about God and religion – besides the appearance of two members of the Jewish priestly strata – it also contains a religious and spiritual message. This is due to the fact that the story is a part of the Gospel, being primarily religious and spiritual literature, and also due to its narrowest context, being the opening and closing dialogues of Jesus with the Law expert.

The meaning of active spirituality is what the parable wants to convey in religious and spiritual senses. The evangelist aims at challenging the purely cultural form of respect for God. By involving the priest and the Levite in the story, Jesus shows a new form of service to God: the worship God desires is the service to one's neighbour (Schürmann, 1994, pp. 144–145). For this reason, those interpretations are misleading which speculate that the priest and Levite preferred the cultic rules over help. These work with the duality of *faith* and *works*, respectively, words and deeds. Similarly, there are inaccurate interpretations that perceive the parable as an appeal to connect faith and works, words and deeds. The essential is expressed by opening and concluding the parable by the dialogue about the greatest commandment of Mosaic Law, and by the fact that the two greatest commandments of Mosaic Law are not mentioned at all: both the commandments of the Law were fulfilled through the Samaritan's *actio* – seeing-stirring-action. If the commandment to love one's neighbour is not seen as important as to fulfil the commandment to love God, then we do not understand the stipulations of Mosaic Law regarding love for God and one's neighbour per se.

5. The parable emphasises the priority of the status gained through active conduct over the status ascribed – socially, culturally or by religion.

If the helping person is a neighbour in the sense in which the Samaritan has become one, this means that one does not become a neighbour through some external definition but only and exclusively on the basis of his attitudes inextricably combined with his conduct. Thus, the identity of one's neighbour is not obtained, for example, by baptism but by a concrete action – whether it regards first aid, as in the case of the parable, or working in helping professions. Even in this case, however, one does not become a neighbour by his education, for example, in care work or social work, but only by his active commitment to others.

Consequently, situations in which a person can manifest his attitudes through actions that show him to be a neighbour are situations in which he is the recipient. He himself becomes a neighbour – the object of love, that is, for example, gratitude and trust – to the person whom he helped. Such situations must therefore be understood as a gift from God – as an opportunity given by God for one to become a neighbour. As man is endowed with neighbourly love in his nature and as this is strengthened by God's grace, those situations when one might respond at the time of the other's need should be read as a sign of the times. That is, be read as a sign – a challenge from God whether one will act in a human or inhuman way (Sander, 2005), whether he will respond to God's offer by *seeing-stirring-action* or by ignoring it. Thus, active helping action might be active spirituality and not merely a self-imposed act.

4. What's left of the story? The public message of the parable

The public message of the parable is based on the anthropological-ethical interpretation that each person is a neighbour and it asks what the story's message is to all people, regardless of their Christian orthodoxy and denomination. In order to relate this message to the practice of contemporary helping professions, we must subject the existing interpretations of the parable for practical use, as described in Chapter 2, to a critical view through the prism of the conclusions of Chapter 3. These new economic and methodological interpretative allegories must be deconstructed, so to speak, purged to the core from the deposits of the praxeological and missionary message contained, but also from the cultic message with which the public message has least in common:

- Therefore, given the *cultic message* of the parable, we will not ask in this chapter how the Church, being a community of Christians, should act. This will be the topic of Chapter 5.
- Given the *praxeological message*, it is necessary to leave out, from the interpretations focused on practice, the specific ecclesiocentric question of how the Church should act, being individual Christians, communities of Christians, ecclesial organisations such as Caritas organisations and Diakonias, etc. The point now is to remain within the general matter of how every person should act in practice.
- Given the *missionary message*, which is linked to the public message by the question of how all people should act, it is necessary to distinguish between the intention to engage the reader or listener and the intention to thus gain him – that he believes that Christ saves also him, the same as the Samaritan saved the ambushed. It is therefore a matter of reducing the communication of the parable's missionary message in the sense of renouncing its missionary claims regarding non-Christians. In a theological book, such an intention may appear controversial, or even worse. But the matter here is not whether Christianity should or should not be a missionary religion. The matter regards what Christianity can bring from this parable to the public space outside the community of shared faith. *This also regards how Christianity's traditional understanding of human need and help in need can be of public benefit.*

The fourth chapter will therefore be based primarily on the diaconic exegesis of the parable (▸ Chapter 2.4), that is, its interpretations which, while adhering to exegetical principles, focus on its caritas and diakonic theme. Such interpretations are not directly determined by the context of their origin, as it is the case of modern allegories – economic, methodological, and pastoral interpretations also described in the second chapter. Taking into account the criteria by which Chapter Three was concluded, the exegetical framework for examining the parable's message will thus be maintained. Thanks to this, it will be possible to subject modern allegories (economic and methodological interpretations) to a critical view in order to purify them in the above sense; this then reveals, in the caritas and diakonic theme of the parable, the core of its public message useful for helping professions.

4.1 Hermeneutical key to and of mercy

In some languages, the parable of the Good Samaritan is called the parable of the Merciful Samaritan (in German *Barmherziger Samariter*, in Czech *milosrdný Samaritán*). Such parable titles refer to the concluding dialogue where the Scribe responds to Jesus that for the ambushed, *it was the one showing him mercy who became his neighbour*: 'The one who had mercy on him' Jesus' answer to the Scribe is to go and do likewise. It can be easily deduced from this that what is emphasised by the whole narrative is merciful conduct, or simply *mercy*: According to the parable, the criterion to be a neighbour is only the mercy that provokes the need. Also, mercy is the main theme of the exegesis that follows from the parable. Mercy is also the central theme of the diaconic exegesis of the parable – it is a rational, thought-through practical conduct that is the response to one's feelings when faced with human need. The fundamental message of the parable, then, is to clarify or define mercy. 'The problem with the Christian interpretation of *Lk* 10:25–37 is that mercy appears so self-evident, while the text tells us that it is not at all self-evident' (Schottroff, 2005, p. 170). However, love, compassion, mercy, and pity are theological categories that do not mean the same. Usually, compassion and mercy are considering synonymous. Another aproaches develop the term closeness (Bonilla, Mora, 2022). With regard to translation of the parable's name (Good Samaritan) in my native language, where *milosrdný Samaritán* means *mercifull Samaritan*, and with regard to smiliar tranlsation in other languages like German (*Der barmherzige Samaritan*) for example, I will prefere the word *mercy*.

In the helping professions and social sciences, however, mercy (especially when associated with Christian faith) is considered a concept that should be criticised, if not outrightly rejected.[1] Although he who emphasises mercy sees the need of another and attempts to change it, he does not consider the matter of whether his help was of any use, whether it was practical and useful. Such mercy and its promoters do not even care whether their help is effective in terms of financial, material, and human resources employed, and whether it can hold while faced with scientific reflection – this concerns especially helping disciplines such as social work, psychology, etc. (Bopp, 1998). As scientific reflection is required because of the professionalisation of helping professions, it is now a matter of course, the critique of the concept of mercy based on the Christian faith is thus understandable. It may not strengthen

---

1 Along with mercy, the same is true also for compassion.

in particular the client's autonomy, it does not consider the boundaries between the client and the helping person, and it does not regard the already mentioned effectivity and other potential clients. Furthermore, the critique of mercy adds that the helping person is concerned with himself, securing his own position, and his own faith. As a result, the helping person instrumentalises the client for his own needs (Bohlen, 2007, p. 51). This has its opposite also in institutionalised help when it is framed by the concept of mercy. Thus, Christian caritas and diakonia tend to be reproached by other helping disciplines and social sciences (Allen, 2017), that their services and socio-political lobbying do not pursue clients' interest but their own benefit, their own business interests, their maintaining of the status quo of accredited social services and facilities, and their stabilising of the situation and securing their 'shares' in the social services market. Thus, instead of addressing them, Christian Caritas organisations and Diakonias stabilise various forms of social need and serve primarily their own social business interests in the social field rather than be bringing about the sustainable personal and structural improvement of the living situation of the people affected by, or at risk of, poverty and social exclusion (Baumann, 2013a, p. 73).

However, the Samaritan, whom the parable regards, was merciful neither to instrumentalise the ambushed for his own use nor to stabilise his business in the social services market. Three important conclusions emerged from the diaconic exegesis of the parable (▸ Chapter 2.4), significantly clarifying the message of the whole story regarding the matter of mercy:

1. Although the parable regards salvation, that is, a religious theme as follows from the dialogue framing the parable, it does not concern the salvation of the helping person. He who is merciful does not pursue his own salvation but the salvation of him whom he is helping.
2. Humanity, which in the parable transcends various social boundaries, is the core of conduct desired by God, that is, the conduct that God expects from man. Love of God takes place in love of man. Such behaviour, as the parable shows very illustratively, cannot be inefficient, without borders, or, conversely, in terms of having power over the client. In the parable, this regards a rational procedure that has clear limits and does not bind the ambushed to the Samaritan.
3. Last but not least, the parable communicates that even one who does not pursue any religious goals acts mercifully. The story does not talk about God; the Samaritan acts without religious interests and motives. And therein lies the core of the contrast between him and those who bypassed the ambushed – the priest and the Levite. While no one expected from the priestly tribe members anything but acting with religious interests and motives, for Jesus' listeners the Samaritan had nothing to do with true religious interests and motives. At the same time, however, it was his actions which corresponded to God's will.

Therefore, both the conclusions of diaconic exegesis and the convergence between theological and human motifs within the Samaritan story (Theißen, 2008), (Bopp, 1998) show that mercy is not an exclusively religious or Judaeo-Christian term – although is important for both religions. This means that mercy is one of the concepts that is important also for *public theology*. The parable per se thus becomes the key source of restoration of mercy in public debate and the interactions of theology with the social sciences and helping professions.

However, the objections to mercy are not thus exhausted:

> In modern society, both the definition of human need and the appropriate authority [to help] are not left to the spontaneous and subjective mercy of individuals but to state laws defining social need and regulating relevant helping measures. Those in need are thus (at least in need as defined by the law) independent of spontaneous mercy because depending on the form of the need, they now have a legal right for help. Given the legal protection of the modern welfare state, it seems that human need no longer needs mercy. (Bopp, 1998, pp. 13–14)

Nevertheless, the ethnographic studies of charity activities show the particular role of emotions besides their importance for the constitution of the local community or the community of immigrants. The role of emotions (compassion, mercy) in helping activities was an important topic for Middle Ages philosophy and theology, and since the 19th century its revival has been observed (Trundle, 2014). It will be, therefore, short-sighted for the helping professions to forbid themselves this anthropological phenomenon. On the contrary, it is true that postmodern man wants to be in charge of his own life desiring to be independent – and this also means to be independent of potential mercy someone of else's (Bopp, 1998). It is therefore also a functional problem which is clearly evident from the fact that there are two thousand years between the time of the origin of the parable and the current developed social care systems as well as the advanced individualisation of man. Simply put, nowadays we think completely differently about topics such as mercy.

Here, therefore, the context of the parable proves to be very important, especially the placement, being the *bloody path* through the wadi *Qelt* from Jerusalem to Jericho. For the ancient readers and listeners of the *Gospel according to Luke*, this was a place where something bad may happen to anyone (▸ Chapter 3). Some works of art expressed this fact using the figure of the ambushed depicted as a strong man, that is, as someone whom not many people dare to harm – and yet it happened to him (▸ Chapter 1). Furthermore, the ambushed is passed by the priest and the Levite without any concern: as practising Jews, both were required to help by Moses' law; as humans, both were required to do this by the ancient social ethos (▸ Chapter 3). Thus, even in ancient times without social security systems, this regards in a certain way an extraordinary situation – an extremely dangerous place as well as an extraordinary omission of religious and social duties. The mercy of the good Samaritan, then, is not a stirring up and an action regarding ordinary human need, but an extraordinary need. So, this is a situation that was not particularly common, which, in a sense, was insufficiently covered by the law of Moses and the ancient social ethos – by staying with the ambushed, the helping person could put himself at risk of being ambushed also.

It is our context of modern society with developed systems and forms of social and other support and assistance that requires reading of the parable within its own historical context. Thus, mercy, as expressed in the parable, is not the answer to the situations addressed by the laws on social services, benefits, and social work. On the contrary, it relates to situations when someone falls through the system – when they lose their legal right to help, when they are not covered by the guarantee given by the welfare state, when for some reason the help does not reach them or the help is not in a suitable, and thus effective, form. Then, it is also clear that these are situations where the person with his individualisation and independence is simply not enough. The parable indicates this by the ambushed being half-dead – unconscious – and therefore unable to take care of himself. Again, this is an extraordinary rather than normal human need. Thus, although modern welfare states – their number being far from all the countries of the world – are trying to completely eliminate poverty and penury, it cannot be expected that this would be fully successful and thus mercy would not be needed at all (Benedict XVI, 2006).

During the Reformation in Basel, Switzerland, when attempts to reform the Church as well as society took place, a statue of a beggar was removed from the sculpture of St Martin in Münster, their local cathedral. Thus Martin, sharing his cloak, remained next to an empty stump on which the beggar used to sit. Here, one of the foundations of the welfare state, as known today, was laid in Switzerland and beggars began to disappear. However, this does not mean that the willingness and will for social reforms and the development of the nascent welfare state could also 'disappear'. Therefore, St Martin remained in Münster. Mercy is therefore still needed also because it is the 'soul' of the solidarity structures of society and it changes them from nationalist and party-based to something broader, it prevents their misuse by both neoliberalism and communism, and it draws attention to the holes that may have remained in solidarity structures (Moltmann, 2018). Thus, mercy will always be needed at least in terms of empathy and acceptance (Zulehner, 2006b). The conclusion that mercy is not simply substitutable, even in a socially just society, agrees with the diaconic exegesis of the parable (▸ Chapter 2.4) and also is not in contradiction with any of the criteria emerging from Chapter 3 (▸ Chapter 3.5).

We can defend mercy with a number of arguments that address the usual objections and also respond to current conditions and forms of help. Nevertheless, it should be added that, at least within Christianity, there is another reason for mercy. 'Our God is a passionate God. He does not observe what is going on like a Stoic. He is not someone whose peace is never disturbed' (Küberl, 2013, p. 18). If the Christian God is as merciful as the allegories of antiquity point out, that is, as is explicitly shown in the Scriptures by the parable of the Prodigal Son (▸ Chapter 3.2), then mercy has its final reason in God himself. Unlike the public message, other parable messages (cultic, missionary, and praxeological) work with this. However, this cannot be overlooked within the search for the public message. For one thing, theology would no longer be theology, and additionally the public message must also face the fact that this justification of mercy is somewhat refuted by the churches and Christians themselves by their life and conduct (Bopp, 1998). This issue will be the subject of Chapter 5.

It is now possible, therefore, to draw one of the important conclusions of this book: The parable is the hermeneutic key to mercy, and mercy is the hermeneutic key to the parable:

- *The parable is the hermeneutic key to mercy:* In the first case, the parable itself illuminates what mercy is. Using social sciences terminology, it can be said that the parable operationalises mercy – literally: it makes the theoretical concept empirically comprehensible, that is, in this case it makes it understandable for the thinking of a common person, and repeatable in the sense of an example that invites imitation.
- *Mercy is the hermeneutic key to the parable:* However, at the same time, understanding the parable and its message can only be achieved through mercy. If we exclude mercy as an unacceptable concept of thinking or behavioural model, we will not understand the parable itself, let alone its message.

This closes the hermeneutical circle: The message of the parable can be understood only through mercy, but the parable itself primarily illuminates mercy. This means that by reading it, researching, meditation, etc., we arrive at better understanding of what mercy is. Although it is a cyclical process, it is not a tautology, a kind of a vicious circle, because it is possible to gradually gain a better and more accurate understanding of the parable message – a better and more accurate understanding of mercy.

4.2 Modern allegory and the hermeneutic key to and of the parable

The conclusion that mercy is the hermeneutic key to the parable and the parable is the hermeneutical key to mercy is essential for the assessment of modern allegorical parable interpretations. Next, therefore, these interpretations will be evaluated *sub specie misericordiae* – from the point of view of mercy while the absolute minimum criteria for the parable interpretation from Chapter 3.5 will continue to be adhered to. This will therefore consist in a necessary deconstruction of economic and methodological interpretations so that a conclusion can be drawn in the following chapter regarding the public message of the parable.

4.2.1 Economic interpretations

Merciful neighbourly love, as introduced by the parable – that is, the neighbour is primarily the helping person (see Criterion 3) – contains non-profit elements and even those of risk and loss. As the helping person, the Samaritan helps at his own costs and risks that he also will be ambushed on the *bloody path*. Precisely with regard to mercy, but also because of the way that the parable perceives the inn, neighbourly love appears to be the exclusive matter of the Samaritan. This however means that in the parable, it is not associated with any other actor. This is essential for a proper understanding of the innkeeper. The differentiation of helping activities into professional and organised on the one hand and spontaneous and voluntary on the other, as it is in economic (as well as methodological) interpretations, is therefore against the intent of the parable. Clearly, the figure of the innkeeper cannot be thus instrumented in favour of justifying professional and organised help. Such an approach to the figure of the innkeeper resembles the understanding of the parable in medieval art (▸ Chapter 1.2), where rulers had themselves portrayed as innkeepers to reserve organised and professional help as exclusive for themselves while leaving spontaneous and voluntary charity to their subjects. The separation of attitudes and actions as well as various forms of helping practice also is against the parable's intention that no distinction should be made between cult (that is, attitudes) and deeds (that is, helping actions) (see Criterion 4). The foundational cultic rule is correct and good conduct: one's good relationship to God cannot be carried out any other way than by correct and good conduct towards people. That is why the parable also priorities the status acquired by action over the status ascribed by others (see Criterion 5). So, the helping person is the one who acts thus. It is similar for institutions. A helping organisation is one that gives its members the space to take stance through good and right conduct.

However, even in ancient times the parable was not particularly ground-breaking. It regards only a specific – that is, Christian – understanding of the Old Testament and ancient ethos of help or it regards a Christian interpretation of the ancient social ethos for a situation of need (see Criterion 1). This Christian understanding is fulfilled in mercy: the Old Testament or ancient ethos of the parable represents the correct answer to God's call within man, in his conscience. Therefore, something unrelated to this intention cannot be deduced from the parable. Concerning economic interpretations, this means that the principles cannot be deduced from it regarding how to finance and manage modern non-profit social service providers – this even applies to Christian caritas and diakonia organisations. Hence, the inspiration in the parable for creating more sophisticated models of managerial and economic management of helping organisations thus appear to be purpose-built. It appears as an effort to mine the story of the parable in order to provide a nicer, or more theological, or more 'pious' justification for ethically and economically responsible forms of managing helping organisations. However, other Old and New Testament parts can certainly serve this purpose just as well or even better, which emphasise man's responsibility for the world that God had entrusted to him,[2] for responsible financial management,[3] and

---

[2] Gen 1:26 Then God said, 'Let us make mankind in our image, in our likeness, so that they may rule over the fish in the sea and the birds in the sky, over the livestock and all the wild animals, and over all the creatures that move along the ground.'

[3] Mt 25:14–30 Again, it will be like a man going on a journey, who called his servants and entrusted his wealth to them. To one he gave five bags of gold, to another two bags, and to another one bag, each according to his ability. Then he went on his journey. The man who had received five bags of gold went at once and put his money to work and gained five bags more. So also, the one with two bags of gold gained two more. But the man who had received one bag went off, dug a hole in the ground and hid his master's money. After a long time the master of those servants returned and settled accounts with them. The man who had received five bags of gold brought the other five. 'Master,' he said, 'you entrusted me with five bags of gold. See, I have gained five more.' His master replied, 'Well done, good and faithful servant! You have been faithful with a few things; I will put you in charge of many things. Come and share your master's happiness!' The man with two bags of gold also came. 'Master,' he said, 'you entrusted me with two bags of gold; see, I have gained two

4.2 Modern allegory and the hermeneutic key to and of the parable

responsible personnel management,[4] as prefigurements of the Kingdom of God. The settlement – being the cost-centre of mercy (▸ Chapter 2.1) – should therefore be based rather on the principle of *patrimonium pauperum*[5], which arises in antiquity only when the Church acquired property permanently in a somewhat significant volume. However, such a situation is not directly addressed in the Scripture because it belongs to the later diaconic tradition of Christianity.

In addition, modern economic allegories also conflict with the 2nd criterion that far-reaching conclusions cannot be drawn from factual data in the parable (especially the inn and the innkeeper). In this case, these are calculated detours from the message of the parable, its eisegesis, which primarily follows the problem of financing

---

more.' His master replied, 'Well done, good and faithful servant! You have been faithful with a few things; I will put you in charge of many things. Come and share your master's happiness!' Then the man who had received one bag of gold came. 'Master,' he said, 'I knew that you are a hard man, harvesting where you have not sown and gathering where you have not scattered seed. So I was afraid and went out and hid your gold in the ground. See, here is what belongs to you.' His master replied, 'You wicked, lazy servant! So you knew that I harvest where I have not sown and gather where I have not scattered seed? Well then, you should have put my money on deposit with the bankers, so that when I returned I would have received it back with interest. So take the bag of gold from him and give it to the one who has ten bags. For whoever has will be given more, and they will have an abundance. Whoever does not have, even what they have will be taken from them. And throw that worthless servant outside, into the darkness, where there will be weeping and gnashing of teeth.'

4 Mt 20:1–16 For the kingdom of heaven is like a landowner who went out early in the morning to hire workers for his vineyard. He agreed to pay them a denarius for the day and sent them into his vineyard. About nine in the morning he went out and saw others standing in the marketplace doing nothing. He told them, 'You also go and work in my vineyard, and I will pay you whatever is right.' So they went. He went out again about noon and about three in the afternoon and did the same thing. About five in the afternoon he went out and found still others standing around. He asked them, 'Why have you been standing here all day long doing nothing?' 'Because no one has hired us,' they answered. He said to them, 'You also go and work in my vineyard.' When evening came, the owner of the vineyard said to his foreman, 'Call the workers and pay them their wages, beginning with the last ones hired and going on to the first.' The workers who were hired about five in the afternoon came and each received a denarius. So when those came who were hired first, they expected to receive more. But each one of them also received a denarius. When they received it, they began to grumble against the landowner. 'These who were hired last worked only one hour,' they said, 'and you have made them equal to us who have borne the burden of the work and the heat of the day.' But he answered one of them, 'I am not being unfair to you, friend. Didn't you agree to work for a denarius? Take your pay and go. I want to give the one who was hired last the same as I gave you. Don't I have the right to do what I want with my own money? Or are you envious because I am generous?' So the last will be first, and the first will be last.

5 *Patrimonium pauperum* was the principle of church property division in antiquity. The phrase itself means 'the property of the poor'. Thus the principle stated that church property is the property of the poor and should therefore be used, after deducting the most necessary operating costs, to help the poor (Svoboda, 2012).

caritas and diakonia activities. This then completely diverges from the interpretation of the parable as the hermeneutic key to and of mercy.

Unfortunately, this means for modern economic allegories that while they provide inspirational stimuli for the practice of charity and helping organisations, they cannot base their arguments on the parable of the Good Samaritan.

4.2.2 Methodological interpretations

The parable of the Good Samaritan is a part of one of the Gospels and is therefore an explicitly Christian text. As such, however, it emphasises an entirely secular fact corresponding to the ancient social ethos that compassion and mercy are manifested exclusively in practical, that is, in helping, conduct. This emphasis also makes the parable unique among most biblical texts. Its methodological interpretations therefore very well understand mercy as practical conduct backed up by one's own decision, that is, which is not enforced or being forced by external circumstances – social control, religious duties, etc. (see Criterion 1). It is therefore paradoxical that at the same time the methodological interpretations read the parable as an instruction manual – they try to apply exactly its individual parts to today's conditions (see especially the triple-step according to Lehner, ▸ Chapter 2.2) rather than to emphasise the principle of mercy while leaving its application open regarding specific historical, cultural, social, and other conditions in which a person decides whether or not he will act mercifully towards someone else's human need. In other words, most methodological interpretations do not actually provide room for interaction between the parable's message and its reader or listener.

At the same time, the parable is a great example of exactly the opposite approach. When the Samaritan came to the ambushed person, he saw his situation and thus a situation arose between the stirring and rational decision to systematically carried out help. It is precisely such an interaction between the stirring in the conscience and the rational decision that the parable aims at evoking in its readers and listeners. In fact, twice – firstly by the story itself, and also by the dialogue between Jesus and the Scribe. Therefore, the triple-step of seeing-stirring up-acting (Baumann, 2013a, p. 82) (▸ Chapter 2.2), as a practical conclusion regarding how to proceed according to the parable, fits into its message; this is because the core of its message is applied without being conditioned through applying other realities, which are a mere context of the parable, albeit an important one. Practical principles based on secondary factual data (▸ Chapter 2.2: Lehner, Kübler) thus overestimate them (see Criterion 2) and although they do not want to be eisegesis of the parable, they become so. On the contrary, Haslinger's emphasis on 'taking care' (▸ Chapter 2.2) – that is, that the Samaritan was taking care for the ambushed at the inn – corresponds to what the parable intends to convey. Namely, it conveys that one becomes a neighbour not merely by seeing the need and being stirred over it but only by a thought-through implementation of the necessary care. This then allows him to move on while not being attached emotionally or otherwise to the person helped – as the situation at the inn shows and, overall, what kind of inn the parable regards.

4.2 Modern allegory and the hermeneutic key to and of the parable

This, in a sense, cold rationality, expressed in the concise, clear, and aptly described way of help provided by the Samaritan is therefore an important message of how the Samaritan acted towards the ambushed. Hence it is necessary to supplement Baumann's (2013) triple-step seeing-stirring up-acting with rational decision, being a reasonable assessment of the situation. Rationality belongs to mercy and the practice of mercy – mercy as the Good Samaritan's method – and therefore consists in the following four aspects:

1. *Seeing* the need of the other,
2. *being stirred* in conscience (by God),
3. *assessing* the situation using reason,
4. and acting.

Thus, this regards that which the helping profession, especially social work, calls the reflexivity of the helping person (Payne, 2005)[6] as it is the Samaritan who is reflexive: the Samaritan sees the ambushed on the *bloody path*, recognises what the situation stirs within him, is able to rationally process this and then acts accordingly. And all of this takes place here and now in an instant of the present moment (Mandl, 1959). Thus, mercy is possible – not destructive – when the helping person approaches help reflexively. This also includes the appreciation of the findings and conclusions of social sciences regarding helping professions. Without such skills and knowledge, reflexivity is not possible.

Methodological interpretations are also based on the incomparability of the helpless ambushed person and the equipped Samaritan, and on the incomparability of the Samaritan as an outcast and the members of the social elite – the clerical strata. This is done to emphasise mercy as neighbourly love transcending various cultural, social, and religious boundaries and barriers (see Criteria 3 and 5). But sometimes this is done to emphasise the relationship between faith and deeds or to stray into a critique of the cultic based understanding of religion. Then, however, these interpretations come into conflict with the fact that the parable cannot be reduced to a critique of the cult (see Criterion 4). On the contrary, the parable emphasises the cult showing very plastically that God expects from man above all his solidarity with other people

---

6   Reflexivity is a fundamental alternative to bureaucratic tendencies which are heavily promoted for the assessment of the life situation and in the whole practice of social workers. Reflexivity refers to the competence of a social worker to consider various perspectives of the client's life situation. Therefore, he also considers both his impact on the client's life situation and also retrospectively evaluates the course and result of his intervention – this takes place during communication with the client. In practice, therefore, the essence of reflexivity is the introspection of the helping person who, during communication with the client, considers how the client with his message is coming across to him, how he reacts verbally and non-verbally to the client, and what response he receives from the client, what external influences affect him and the client, etc. Reflexivity thus means checking and providing feedback that the helping person gives to one's own self regarding the preconditions and circumstances of his work which should strengthen the quality of his work with clients (Navrátil, Punová, Bajer, Navrátilová 2014).

in need (▸ Chapter 3.2). *The true cult is to be a neighbour.* Therefore, the fact of the Samaritan being the main parable's character is not a mere factual piece of data but a decisive content part. This expresses that every person is capable of true cult through action – even those who are heretics, schismatics, or enemies in the eyes of others.

Thus, methodological interpretations work also with the theme of the Samaritan as a heretic and schismatic, that is, as a person who differs in the conception of piety from the priest and the Levite. This underpins the parable's message that the true cult is to be becoming a neighbour. Thus, in the story, the issue of incomparability is its narrow context through which mercy is being clarified. The story, where the Samaritan was stirred when he saw the ambushed man and his thought-through action was to save him, gains sharper contours by repeatedly emphasising the incomparability of the actors. The message of what mercy is, is thus expressed even more precisely. Although the methodological interpretations are ecclesiocentric in the sense of relating the messages of the parable to Christian caritas and diakonia, they also emphasise, through incomparability, that anyone can be the helping person in the sense of the parable. The application of the message of the parable only to Christian caritas and diakonia is therefore actually its reduction, in a sense it contradicts itself, when emphasising the incomparability of the figure of the Samaritan and the Israelite elites. That is why it is also possible to examine the public message of the parable which is not limited only to Christian caritas and diakonia. The interactive and functional legitimacy of caritas and diakonia entailing from the parable (▸ 2.2) therefore regards every helping activity; every helping activity regardless of spiritual motives – because the parable says nothing at all about these regarding the Samaritan – can correspond to the message of the parable. This is also because every person is loved by God and therefore is enabled to love his neighbour. So, he is able to be stirred when seeing the need of the other, and act rationally to help him. (This corresponds to the 1st, 3rd and 5th criteria for the interpretation of the parable.)

Methodological interpretations, especially the triple-step according to Lehner and the quintuple-step according to Haslinger, and other conclusions (Rügger, Sigrist), undoubtedly entail a number of interesting observations for the practice, while none of them overlook the Samaritan's mercy – love of neighbour and orientation to those that others have bypassed – as an important principle or a part of the 'method'. In addition, however, methodological interpretations often place too much emphasis on factual data which create the context for the better expression of the parable's message. However, such observations cannot be absolutised as if there could be no alternative to them, such as the inspiration of caritas in social work as a sign of the times (Opatrný, 2013). Similarly, they cannot be employed to formulate a method of caritas and diakonia work when they emphasise the importance of the story's contextual facts above the very core of its message.

The parable wants to show, above all, that mercy consists in the rational decision of how to help effectively when feeling the stirring over the need of another. In order to emphasise this core of the message, several contrasting situations in the story are deliberately created. At the same time – perhaps paradoxically in the religious text – emphasis is laid on rational action. The neighbour is not simply anyone, as could be easily answered to the Scribe's question 'And who is my neighbor?'. If the parable rejects as inappropriate the answer that only some people are, then it must also reject the question posed in this way. According to it, only the one who *is* merciful is the neighbour, this thus being he who has shown not love of neighbour but *neighbourly love*. Thus, the parable prefers ortho-praxis (good practice) to orthodoxy (purity of faith). This is because every person is capable of neighbourly love, which is manifested by mercy. He was created by God in such way as to see the need of another and God calls him, in his conscience through being stirred over the need, to help as well. The way to help so that it is effective is then a matter for human reason. Rational reflection of the situation is therefore a human contribution to solving the issue of need. Thought-through conduct, as shown by the Samaritan, is therefore a human response to God's voice in man's conscience.

4.3 The public message of the parable

While the so-called economic interpretations are virtually non-useable for the public message of the parable because they do not respect its foundational message, methodological interpretations need to be seen in a more differentiated way due to the same reason. They understand the parable as the hermeneutic key to mercy and, in a certain way, they could not have emerged had they somehow excluded mercy. At the same time, however, to the detriment of mercy, they emphasise those elements of the parable context that have precisely opposite purpose – they are to emphasise mercy. Thus, based on the previous contrast of modern allegories with the exegetical analysis of the parable, it is clear especially that:

- The problem of mercy must remain an essential part of the public message of the parable.
- Besides this, the message of the parable also includes its cultic statement, being the emphasis on mercy as the true cult: the real cult is to be becoming a neighbour.
- This is then framed by another important message that even a person who is considered by others to be an enemy or an outcast – precisely due to the cult (a schismatic) and orthodoxy (a heretic) – is also capable of this true cult.

With regards to other messages of the parable, captured in both its exegeses and its allegories, in the third chapter and at the beginning of this chapter the public message as such was defined, communicating how each person should act in practice, that is, what approach Christianity can offer to the public debate regarding human need and helping in it – to be without ambition, to use this entry into the public debate as a tool for gaining new believers, or to approach churches and their caritas and diakonia in public space.

Thus, the main issue for the public message of the parable is the fact that the parable is the key to mercy in the sense of how God understands it. Although the parable itself does not mention God at all, its context in the dialogue between Jesus and the Scribe, as also in the whole Gospel of Luke, closely connects the theme of mercy with the God of Jews and Christians: '...loving one's neighbour is not merely a universal ethical principle but also an emblem of the true people of God' (Brown, Yamazaki-Ransom, 2021, p. 246). Mercy, as understood by humans (see, the ancient ethos of help), is the hermeneutic key to the parable. However, the parable itself is the hermeneutic key to mercy as understood by God – and therefore it is also the true cult to be becoming a neighbour. Therefore, if the previous chapters concluded that the parable seeks convey the message, through the Samaritan's inward stirring while encountering the ambushed, that he is called by God to act rationally, it is not possible to separate God and mercy. Moreover, the figure of the Samaritan as a heretic and schismatic (with regards to the Jerusalem cult) shows that this stirring is not conditioned by the orthodoxy of the helping person. This means that even if one does not believe in God, he still responds to Him when stirred within by the human need he perceives and acts rationally to change it. However, this is a fundamental problem for human autonomy so valued by the postmodern period. This problem remains unsolvable for theology, including public theology, in the sense that it cannot resign in its loyalty to God or in its critical relationship with the social and academic public (▸ Chapter 1.3.1).

More precisely, this does not actually constitute a problem for theology. Rather, *how to speak of God* is a cardinal question of public theology so that its statements are publicly at least comprehensible and understandable and, ideally, possible to be accepted. This is possible either in an apologetic way (to show the usefulness of the Christian view of the matter) or in a way of the approach of profession of faith (to create a provocative prophetic edge regarding the public). However, the ideal approach is the synthetic one (▸ Chapter 1.3.1), where Christian theology remains rooted in the tradition and narratives of the Christian community while at the same time being deeply involved in current problems without desiring to privilege the Christian tradition in them (Paeth, 2016, pp. 480–483). Therefore, there is no need to seek an ultimate solution to the problem of the parable as the hermeneutic key to mercy as understood by God. The message of the parable that the stirring over human need that one feels in one's conscience, which is according to Christianity the place of encountering God (Gaudium et Spes 16), is the provocative prophetic edge regarding the social and academic public. If this message is not perceived as the reason and the tool how to privilege the Christian view, it can be approached as a contribution to the debate on how the story of the Good Samaritan can be useful to humanity for its own self-understanding. If, on the other hand, that prophetically provocative edge was not to emerge, such an interpretation would disjoint the parable from its message. After all, the parable itself creates several prophetically provocative edges. At the same time, however, these are understood in the way that the person retains his freedom to decide regarding these – just as the priest and the Levite decided not to help, so can the reader and listener of the parable reject its message. The narrow context of the parable, being the dialogue between Jesus and the Scribe, also ends with the fact that the Scribe confirms Jesus' words, but it remains open whether he has changed his conduct. The readers of the parable, too, must therefore retain this freedom if we are to consider the public message of the Samaritan story.

Thus, in the current debate on the socially just state organisation and global justice, the parable, in its specific apologetic way of not giving ultimata, brings the theme of mercy predominantly as a rational reaction to the emotional stirring when encountering human need. Even if a socially and environmentally just world could be built, mercy as a will to this would not remain waste. Without mercy, as presented by the story of the Good Samaritan, such a world would immediately turn into a totalitarian implosion. This makes the theme of mercy all the more important for helping professions.

The public message of the parable then consists in the restoration of mercy. This is restoration in the sense that it is first and foremost theology which must restore mercy. Its systematisation in the period of scholasticism led to a significant narrowing of the meaning of mercy. Mercy has become a legalistic principle to guide human life (Bopp, 1998, pp. 139–147). As a result, such an approach has led to a psychologically and socially unhealthy understanding of the mercy by which modern social sciences and philosophy have justly defined themselves. If mercy is to be restored, Christianity itself must first think of it differently – as mercy is so important for Christianity due to its connection with God, Christianity must communicate it in a different way (see Chapter 5). Otherwise, the prophetically provocative edge cannot emerge, let alone the apologetic presentation of the usefulness of the biblical understanding of mercy. This book also wants to contribute to this, having presented mercy in previous chapters as the 'Samaritan's method' – as a complex reaction to encountering the need of another person. The public message of the parable, then, is that mercy consists both in one's stirring when encountering human need, and in acting that is thought-through. It is the pure rationality and matter-of-fact approach of the Samaritan's action that is the parable's contribution to the ancient ethos of helping a person in need. The parable, which is also referred to as instructive narrative (▸ Chapter 3.5), thus shows that it is beneficial to involve human thinking and critical reason in helping activities. At the same time, with its specific connection of compassion as a stirring within, in man's conscience, with the Christian God, the parable creates the prophetically provocative edge with regards to the public helping professions. This is at least in the sense that the story challenges the idea that the role of conscience and emotion is always negative in providing help. But such a challenge is not only because the parable says that the Samaritan was stirred. As his story, along with emotions, expresses his pure rationality and matter-of-fact approach, it is an example of the involving of human thinking and critical reason in the process of help, thus showing that stirring and rationality are not necessarily opposites but parallelisms. The literary genre of the Old Testament, which the author of the Gospel according to Luke knew well, employs especially in poetry the element called *parallelism membrorum*, when one statement is immediately repeated in other words. In the story of the Good Samaritan, in the way of *parallelism membrorum*, the stirring and rational action are coupled. Stirring is in vain without rational action, and rational conduct without stirring would be as dangerous as a socially perfect world without mercy. According to Spencer, the parable was raised in today's public in the first decades of the 21st century: in '...good Christian fashion, what looks like it is dead is in fact surprisingly and strangely alive' (Spencer, 2017, p. 134). The parable thus says that being merciful is a process of interpersonal interaction which, regardless of cultural, social, religious, and other boundaries, establishes new relationships between people.

According to the parable, however, even a man who is considered by others to be an enemy and an outcast is capable of such mercy. The restoration of mercy therefore necessarily leads to 'merciful restoration' – to using mercy as a tool of social restoration, client's empowerment, or personal and social change. The parable communicates that one who acts mercifully becomes a neighbour and thus prefers the status acquired over the socially ascribed, and the interactive and functional legitimacy of help over its formal legitimacy. This does not concern merely the person defining the help. This mainly regards the helping and the helping person. Helping must consist in creating and giving space for the clients to take stances through good and right conduct. If the parable regards a statement that every person can rationally decide how to help on the basis of their stirring when encountering suffering, then the parable speaks, among other things, of those people that are called 'clients' in the field of helping professions. The change in perspective with which the parable works in its conclusion ('Which of these three do you think was a neighbor to the man who fell into the hands of robbers?') must, in the end, also concern the perspective of how the client is perceived. In the story, it was the Samaritan who became a neighbour, being considered a heretic and schismatic, an enemy, and of a problematic minority. It follows that even he, who is to be 'corrected' through some specific form of help – for example, to restore his social functioning – can become a helping person. Furthermore, he can, and should, become this before being 'corrected,' because according to the parable, the 'correction' takes place through a merciful conduct and does not consist in changing the acquired status but in the status acquired. The parable thus expresses the preference of what we now call the participatory concept of help and empowerment to self-help. When the fundamental message of the parable is mercy, it means that help takes place primarily by participating in merciful conduct, by empowering to the merciful conduct, and by similarly set self-help in a group: to see the need of the other – to be stirred in one's conscience – to evaluate the situation by reason – to act. Here, this does not regard an idealistic and utopian wish using a biblical text for its support. For example, there are already organisations in place where imprisoned women work as medical orderlies in a nursing home.[7] There are projects in which clients of hospices or Alzheimer centres regularly meet kindergarten children, and in more advanced stages these organisations are directly interconnected.[8] We can therefore understand these and similar activities as the application of the public message of the parable.

Regarding the public message of the parable, we can therefore draw the following conclusions correlating with the criteria of the third chapter:

1. Modern allegories of the parable, that is, its economic and methodological interpretations, are mostly problematic in its core from the point of view of exegetical, historical, and archaeological research – it is not possible to say that they follow

---

7   Saint Charles Borromeo Home: Four worlds under one roof (https://www.domovrepy.cz/index.php/odsouzene-zeny/projekt-odsouzene-zeny/item/75)
8   Bürgergemeinschaft Eichstetten e. V. (https://www.buergergemeinschaft-eichstetten.de/site/buergergemeinschaft.html)

from the message of the parable. At the same time, however, they cannot be denied that their observations can inspire the practice of helping professions and organisations.
2. The status of neighbour is obtained only by mercy, being a stirring that is manifested in thought-through actions: to see – to be stirred – to assess – to act.
3. It is essential for helping professions today to read the parable as a restoration of mercy, in the sense that the story of the Good Samaritan is an apologia of mercy for every period of time and for every person.
4. In this sense, help means in particular the participation of the clients, patients, etc., in merciful conduct by being empowered to self-help in the sense of mercy – the stirring that is manifested through thought-through action.
5. Mercy, which consists in connecting seeing and stirring, with the reasonability and action, has worth in itself. From the point of view of Christianity, this is precisely what is expected from man by God, who himself is compassionate – merciful; however this does not add any further or hidden meaning to mercy.
6. Mercy, which is manifested by works, is the true way of following Jesus Christ in man's life; it is what man needs to do in order to obtain eternal life. Man has his freedom to choose this path.

5. What's left of the story for Christian caritas and diakonia?

My intention for this book was to find and describe the public message of the Good Samaritan parable. In the previous chapters, I tried to show in steps that the parable itself has a public character, being written in the way to be understandable in antiquity to those outside the circle of people familiar with Jewish and early Christian literature. It is a story where the message is striving to overcome various national, social, cultural, and religious boundaries. The previous chapter concluded that the public message of the parable is – to speak from today's point of view – the restoration of mercy. While in antiquity this originally regarded its defining and strengthening, nowadays we can talk about its restoration. This chapter will be a kind of epilogue to this, the second ending of the whole book, and will focus on what the restoration of mercy means for Christians, their local communities and churches, and their life practice, especially for Christian caritas and diakonia.

Therefore, this chapter will no longer regard the public message itself. It will concern an important addition to the three other types of messages contained in the story of the Good Samaritan, which were described at the end of the third chapter:

- Considering the *cultic message* of the parable, I will be asking here how the Church should act as a community of Christians, because the true cult is to help those who – unlike God – need the help of others;
- Therefore, due to the *praxeological message*, it will be necessary to return to the parable interpretations focusing on practice and to think again more ecclesiocentrically, that is, how the Church should act as well as individual Christians, communities of Christians, church organisations such as Caritas and Diakonia, etc.
- Due to the *missionary message*, which is related to the public message by the question of how all people should act, it is necessary to pay attention to the intention of the Gospel's author so that the parable interests the reader or listener and wins him over to its approach to the world.

However, once the parable has its public message, it is not possible to ignore it while considering the remaining types of messages in the sense that they cannot come into conflict with it. Therefore, all that was said in the fourth chapter must be factored out before what will be said here. The *hermeneutical key to and of mercy* therefore also applies to its other messages.

If the public message of the parable today consists in the restoration of mercy, it must therefore be restored first and foremost by theology itself. Thus, this second conclusion of the whole book is not insignificant. It was the former approach of theology that led to the psychologically and socially unhealthy understanding of mercy, against which modern social sciences and philosophy rightly defined themselves (▸ Chapter 4). This is not a matter that would be forced merely by the contextual reading of the parable, that is, by its reading in the actual – today's – context. If the Christian God is merciful as the ancient allegories showed in parables, that is, how the parable of the Merciful Father explicitly shows in the Scriptures (▸ Chapter 3.2), then mercy has its final reason in God himself: 'So, the ethical implications for Christians of this parable are clear – we are required to provide mercy and aid to those who are in need of it. The allegorical interpretation explains the underlying reason *why* we should do so' (Blackshaw, 2021, p. 161). Understanding the parable as a restoration of mercy is therefore necessary also here because the story of the Samaritan was originally intended to define and strengthen mercy as an integral part of the life practice associated with the Christian faith. In contrast to the public message, the other messages – cultic, praxeological, and missionary – work with this very issue.

Therefore, in this chapter I will first focus on the cultic and praxeological messages of the parable and then on the missionary message. First of all, I aim at carrying out a certain revision of the methodological and pastoral interpretations described in the second chapter, respectively, their *relecture* (rereading) in relation to the parable's cultic and praxeological messages. This means nothing other than reading the parable on the basis of the critical exegetical examination described in the third chapter with regard to the contemporary practice of Christian caritas and diakonias, and also of church communities, and individual Christians. In the second part, I will address the problem of how Christians should grasp the parable's missionary message in the current post-secular context. This refers to the way how the parable's missionary and public messages are related. Again, diaconal exegesis will not be understood here as a modern allegory which must be subjected to relecture (rereading). Its view will permeate also the entire fifth chapter.

It should be added that economic interpretations (see Chapter 2) will be completely left out here. Their approach is actually an eisegesis of the parable, being a subjective reading that pursues predetermined goals. These regard the maintenance of helping organisations established by churches in state-funded social service systems so that they can remain a caritas or diakonia organisation at the same time. This is characterised by separate thinking about the organisations per se and the helping professions at work in them. But this is precisely how economic interpretations diverge from the parable and its exegesis. While in the parable it is the Samaritan and his actions that are presented as the effective help, organisations are identified in economic interpretations with the innkeeper and his tavern. But the parable did not intend to communicate anything like that and thus, in the end, economic interpretations cast doubt over themselves when trying to prove that the inn is a form of caritas or diakonia help. There is only one caritas and diakonia and therefore Christian helping organisations themselves must apply the standard of the Good Samaritan to themselves. It is not possible for them to refer to and relate to the person of the innkeeper. However, this does not mean that church caritas and diakonia organisations are superfluous or even undesirable as a part of modern social service systems. Rather, it entails a special commitment for Christians, so that the leitmotif of their activity is not survival in the social services system but a specific grasp of the ethos of help in the parable's sense. More precisely, this means for churches who establish caritas and diakonia organisations as providers of social services that these are not means of outsourcing neighbourly love (Opatrný, Morongová, 2016) but a tool for its realisation. And this is exactly what the first part of this chapter will be devoted to, focusing on methodological and pastoral interpretations of the parable with regards to its cultic and praxeological messages.

5.1 Cultic and praxeological messages of the parable

This first part of the book's second conclusion will be devoted to *relecture* (rereading), that is, a new reading of methodological and pastoral interpretations of the Good Samaritan parable. These were described in more detail in the second chapter. They will now be evaluated from the point of view of the parable's cultic and praxeological messages, on the basis of its exegesis (▸ Chapter 3), including diaconal exegesis (▸ Chapter 2.4).

The chapter will therefore focus on what remains of the parable for the practice of Christian caritas and diakonia, respectively, for the practice of churches and their communities (parishes, congregations, religious communities, helping organisations) and individual Christians, if we rid the interpretations of the Samaritan's story of the ballast of various modern allegories. At the same time, however, the chapter will strive to preserve the essence of the message of ancient allegories, as defined in the third chapter. In the second part, this chapter will focus on practical implications. It will therefore aim to present a certain update of methodological and pastoral interpretations which, as in previous chapters, will be summarised in a few clear points at the end.

5.1.1 Caritas and diakonia in the spirit of the parable as public theology *par excellence*

Considering the understanding of the *Gospel according to Luke* (▸ 3.2), Jesus Christ is not only the end or climax of history, and the salvation of man is not only a matter of the future. This is how the Old Testament understood the Messiah, and in the New Testament we can find this concept with John the Baptist. For Luke's writings, Jesus is the centre of history while the salvation is rooted in and grows out from Jesus' time. It therefore regards a different understanding of history and a different interpretation of its significance for the present. The Christian teaching on the last things of man, that is, the eschatology, became separated from the original Jewish teachings precisely because of Luke's writings. In Christianity, this no longer regards mere waiting for future, waiting for salvation – one day, sometime in the next world, in the Kingdom of God. Besides this, this also regards reminding oneself about the salvation which took place in the person of Jesus Christ and which is still happening. Such belief and awareness of this was present in all Christian confessions from the beginning, but only the author of the *Gospel according to Luke* made them explicit (Pokorný, 2004, p.

22). The experience of salvation which is to be evoked happened not only at the time of Jesus through his person but continues in the community of his disciples and actions of the Holy Spirit in the world. This experience of salvation in the community of Christ's disciples is already foreshadowed in Luke's Gospel in the Chapter 17: 'The coming of the kingdom of God is not something that can be observed, nor will people say, "Here it is," or "There it is," because the kingdom of God is in your midst' (*Lk* 17:20–21). When we read the parable of the Good Samaritan in this context of Luke's writings, then caritas and diakonia practice proves to be above all a reminder and experience of salvation – not only in the exegetical interpretation but above all in the allegorical interpretation.

Historical allegorical interpretations of the Good Samaritan story went far beyond the literal meaning of the parable's text (Benedict XVI, 2007a). However, from the point of view of today's Christianity, we can also consider a post-secular[1] allegorical interpretation: it preserves essential exegetical findings while it does not reject the allegory of Christ as the Samaritan saving man due to the allegory's unscientific nature; on the contrary, it accepts it because it expresses an essential part of the Christian faith and does not contain anything that would be contrary to the exegesis of the text by the historical-critical method. After all, medieval authors (Bonaventure, 1990) already distinguished between literal and allegorical (referred to as spiritual) interpretations. As Benedict XVI stated:

> We can pass over the individual features of the allegory which the Fathers presented differently. But a great vision about an alienated and helpless man lying by the path of history and about God Himself becoming his neighbour in Jesus Christ can be easily kept as a profound dimension of the parable that concerns us. For, the powerful imperative present in the parable is not thus weakened by it but only then reaches its full size. (Benedict XVI, 2007a, p. 144)

In principle, we do not need to talk even about allegory here because Christ compassionately embracing a person wounded by evil and sin is exegetically clearly provable as an essential theme of the *Gospel according to Luke* (Moessner, 2016), (Hoppe, 2006), (Pokorný, 2004) as well as other Gospels.

Caritas and diakonia, their practice and its various forms, personal or institutional, thus become an experience and a reminder of what God does for man. The allegorical interpretation, or reconstruction of the original narrative which inspired the author of the *Gospel according to Luke*, thus does not lose its validity and relevance for life practice even today. The exegetical view adds important practical context to this, which cannot be overlooked or separated from this allegory. It is precisely in this that the close connection between the parable's cultic and praxeological messages lies.

Ecclesiocentric interpretations of the parable (▸ Chapter 3.5), on which this chapter focuses, cannot therefore separate the parable's cultic and praxeological messages. In the practice of human life and conduct, the Christological-soteriological interpretations of the parable cannot be separated from their anthropological-ethical

---

1   For more regarding the term 'post-secular', see Chapter 5.2.2.

interpretations (▸ Table 1 in Chapter 3.5). On the contrary, it is necessary to keep them as close to each other as possible because what people are supposed to do is related to what God – Jesus Christ – does.

If a person is faced with the ethical challenge of becoming a neighbour, then, according to the Samaritan's story, a positive answer means not only the practical implementation of help but also saying yes to God (Wright, 2016) (Söding, 2015). This assent takes place, in the effect, by the conduct itself – not only when using religious vocabulary but also without it. This conclusion from the parable is of no less importance for non-Christians than it is for Christians. That is why I want to emphasise it also in this chapter. The cultic message, if understood as closely connected with the praxeological message, turns away from what it was so fiercely focusing on – from the actions of the Church as a community of Christians, or the actions of various parts and components of different churches such as parishes and congregations, religious congregations, and various helping organisations, etc. Thus, the pure cultic respect for God is challenged which without corresponding life experience (that is, also a helping life practice) becomes unfeasible. However, a helping life practice can become a path to the true cult (▸ Chapter 3.5). *An ecclesiocentric interpretation must therefore focus on making sure that the Church herself is not the centre of its own interest.* An ecclesio-centric interpretation of the parable is therefore only the one that focuses on the mission of the Church in the world (Verstraeten, 2011, pp. 317–318) (Gaudium et spes, 40–45), not on the Church herself.

Ancient allegories (Zimmermann, 2007a) saw the Church as the inn and the innkeeper (Erasmus, 2003–2016) taking care through the Sacraments of a person beaten by sin (Bonaventure, 1990) (▸ Chapter 3.1); modern allegories have adopted this motif when seeing in it ecclesial helping organisations (▸ Chapter 2.1 and 2.2) that take care of people in need within the framework of public social service systems, etc. However, this interpretation is problematic. If we confront it with exegetical findings (▸ Chapter 3), the inn as an image of the Church suffers serious cracks and the allegory of the inn as the Church is not compatible with the exegesis, at least not in its original concept and in the concept of modern economic and methodological allegories. The text of the Samaritan story clearly states that it regarded a *pandocheion* – an inn of dubious reputation. Thus we must mention that the Samaritan paid the innkeeper (Zimmermann, 2007a, pp. 545–546). Therefore, he cannot be regarded a counterpart to the helping action of the Samaritan.

If we were to apply this exegetical conclusion to the allegory of the Church, then the Church also acquires the features of a place with a dubious reputation, the keeper of which can expect mainly dislike and contempt from those around him and who can only dream of social esteem or respect. But if we think about the consequences of this combination of allegories and exegesis, it means that it is to such a Church that Jesus Christ entrusts a person who lies alienated and helpless on the road of history (Benedict XVI, 2007a). An inn like a *pandocheion* – i.e. a tavern open to all or just a dive – is thus not some kind of a torn and stained and therefore unacceptable image of the Church, but an it is an image of how Jesus, the Master and the Lord, perceives the Church. In this image, we are, therefore, also dealing with a Church that Benedict's successor, Pope Francis, compared to a sheepfold in which the shepherds smell of their sheep. Jesus Christ expects that such a Church will accept the person picked up along the path of history – and that is because he himself pays for him in advance. After all, a *pandocheion* is an inn to where anyone can come.

The *relecture* (rereading) of the Good Samaritan parable, which is based on exegetical findings and does not reject the foundational principle of early Christian allegories, seeks to restore mercy. The understanding of the Church as appears in the parable must therefore be factored out before any methodological reflection on Christian caritas and diakonia. It is the Church which does not care for herself, which is like a *pandocheion* open to anyone, and which therefore sees the path and the gate to the true cult, as depicted by the parable, in *every helping practice*, not only in her own: he, who is interested in the salvation of the other, acts mercifully; he, who does not need to ask how he is to fulfil the Law because he asks what he can do for the humanity of the other (▸ Chapter 2.4). This mercy of the Merciful Samaritan is not instrumental (▸ Chapter 4) because: (1) it is not done out of one's own religious interests, (2) it is to-the-point and effective, (3) and even one who does not pursue any religious goals acts mercifully in its sense. Such mercy is therefore not exclusively Christian. Christians, ecclesial communities, and the churches themselves and their helping organisations cannot therefore make any special claim to it. This mercy is the *public theology of the Gospel according to Luke* (▸ Chapter 4). In the context of the parable and its contrast between the Samaritan on the one hand and the priest and Levite on the other, this means that it is necessary to recognise that what Christian caritas and diakonia do, others do also. This regards even those who are strangers or even enemies, and it needs to be taken into account and, according to possibility, supported. At least in Catholic theology, this is not a new conclusion (Haslinger, 2009, pp. 260–261), because Paragraph 44 of the constitution *Gaudium et Spes* of the Second Vatican Council from 1965 says exactly this (Opatrný, 2013), that the Church receives help from all who do what she wants to do, even its opponents and enemies thus help her. *A small but significant difference then consists in the fact that Christian caritas and diakonia cannot renounce this mercy due to being bound by the biblical story of the Good Samaritan.*

It is also important for caritas and diakonia practice itself that the persuasiveness of the Samaritan's story is also brought about by his to-the-point or rational approach to help (▸ Chapter 3.5). The authenticity and persuasiveness of Christian caritas and diakonia therefore also depend on the nature of the help whether it is to-the-point and rational. Due to the cultic and praxeological messages of the parable, the *demonstratio Christiana* should therefore be avoided and not used for a recruiting self-presentation of Christians and the Church. Indeed, what the Samaritan's story really is not, is a sermon about obligatory belonging to a religious community (Haslinger, 2009, pp. 260–261). However, this issue will be addressed in detail in the next part of this chapter.

For now, the most significant problem here appears to be the fact that caritas and diakonia often are not a to-the-point, or a rational, form of help. More precisely, they are not understood as a to-the-point and rational form of help, not only on the outside but also – much more importantly – by those involved and those supporting. This problem has already been named here in the first chapter as a preference for such a helping practice: those

...that practice charity are largely unreflexive about the manner in which it buttresses their privilege and maintains oppression. Conversely critical social science requires its practitioners to be reflexive about the manner in which their own privileged standpoints infuse their episteme and understanding of the oppressed, i. e. they are required to exhibit epistemic humility. (Allen, 2017, p. 231)

Theological investigation of Christian caritas and diakonia does not address this issue if it remains in its original denominational paradigm (which is hagiological and doxological), presenting examples of the caritas and diakonic activity of saints and other Christian personalities, and which clings to the simple emphasis of Christian caritas and diakonia, often without relation to the carrying out of a specific helping practice (▸ Chapter 1.3.2). It seems, that such an approach is to a significant extent caused by the normative or objectivist nature of theology, which does not emphasise the reflection of practice and thus is not even reflexive to its own preferred starting points and how they affect its knowledge and understanding of those oppressed (▸ Chapter 4.2.2). If theological thinking is based only on deductive arguments, it can hardly be reflexive about the way in which its own preferred starting points influence its knowledge and understanding of the oppressed.

As was already shown in the first chapter, the theological view on human need and social problems in the *sense of public theology* leads to being a person who is for others, to caritas and diakonia as pro-existence. Public theology uncovers the fact that this has similar normative consequences for helping practice as the epistemic humility of the social sciences (▸ Chapter 1.3.3). Charity pro-existence leads to service and voluntary poverty; the epistemic humility of the social sciences leads towards options for the marginalised, and the concept of help as a co-solution for social problems and need by helping people, clients, and the community or society (Verstraeten, 2011, p. 327). The view of theology and the social sciences connect in the cross-narrative of 'being for' the marginalised, *which is at the same time also 'being with' the marginalised*. This, however, cannot be achieved by mere words. This cross-narrative compels radical practice – regardless of it being caritas and diakonia or a social scientific conception of help (Allen, 2017, pp. 233–234). This entails the important conclusion that the caritas studies or the diakonics are not public theology only because of their reflection of practice, respectively, hermeneutics of social scientific findings (▸ Chapter 1.3.2). Public theology in its synthetic approach (▸ Chapter 1.3.1) shows that more is needed. It is not enough to stand firmly in the tradition of the Christian faith and from this position to think about the social scientific knowledge of helping professions, their work, and clients. It is necessary to create a provocative prophetic edge of the caritas studies and the diakonics, that is, to enter into a much closer interaction with other disciplines that also regard helping. Only in the synthesis of the apologetic and prophetic approaches is it possible for the caritas studies and the diakonics, with their themes, theories, and methods, to become a partner also for other disciplines. Practically speaking, this means nothing other than having influence on the practice of helping in the sense that they will bring important feedback and new stimuli which can also be used by their social scientific understanding *et vice versa*. A good prerequisite for this is the readiness of both disciplines to work hermeneutically with social-scientific knowledge of structures, processes, and partakers in help. Mercy, as presented by the parable, therefore ultimately changes caritas and diakonia in the sense that an asymmetrical helping relationship becomes a symmetrical one (Mieth, 2012, pp. 183–184). The cross narrative, where 'being for' the marginalised and 'being with' the marginalised overlap, is ultimately help where the basic methodological approach consists in changing the client into the helping person – so to speak, drawing him into the tissue of mercy (▸ Chapter 4). It becomes apparent from this that mercy understood thus must be the foundation for the theological grasp of caritas and diakonia, which does not renounce the reflection of existing practice but founds its theological hermeneutics on the primary social-scientific reflection of practice (▸ Chapter 1.3.2). This also becomes the true theology of caritas and diakonia, as it is founded on the Biblical understanding of mercy, only when the theological hermeneutics of the reflection of social scientific knowledge about diaconical practice and the life practice and problems of their clients stems from pro-existence as a combination of 'being for' and 'being with'.

5.1.2 Practical implications

If we apply this conclusion resulting from cultic and praxeological messages to the methodological interpretations (▸ Chapter 2.2), then their foundational starting point is confirmed, that mercy consists in compassion, which was manifested in practical and effective conduct. As already explained, every person can be capable of such mercy. However, on the basis of the previous examination of cultic and praxeological messages, it is necessary to add that this does not regard a mere adaptation of the methods of helping professions under the banner of Christian caritas and diakonia. Although this is certainly correct and effective, the starting point is important also, not consisting so much in the Christian motivation of the helping person, as is often conceived in caritas studies and the diakonics, but in mercy as 'being for' and 'being with' the person who needs help. It is precisely for this mercy that man is being made capable within his own self by God, as the parable shows. Hence, Christian caritas and diakonia should adopt the epistemic humility inherent to the social sciences and also participatory forms of help. As already explained, the same applies to their theological reflection. The praxeological message of the parable, which presupposes that every person is a neighbour and that the mission of the Church in the world is to support the good, that is, the neighbourly love of all people, must therefore lead to service as participative cooperation to solving problems and to voluntary modesty in the sense of epistemic humility towards lives and problems of people in various forms of need.

From a practical point of view, therefore, this cannot be a matter of dividing help between parishes, congregations, church communities, etc., on the one hand, and professional caritas and diakonic helping organisations, whether voluntary or participating in social service systems, on the other hand. Just as in the parable the help cannot be divided between the Samaritan and the innkeeper, the principle of mercy cannot be applied only to local church communities or only to organisations, while maintaining their professionalism from the point of view of the social scientific concept of helping professions. Therefore, methodological interpretations ascribing spontaneous and voluntary help to Christian communities and professional help to Christian helping organisations are not relevant for Christian caritas and diakonia. In the same way, it is not possible to make professional helping organisations into caritas and diakonia organisations by making spontaneous and voluntary help conditioned by their high level of expertise. Both of them are misunderstandings of the parable's message. Such a misunderstanding is caused by its eisegesis which stems from the interest to maintain at all costs the current form of caritas and diaconal organisations as a part of the system of social services supported by public funds.

The parable of the Good Samaritan knows only one form of help, only one form of mercy: the Samaritan's help and the Samaritan's mercy. *Everything must therefore regard voluntary modesty in the sense of epistemic modesty and service in the form of participatory forms of help – both in church helping organisations which are highly professional, and in parishes, congregations, and communities, as well as in the caritas and diakonic dimension of the life and conduct of every Christian.*

This has consequences not only for modern methodological allegories, but also (and especially) for the pastoral ones. Their reflection in the second chapter brought about the finding that, in addition to pastoral interpretations, there are also more radical interpretations, so-called spiritual-pastoral. They emphasise solidarity lived out over professional help, which also leads to a critical view of helping professions. This approach can therefore appear seemingly identical to the cross-narrative of caritas or diakonia with the social sciences, from which a participatory conception of help follows. The problem is that the parable's spiritual-pastoral interpretations reject the social scientific concept of help. In doing so, however, they also reject the autonomy of the helping professions, attributing to them the role of so-called *soft cops*, that is, of 'useful idiots' who serve the system by providing help which is trying to adapt and fit the marginalised and all needing help into the system. However, from the theological point of view, the so-called justified autonomy of earthly affairs (*Gaudium et spes*, 1965, 36) is denied. It is the pastoral interpretations that count on it, being open to mutual inspiration of the helping professions in their social scientific concept with Christian caritas and diakonia. In their view, the help provided by the local Christian community or helping organisation is a part of pastoral care in the sense of Christians' responsibility for the world. This is not in the sense of pastoral care for those who need help as if they were its object but in the sense that the community or organisation is the subject and therefore also the object of pastoral care: *Christian communities themselves undergo development, change, and maturation when they are dedicated to helping* – which does not exclude, but rather presupposes, inspiration by helping professions so that the help is to-the-point, rational, and effective, as in the case of the Samaritan. Christian communities thus become a place where salvation is remembered and experienced, as was explained at the beginning of the this chapter. That is why their concern should be service in the sense of developing participatory forms of help and voluntary modesty in the form of epistemic humility towards the lives and problems of people who need help. This is what, according to the Good Samaritan parable, mercy consists in as a practical and to-the-point conduct for the benefit of others, being a response to God's call which the person experiences in his heart as compassion for their lives and problems.

We can therefore draw the following conclusions regarding the cultic and praxeological message and its meaning and practical implications for Christian caritas and diakonia:

1. Christian caritas or diakonia, understood as the task of each Christian and as the constitutive element of the Church, 'narrate' public theology *par excellence* through their practice in the sense of the parable. This is because they focus the Church's attention outside of itself. An ecclesiocentric interpretation of the parable, that is, one that addresses what the Church should do, necessarily leads to focusing attention outside the Church. Caritas and diakonia, as the task of every Christian and a constitutive element of the Church, actualise this focus. Thus they are also the true cult when they worship God by imitating the image of man that, according to the parable, God has in his eyes and also by imitating God in the sense that, according to allegorical interpretations of the parable, it is God himself in the person of Jesus Christ who receives the alienated and helpless man lying by the way of history.
2. Christian caritas and diakonia are carried out both by individual Christians and by their community, being the Church. In the spirit of the parable, this Church is to be a 'sheepfold where the shepherds smell of the sheep,' and where anyone can come to rest and recover. This exegetical actualisation of ancient allegories changes the ideal image of church caritas and diakonia, to which they should relate in their practice, ranging from paternalistic help that provides alms, good advice, etc., towards participatory forms of help.
3. In the Good Samaritan story, only one mercy appears – the mercy of the Good (Merciful) Samaritan – which is not carried out from one's personal religious interests, which is to-the-point and effective, and in the sense of which even he who does not pursue any religious goals acts mercifully. Such mercy is not exclusively Christian and is therefore also public theology presented by the Gospel itself, and which Christians and churches can also present when they act in this sense – when they are focused on others. And since the mercy of the Good (Merciful) Samaritan is only one, individual Christians and their communities (parishes, congregations, religious houses, etc.), as well as professional Christian help organisations should act in this way.
4. This public theology of the parable, which speaks of the focus on others by a man, a Christian, and the church with its helping organisations, has *normative consequences* for the practice of caritas and diakonia. It takes place – it can be 'spoken' and 'heard' only through practical conduct for the benefit of others. According to the story of the Good Samaritan, mercy is manifested by action which must be effective, that is, socially scientifically informed. Christian caritas and diakonia must therefore be effective as the Samaritan's action. For this, they need an important reference point of the social sciences (especially social work), which can describe and assess this effectiveness.
5. The one mercy of the Good Samaritan therefore means help as participation in solving problems and also modesty as epistemic humility towards others – towards clients as well as towards social scientific perspectives on helping. This is also why

Christian caritas and diakonia are public theology that can create the provocative prophetic edge on the border between social sciences and theology and their mutual definition and inspiration. Both the mutual inspiration and mutual definition are important for Christian caritas and diakonia to be a truly public theology in the same way as the parable itself.
6. This means that in the Good Samaritan's methodical process of *seeing* the need of another – being *stirred* within the conscience (by God) – *judging* by reason – *acting*, the steps reserved for epistemic humility towards the social sciences are especially those of *seeing* and *judging*. Here, Christian caritas and diakonia should be especially inspired by the social sciences, respectively, by helping professions, that is, should be inspired by their theories and current analyses. For theological hermeneutics in the sense of the parable – the hermeneutic key to and of mercy – however, it is not just the step of *being stirred* that is reserved, but all of the steps. Mercy in the sense of the parable (compassion connected with effective conduct) must be a part of the situation's solution from *seeing* it – cf. Lk 10:33: 'But a Samaritan, as he traveled, came where the man was; and when he saw him, he took pity on him.'
7. Through all of this, Christians and the Church, respectively its communities (parishes, congregations, religious houses, helping organisations) not only realise, or more precisely live out, their pro-existence in the sense of the parable but they also undergo – again in the sense of the parable – the change which is necessary for eternal life because they are becoming neighbours. This change has its origin in God, who calls a person to this change within himself, in his conscience, when he is not indifferent to the fate of other people, and thus also enables the person to act. Therefore, the true cult is not Christian-motivated help but merciful help in the sense of the parable.

5.2   The missionary message of the parable

In this chapter we arrive at the most difficult theme regarding the interpretation of the parable, more precisely, at the problem which is revealed due to the current socio-cultural context. The current concept of human autonomy is, in fact, hardly compatible with the missionary message of the parable, respectively, with any topic related to missionary work. The fourth chapter regarded only the matter of what aspects in the parable might be interesting for a non-Christian environment. It was therefore necessary to reduce the parable's missionary message in such a way that it was possible to say in what the public message of the parable consists – that is, its contribution to a better understanding of human need, suffering, and appropriate help in general. This fifth chapter, which is focused on Christian caritas and diakonia, regards the contribution that the parable has for these and therefore also its missionary message. What does the fact that one of the main purposes of this parable was to engage and win the listeners or readers for its narrator – Jesus Christ – mean for Christian caritas and diakonia, respectively for Christians, their churches and communities, and helping organisations who feel bound by the Samaritan's story?

5.2 The missionary message of the parable

The missionary message of the parable results from interpretations focused on the whole creation and human nature, and from Christological-soteriological interpretations (▸ Chapter 3.5). These are therefore interpretations according to which the parable tells how every person should act, and which at the same time sees in the parable a message about God who in the person of Jesus Christ saves man wounded by the sins of others and his own sins, and who is lying on the edge of his life's journey through history. As was explained above, such an understanding of the parable is not just a matter of ancient and medieval allegories and of those who like to find themselves in them even today. The original, orally transmitted matter which the author of the *Gospel according to Luke* used as a foundation, might have had this form (▸ Chapter 3.1) and only during the writing of the Gospel might this have been redacted to the form as we know it (▸ Chapters 3.2 and 3.3). However, these allegories and their authors mostly did not exclude the normative-ethical significance of the parable for the lives of its listeners and readers. They therefore emphasised the challenge contained in the Good Samaritan parable as well as in every other parable as a genre, that the way God or Jesus Christ acts (or the Samaritan), people are to act too. This is why some exegetes working with modern methods consider ancient and medieval allegories to be compatible with the current exegetical approach to the parable's text (▸ Chapter 3.1).

However, the Gospel writer's intention was not normative in the sense that he understood one's conduct according to the Samaritan's example to be a condition of salvation *sine qua non*. He did not want to say what a person must *fulfil* to be saved. From the dialogue between Jesus and the Scribe, it is clear that the author's aim was to show how Jesus interpreted the Law of Moses and the commandment of love for God and neighbour in order to interest his listeners and thus win them over to Jesus' side (▸ Chapters 3.3 and 3.5). Perhaps it would therefore be more appropriate to speak of the parable as an illustrative narrative rather than a didactic or instructive narrative (▸ Chapter 3.1). His intention is not to give precise instructions to others regarding how to act (▸ Chapter 4) but to help better understand what Jesus wants to convey – just as an illustration draws the reader even more into the text and its message through visual perception. The story was thus intended to interest and subsequently win over to Jesus Christ even those who stand on the fringes or outside of Christianity and who might have considered Christianity to be merely a certain offshoot of Judaism. It is possible that the Gospel writer wanted thus to address the Samaritans (▸ Chapter 3.5). This means that the missionary message of the parable is not normative – it does not tell what non-Christians should or must do in order to become Christians, or what Christians should do to win non-Christians to their faith. The missionary message of the parable is much more descriptive, intending to interest non-Christians with its description, its telling of the Samaritan's story. And it wants to interest especially those non-Christians who can identify themselves with the story and its point because in their lives they approach others similarly to the Samaritan. This interest should then lead to further interest in the person of Jesus Christ, to openness to Jesus Christ. Salvation is not one's own action procured by helping others. He who is open to Christ can be saved. The parable therefore shows how this openness can be realised in everyday life (Benedict XVI, 2006, 18).

However, such operationalisation of the parable's missionary message does not solve the difficulty of its theme. As already said, these difficulties do not arise from the parable or its missionary message but from the current socio-cultural context. Therefore, it is necessary to address the parable's missionary message in view of this context. Therefore, this second part of the fifth chapter first pays attention to the close connection between the missionary and the public messages of the parable. Both of them are linked by their focus outside of Christianity, outside of the ecclesial community. They do not ask how the Church should act, or Christians, but how all people should act, how every person should. The public message of the parable is therefore, actually, the foundation for the missionary message, and this must not only be based on the public message, but also must not be in contradiction. Thanks to this understanding of the parable's missionary message, it will then be possible to pay attention to the current socio-cultural milieu, being the context in which the parable's missionary message should echo. This will again have practical implications especially for Christian caritas and diakonia but also for Christians in general, as well as for churches and their communities (parishes, congregations, religious houses, etc.).

5.2.1 Missionary and public messages of the Samaritan's story

As has now been emphasised, the missionary message of the parable cannot do without its public message. Only when the public message captures interest by its perspective on human need and help – it is useful and beneficial – is it possible to consider whether and how the parable can also win its listeners and readers for its narrator. The Christian mission is not a recruitment campaign for the Church or churches but rather following Jesus Christ on his journey to the person to whom he himself wants to come close. At the same time, the parable of the Good Samaritan does not expect to appeal to everyone *en bloc*, that its narrative alone will be sufficiently attractive. It works purposefully with the idea of reaching out to those who share Jesus' understanding of the Law of Moses as presented in the *Gospel according to Luke*. It therefore focuses on those who prefer the existential reading of the Torah over its legalistic reading, lived ethics over declared, status attributed over acquired (▸ Chapter 3). It focuses on those who are not offended that the Samaritan helped the ambushed person and that the one who helped was the Samaritan. Therefore, it is not possible to say without further details that the missionary message of the parable is applicable under all circumstances. In order for it to resonate with its listeners and readers, these must be attuned similarly to the Samaritan in the story, or like Jesus Christ who tells the parable. That is why the missionary message of the parable is conditioned and limited by its public message.

However, the parable's public message can interest anyone who has not dulled his conscience enough to pass by the ambushed person as the priest and the Levite did. Anyone who does not resist reacting to his stirring within over the fate of the other with to-the-point and effective conduct is also open to being interested in the public message of the parable, and thus is also prepared for its missionary message. Whoever is thus prepared to unlock the parable with the hermeneutic key of mercy is also prepared to be interested in its concept of mercy and thus to understand mercy better. As already explained here, love of neighbour is not exclusively Christian; Catholic theology justifies it through human nature (Benedict XVI, 2006, 31) while Protestant theology through the theology of creation (Theißen, 2008, p. 108). A certain ecumenical link is the Christian faith in the triune God, and not only in the sense that it is shared by Christians of various denominations. Indeed, if love for one's neighbour is based on Trinitarian theology, denominational differences especially regarding human nature disappear.

This is how Pope Benedict XVI gave his reasons for neighbourly love in his inaugural encyclical regarding Christian caritas (2006, 7–19). More than a decade earlier, however, the prominent Protestant theologian Wolfhart Pannenberg had justified neighbourly love in a very similar way (Pannenberg, 1993). Ancient Christianity wanted to express the complexity and relationality of God with the doctrine of the Divine Trinity. God does not only relate to his creation and man in it. God is so complex that not only can he be expressed by different persons – Father, Son, Holy Spirit – but the relationships between these divine persons are also a part of God's fundamental characteristics (Pannenberg, 2009, pp. 192–193). And into the web of these relationships, man is being invited by God, we might say he is being drawn in, to participate in them and to experience them towards other people and the entire creation. The story of the Good Samaritan is actually a kind of a narrative form of this invitation: Man is being drawn into the fabric of the relationships in the divine Trinity by being invited to identify himself with the Samaritan's conduct and thus with the image of man as understood by God. Parables, especially those in the *Gospel according to Luke*, are part of the Kingdom of God (▸ Chapter 3.5). That is, they are not only a story about God's kingdom, but also its action here and now (▸ Chapter 5.1.1). Hence, they are also inseparable from Jesus Christ. And that is why the parable of the Good Samaritan ultimately brings neither the radicalisation of old ideas nor new ideas, but brings Jesus Christ himself. In the dialogue with the Law expert and in the telling of the Samaritan's story, Jesus primarily expresses himself and thereby reaches out to his listeners.

However, Trinitarian theology, which grew out of ancient disputations and philosophy, wants to communicate nothing less important than that neighbourly love is not specifically Christian; one does not need to be a Christian in order for a person – just like the Samaritan who was not a Jew – to become a neighbour. But this statement is only possible thanks to God, that is, only thanks to the fact that the origin and foundation of neighbourly love is God himself (*Romans* 5:5) who invites man to participate in it and thus God also enables man to neighbourly love (Pannenberg, 2009, pp. 183–184), (Benedict XVI, 2006, 31).

From the definition of the public message of the parable in the fourth chapter, it emerged that the main method of caritas and diakonia must be, according to the parable, merciful restoration, being the involvement of the client in the fabric of mercy where he himself becomes a helping person, that is, a neighbour, just as the Samaritan did (▸ Chapter 4.3). This merciful restoration is ultimately based on the same principle as God acting towards man. When the divine Trinity invites man to participate in its relationships and to live them also towards other people, it is actually nothing other than a merciful restoration as presented in the Samaritan's story: God involves man in the fabric of his relationships so that he can also be merciful. This is expressed in the *Gospel according to Luke* by its focal points, being the parable of the Merciful Father and the Good Samaritan – the image of God and the image of man which God has about him (▸ Chapter 3.3). The parable is therefore the hermeneutical key to mercy as understood by God (▸ Chapter 4.3): whoever understands the essence and point of the parable also gains understanding of Christian God. However, at the same time, mercy is also the hermeneutical key to the parable. Therefore, if it is rejected and excluded, the parable cannot be understood and nor can the Christian God. Thus, the restoration of mercy in the sense of the Samaritan's story is an important task for Christians, respectively, Christian caritas and diakonia. Mercy is restored above all where Christians themselves act mercifully, that is, where merciful restoration is the main method of Christian caritas and diakonia. Caritas and diakonia, respectively Christians, their communities (congregations, parishes, religious houses), and helping organisations thus actually unlock the parable opening the way to the understanding of Christian God. Therefore, if merciful restoration, as the involvement of as many people as possible in the fabric of mercy, is not important for Christian practice, the restoration of mercy will not be possible thus the effectiveness of the parable's missionary message will continue to be limited.

It is obvious that the effect of the parable's missionary message, or the Gospel in general, is always limited by Christian practice. This regards the life practice of individual Christians, the public action of Christian communities, or the organisation and provision of help by professional providers of health and social services established by churches. Bad or poorly thought-out practice can then cause serious complications to the missionary message of the Good Samaritan parable. The beginning of the 21st century seems to be a time particularly sensitive to this issue; it is a time when complications for the work of the Gospel are piling up rather than breaking away. It follows that what was said in the previous section (Chapter 5.1) about the cultic and praxeological message of the parable becomes a necessary condition for the audibility of its missionary message.

5.2.2 Missionary message of the parable in the post-secular environment

Already the first chapter mentioned the problem of the historical context in which this book addresses the Good Samaritan parable. It is a set of social and cultural conditions that influence our thinking and perception of the biblical text, such as the Samaritan's story, and also of Christianity, or religion as such. This problem was in steps touched upon by other chapters also, each according to its focus, more specifically the second and fourth chapters. They, like the first chapter, had to address directly the context in which this book was created, being the second decade of the 21st century. This context has long been understood and characterised as the so-called postmodern era. It included the shaking of the pillars of former modernity and wide individualism of opinions and values. The covid-19 pandemic, which began in 2020, as well as Russia's war against Ukraine, which has become in 2022 the largest European war since World War II, brought about considerations regarding a change of epoch.

However, the idea that humanity is entering a new – post-secular – era was supported by the authority of the world-famous philosopher Jürgen Habermas already at the end of the first decade of the 21st century (Habermas, 2008). It is apt that a left-oriented agnostic thinker talks about the topic of the 'time after secularity'. The epoch transformation from postmodernism to post-secularity consists in the fact that, even though the wide individualism of opinions and values and the pluralism associated with it continue, some topics that were in postmodernism considered overcome or at least greatly shaken are returning to the public debate (Beaumont, Eder, Mendieta, 2020). This includes religion, religious values, the influence of religion on the concept of family, personal freedom, etc.; hence the term *post*-secularism. As mentioned in the first chapter, in this context, a religious point of view can be heard in public discussions, but attention is paid to it not because religions or churches have a claim to the truth but because in a post-secular environment everyone has the right to express themselves and defend their views and values (Bradstock, 2012). This then creates conflicts in the media, social networks, universities, and in politics (Dinham, 2020), which we became accustomed to call culture wars. The solution to these, according to Habermas and thinkers close to him (Hoyeck, 2021), is the adherence to strictly religion-wise and ideologically neutral language and democratic rules of discussion and negotiation.

In this sense, then, this whole book is also strictly post-secular as it enters the public debate since its aim is to reach out even to non-Bible readers with the theme of the inspiration in the biblical narrative for the helping professions and philanthropy in general. In this chapter the book finally arrives at the issue of the missionary message of the parable. So, it is easy to see in what consists the already mentioned problem between the human autonomy and the missionary message of the Good Samaritan story. In a post-secular environment, an attempt, such as this book, can be made to turn a religious point of view into a public issue, but at the same time, a wide plurality of opinions and values combined with an emphasis on individualism leads to an a priori defence against any missionary activity. This attitude is shared in the post-secular era also by many Christians. If we were to choose the solution proposed by Habermas, this book should speak about the parable's missionary message and other matters in strictly neutral language regarding religion. This is not impossible. The first chapter of this book proceeded in exactly this way, relying primarily on visual arts to bring the Samaritan's story to its readers in as secular a language as possible. In the same way, the entire book in its first half seems to be postponing the moment when the biblical text of the parable itself is being presented (▸ Chapters 1–3). However, this was only possible until the four main messages of the parable were identified – cultic, praxeological, missionary, and public. Since these four messages are interconnected, and the missionary message also belongs to them, it was necessary to abandon the religion-wise neutral language. In other words, the efforts to cling to it at almost any cost would end up going against the meaning of the parable itself.

Therefore, rather than looking for ideologically and religion-wise neutral language at all costs, it appears to be a more appropriate approach (Hoyeck, 2021), (Beaumont, Eder, Mendieta, 2020) to transparently articulate one's own starting point in the debate according to democratic rules. This is how Charles Taylor (Taylor, 2018) proposes to approach the post-secular era, emphasising openness regarding one's own religious, ideological, ontological, or ethical starting points as a necessary condition for democratic debate on public topics. It is therefore a kind of reconciliation between religion and reason (Graham, 2017) which is a part of the specific ethos of the post-secular era (Baumont, Eder, 2020). The Good Samaritan parable communicates its theme and therefore its missionary message in a similar way. Thanks to the combination of the parable's content with the dialogue between Jesus and the Law expert about the greatest commandment, it is clear that Jesus' starting points are his ontology and ethics. Thus, it is clear on which understanding of the Torah, or on what understanding of the Old Testament, his positions are founded. The parable itself clarifies how Jesus' understanding of the Torah is applied in life practice in a language that is generally understandable, in fact a language that is completely religion-wise neutral, since it does not directly mention religious topics. The telling of the parable in connection with the dialogue therefore shows the connection between religion and life practice which is rationally accessible, comprehensible to everyone. And therein also lies the connection between the missionary and the public messages of the parable. The public message is accessible and understandable to everyone. Thanks to the fact that it also openly communicates its ontological and ethical starting points, it also becomes a missionary message. However, it still maintains what we now call the democratic principles of public discussion. The parable's message does not coerce, manipulate, or attack its listeners and readers in advance, nor any of the figures. Neither the priest nor the Levite are actually evaluated negatively in the parable and therefore their motives should not be speculated about. And even the robbers, who had caused the whole situation, are not attacked in any way by the parable, thus giving no reason for eisegesis that it is necessary to punish them, establish a different social order, etc. (▸ Chapter 3.5). In the context of the dialogue about the greatest commandment, the Gospel writer's presentation of the parable is actually a *Paradebeispiel* (an object lesson) of what a Christian mission should look like. The current post-secular context, with its emphasis on individuality and human autonomy, only helps (Speare, 2020) to better uncover the missionary message of the Samaritan's story as well as its timeless significance for Christianity which, although feeling bound by its missionary mission, at the same time blunders through the ways how to fulfil it in the postmodern and post-secular era (Taylor, 2018).

5.2.3   Practical implications

However, it would be a gross mistake to think that the most important thing that Christian caritas and diakonia should do in a post-secular environment is justifying its ontological and ethical starting points. However, this is what we often see in practice when Christians believe that it is necessary to demonstratively show, for example, through clothing, corporate design, or verbally, what the ontological and ethical starting points of Christian caritas and diakonia are. The exact opposite is necessary.

5.2 The missionary message of the parable

As the close connection between the public and missionary messages of the parable shows, the public message must precede the missionary one. Moreover, in the case of caritas and diakonia, this is not possible without their activity respecting the cultic and praxeological messages of the parable (▸ Chapter 5.1).

Practically speaking, this means that any caritas or diakonic activity must be based on the public message of the parable. As this is the foundation, the starting point for its correct understanding, both the praxeological and cultic messages and the missionary message must be built on it. The practice of caritas and diakonia, as well as caritas and diakonia as the true cult, must have their foundation in the public message of the parable (▸ Chapter 5.1) and must not be in contradiction to it. The same applies to the missionary message (▸ Chapter 5.2.1). Therefore, in order for caritas and diakonia to restore mercy, their main method must be merciful restoration, that is, participatory forms of help. If caritas and diakonia will be restoring mercy, the link between their activity and their Christian ethics and ontology, on which they are founded, will be becoming understandable and therefore communicable. This will be taking place without manipulating anyone, having to attack him, create pressure, or be delimiting oneself. Self-help groups, peer programmes, revitalisation of primary sources of help such as the community or the family, all of these are already well-established and described procedures which merciful restoration can use as the main method of caritas and diakonia. Christian caritas and diakonia do not need political lobbying or more public money, etc., but consequent effort consisting in helping to help one's own self. Only on such a basis can the ontological and ethical starting points of caritas and diakonia be openly communicated because only this basis makes them comprehensible and graspable even for those who do not share them. Help to self-helping is open to everyone to become involved and participate in it – to accept help and to become a helping person. He who acts like this becomes a neighbour in the spirit of the Samaritan's story. And he who is a neighbour is open to Jesus' understanding of the world and man in it, which led him to tell the Samaritan's story (cf. Benedict XVI, 2006, p.18).

For *helping organisations established by churches*, at least in the European environment, this means the necessity to deviate from the current form of their connection to the welfare state system in favour of merciful restoration. In order for Christian caritas and diakonia to once again become the driving force of social care, as they used to be in history, they do not need to be like any other helping organisation. They need to be innovative in merciful restoration just as the Samaritan was innovative in the parable. The missionary activity of Christian caritas and diakonia is thus not excluded, however it consists in proving itself with practical and effective help in the form of merciful restoration, which can only then be followed by the defence of one's own ethical and ontological starting points. The parable itself says nothing about the issue whether there should be a professional caritas and diakonia and how it should be organised. However, the parable's inspirational value does not lose its worth regarding the ways how to carry out caritas and diakonia even in the form of professional organisations.

For *Christian communities* such as congregations, parishes, or religious houses, etc., the parable brings a call for them to become foci of restoration of mercy. This means, first of all, to act mercifully towards each other, to apply merciful restoration also within the framework of pastoral care and community management. In other words, this means involving individual members of the community through delegating responsibility. And the same principle is to be applied to public or political communities, that is, municipalities and urban areas where Christian communities operate. However, this also means the participation in the merciful restoration of professional church helping organisations, as described in the pastoral interpretations (▸ Chapter 2.3). This is however the way how church communities can also be active as missionaries in the sense of the parable. Christian communities should in the first place regard not exclusion but precisely the inclusion of those who are not dogmatically thoroughbred Christians. What the parable says in connection with an individual (the Samaritan) about the priority of acquired status over attributed status (see the 5th criterion from Chapter 3.5) also applies to church communities. The space of church communities should not only be a space of faith in a selflessly or gratuitously merciful God, but also and precisely for this reason the space of selfless, gratuitous help.

For *individual Christians*, the missionary message of the parable means not only an invitation and motivation to participate in caritas, diakonic, and pastoral activities. The environment that enables and develops the participation will understandably shape the individual Christians who make it up. Therefore, they should carry this experience further, outside the purely church environment. Mercy and its restoration, or compassionate restoration, should become their life project, the spiritual path of their life, because, as the parable shows, it is precisely in the way of experiencing everyday events that a change occurs in a person which makes him a neighbour: he who is becoming a neighbour accepts Jesus' view of the world and the man in it, and also of God; he is open to the salvation that comes in Jesus Christ. A person who thus becomes a neighbour then makes public and missionary messages of the parable more understandable.

This ultimately has consequences for *church leadership, clergy, and ecclesial superiors.* The parable's missionary message shows that the Christian mission can take place in a completely different way than customary and that this form of mission is already contained in the Gospels. For the current post-secular time, in which churches are finding it so difficult to discover ways to carry out their missionary mission, the parable's missionary message is therefore an invaluable help. It means abandoning all activities in the form of overt conflict or hidden pressure, to which church leadership sometimes likes to resort. On the contrary, it prefers a humble openness based on practical actions that proves to be effective. This means that only when merciful restoration is not only a method of Christian caritas and diakonia, but also a method of pastoral work in Christian communities and especially a method of church management, it is possible to talk – with humility and openly in the sense of democratic principles – about ethical and ontological starting points of merciful restoration, that is, about the Christian faith.

Thus, the missionary message of the parable ultimately turns out to be the necessary conclusion of its entire interpretation, which cannot quite be avoided. Its importance for Christian diakonia and caritas as well as pastoral care can be summarised in the following points:

1. The parable's missionary message is based on the public message and cannot conflict with it. Therefore, it is also related to the cultic and praxeological messages, for which the public message is similarly important. This means that the missionary message becomes comprehensible only when the practice of Christian caritas and diakonia, as well as pastoral care, correspond to the parable's public message.
2. Therefore, the missionary message ultimately communicates the main purpose of the parable which is intended to bring closer to the listeners and readers the person of Jesus Christ and his understanding of the Mosaic Law, respectively, his view of the world and man in it. Connecting the narrative with the dialogue between Jesus and the Law expert, it becomes clear what the image of man in God's eyes is, and that the man who acts like the Samaritan is also open to God.
3. This turns out to be very important for the socio-cultural context of the beginning of the 21st century, often referred to as the post-secular era. The parable shows how to grasp the missionary task of Christianity in an environment that emphasises pluralism of opinions and individuality. But the message of the parable here is much more general and reaches beyond the specific historical conditions in which it is read. The missionary task of Christianity cannot be accomplished by coercion, confrontation, or manipulation. According to the parable, it is only the restoration of mercy that refers to God as a merciful Father. In this, the missionary activity of Christian caritas and diakonia or pastoral care consists because that is how the provocative prophetic edge is created which, at the same time, remains apologetically rooted in the Christian faith (▸ Chapter 1.3.1).
4. To speak about God in such a way that is understandable in the post-secular era and in the way that may be accepted, that is, according to the parable, means first to *see* the need of the other – to be *moved by conscience* (God) – to *judge* with reason – to *act*, and only then to defend ontological and ethical starting points of one's decisions and actions, being the Christian faith. The opposite approach can never be trustworthy – although being widely practised as it actually says that Christians know in advance how to act, and therefore others should act that way also. The parable's missionary message, on the other hand, shows that only practical action makes the ethical and ontological starting points comprehensible to others.

Instead of a conclusion, the Samaritan's story continues

The book about the Good Samaritan began with the search for the answer to the question of why this ancient narrative is still relevant at the beginning of the 21st century. Using the approach of public theology, I tried to show why and how the story of the Good Samaritan can be inspiring for the helping professions and interpersonal philanthropy. For this reason it was necessary to identify the public message of the story, that is, one accessible to every person regardless of their cultural, denominational, religious, or spiritual background. Various interpretations of the parable, which have inspired Christian caritas and diakonia for centuries, have thus been subjected to criticism by biblical exegesis, which critically examines biblical texts using linguistic criticism and utilising findings from historiography and archaeology. So, it was possible to clean the parable's various interpretations from the ballast of the so-called eisegesis, that is, secondary or actual intentions of a parable's interpreter which influenced him thus distorting the parable's message. The fourth chapter could therefore name the public message of the parable which consists in the restoration of mercy. This concludes the search for the answer to the question of how the story of the Good Samaritan can be useful for contemporary philanthropy and especially the helping professions. The fifth chapter added several observations intended primarily for Christians, which regard the remaining three messages of the parable – praxeological, cultic, and missionary.

The book was thus very critical of a number of modern interpretations of the parable (economic, methodological, pastoral) which, actually, resign themselves regarding human responsibility and the search for historically conditioned – being currently the most suitable – procedures for providing help, that is, using common sense and already proven procedures which can include, for example, social work methods. I wanted to show that the parable demands the exact opposite from its readers and listeners. It shows that in a specific situation it is necessary to find an adequate solution to the situation, and that it is precisely this search that God expects of man, because he, too, is looking for man as his merciful Father (Lk 15:11–32).

Thus, I have tried to show that, even for Christians, and especially for Christians and their churches, those aspects that have already become apparent from the public message of the parable are true:

a) The method of mercy is the four-step process of *seeing* the need of another – *being moved* by the conscience (God) – *judging* the situation and its possible solutions with reason – and *acting* accordingly; this culminates in merciful restoration, that

is, involving the person to be helped into the process of helping – so that he himself becomes a neighbour, just as the Samaritan did in the parable.
b) Because of the restoration of mercy, it is not only possible but also important for non-Christians to be involved in a church's caritas and diakonic activities, and similarly for the Christians and churches with their communities (parishes, congregations, religious houses) and organisations to be involved in secular helping activities.

Finally, the fifth chapter inevitably arrived at the missionary message of the parable, which cannot be denied and which must be grasped in the context of the current socio-cultural context, being post-secularity. In this sense, Christian caritas and diakonia as well as pastoral care should be a witness (in Greek *martyria*) to Jesus Christ as presented in the parable in the sense of allegorical interpretations: this means carefully caring for the 'wounded' person, not being a witness to the 'ecclesial Christ' as a legalisation of the Church per se, that is, regardless of the parable's message and its requirements for change (▸ Chapters 1.1, 1.3.2, and 2.4).

The careful care of Jesus Christ, faithfully imitated by the Samaritan in the parable, ultimately leads to an overall change of perspective. Diakonia and caritas are in God's eyes help to the one whom others have bypassed, that is, the one whom others have forgotten and are unwilling or unable to help. So, if anything determines what Christian caritas and diakonia are, then it is precisely the concern for the one who lies wounded and unnoticed beside the path of his life's journey. The story of the Good Samaritan thus remains open for everyone passing by to also become a neighbour.

References

1965. *Gaudium et spes. Pastoral Constitution on the Church in the Modern World*. Rome: Libreria Editirce Vaticana.
ALLEN, C., 2017. Social Science versus Christian Theology, Reconsidered: The Case of British Social Policy Studies [online]. *International Journal of Public Theology*, **11**(2), 211-235. Available from: 10.1163/15697320-12341483
BASU, K., 2022. The Samaritan's Curse: moral individuals and immoral groups [online]. *Economics and Philosophy*, **38**(1), 132-151. Available from: 10.1017/S0266267121000067
BATZ, R., 2017. *Bibel, Barmherzigkeit und Bilanzen. Kirchliche Sozialunternehmen im Spannungsfeld von Nächstenliebe und Markt*. Kallmünz: Oberpfalzverlag Lassleben.
BAUMANN, K., 2013a. Wieso „Barmherzigkeit"? Gerechtigkeit als Mindestmaß der Liebe. In: E. KOLLER, M. ROSENBERGER, and A. SCHWANTNER, eds. *Werke der Barmherzigkeit. Mittel zur Gewissensberuhigung oder Motor zur Strukturveränderung?* Linzer WiEGe Reihe: Beiträge zu Wirtschaft - Ethik - Gesellschaft. Linz: Katholisch Theologische Privatuniversität Linz, pp. 72-83.
BAUMANN, K., 2013b. Wieso „Barmherzigkeit"? Gerechtigkeit als Mindestmaß der Liebe. In: E. KOLLER, M. ROSENBERGER, and A. SCHWANTNER, eds. *Werke der Barmherzigkeit. Mittel zur Gewissensberuhigung oder Motor zur Strukturveränderung?* Linzer WiEGe Reihe: Beiträge zu Wirtschaft - Ethik - Gesellschaft. Linz: Katholisch Theologische Privatuniversität Linz, pp. 72-83.
BAUMANN, K., 2018. Zwischen vielen Stühlen [online]. Caritaswissenschaft als interdisziplinäre Disziplin Praktischer Theologie. *Caritas et veritas*, **8**(1), 18-25. Available from: doi.org/10.32725/cetv.2018.004.
BAUMONT, J. and K. EDER, 2020. Concepts, processes, and antagonism of postsecularity. In: J. BEAUMONT, ed. *The Routledge Handbook of Postsecularity*. [S.l.]: ROUTLEDGE, pp. 3-24.
BEAUMONT, J., K. EDER, and E. MENDIETA, 2020. Reflexive secularization? Concepts, processes and antagonisms of postsecularity [online]. *European Journal of Social Theory*, **23**(3), 291-309. Available from: 10.1177/1368431018813769
BENEDICT XVI, 2006. *Deus caritas est: Encyclical Letter on Christian Love*. Rome, December 25, 2005.
BENEDICT XVI, 2007a. *Ježíš Nazaretský*. 1st ed. Brno: Barrister & Principal.
BENEDICT XVI, 2007b. *Spes salvi: Encyclical Letter on Christian Hope*. Rome, November 30, 2007.
BERNHARD OF CLAIRVAUX, 1990. *Bernhard von Clairvaux - Sämtliche Werke*, Über die Gottesliebe 1, 1: „Der Grund, Gott zu lieben, ist Gott. Das Maß ist, ohne Maß zu lieben.". Innsbruck. 1.
BLACKSHAW, B.P., 2021. Is Pregnancy Really a Good Samaritan Act? [online]. *Christian bioethics: Non-Ecumenical Studies in Medical Morality*, **27**(2), 158-168. Available from: 10.1093/cb/cbab004
BOHLEN, S., 2007. Profesionalität und Barmherzigkeit in der Sozialen Arbeit. In: E. KÖSLER, ed. *Arbeit an den Grenzen. Zur Professionalisierung von Sozial- und Gesundheitsberufen ; eine Weg-Gabe für Christoph Steinebach*. Konstanz: Hartung-Gorre, pp. 50-58.
BÖHM, M., 1999. *Samarien und die Samaritai bei Lukas. Eine Studie zum religionshistorischen und traditionsgeschichtlichen Hintergrund der lukanischen Samarientexte und zu deren topographischer Verhaftung / Martina Böhm*. Tübingen: Mohr Siebeck. Wissenschaftliche Untersuchungen zum Neuen Testament. Reihe 2. 111.
BONAVENTURE, B., 1990. *Opere di san Bonaventura*. Roma: Città nuova.

BONILLA, D.F.B. and C.A. MORA, 2022. From Persuasion to Acceptance of Closeness: La Projimidad as an Essential Attribute of God in Luke 10:25-37 [online]. *Open Theology*, **8**(1), 95–113. Available from: 10.1515/opth-2022-0195

BOPP, K., 1998. *Barmherzigkeit im pastoralen Handeln der Kirche. Eine symbolisch-kritische Handlungstheorie zur Neuorientierung kirchlicher Praxis*. 1. Aufl. München: Don Bosco Verlag. Benediktbeurer Studien. Bd. 7.

BOVON, F., 1989. *Das evangelium nach Lukas. EKK III/2*. Evangelisch-Katholischer Kommentar zum Neuen Testament. Plancherel, Zurich: Benziger Verlag.

BRADSTOCK, A., 2012. Using God-Talk in a Secular Society: Time for a New Conversation on Public Issues? [online]. *International Journal of Public Theology*, **6**(2), 137–158. Available from: 10.1163/156973212X634902

BROWN, J.K. and K. YAMAZAKI-RANSOM, 2021. The Parable of the Good Samaritan and the Narrative Portrayal of Samaritans in Luke-Acts [online]. *Journal of Theological Interpretation*, **15**(2), 233–246. Available from: 10.5325/jtheointe.15.2.0233

CADY, L.E., 2014. Public Theology and the Postsecular Turn [online]. *International Journal of Public Theology*, **8**(3), 292–312. Available from: 10.1163/15697320-12341352

CARTLEDGE, M.J., 2016. Public Theology and Empirical Research: Developing an Agenda [online]. *International Journal of Public Theology*, **10**(2), 145–166. Available from: 10.1163/15697320-12341440

CAVANAUGH, T.A., 2020. Relating Hippocratic and Christian Medical Ethics [online]. *Christian bioethics: Non-Ecumenical Studies in Medical Morality*, **26**(1), 81–94. Available from: 10.1093/cb/cbz017

CLEMENT, M., 2015. „Genau das will ich: kein Mitleid!". Interdisziplinäre Überlegungen zu einem angemessenen Verständnis von Mitleid heute. *Münchener Theologische Zeitschrift*, **66**, 98–115.

CONGAR, Y., 2014. *Pour une Église servante et pauvre*. Paris: Les Éditions du Cerf.

CORDES, P. J., 2007. Hlavní referát prezidenta Papežské rady COR UNUM. In POMPEY, H. and DOLEŽEL, J. *Mezinárodní konference Deus caritas est: Církev jako společenství lásky: Charitní idea a hodnotová orientace v zemích transformace*. Olomouc: Univerzita Palackého.

DARRAGH, N., 2010. Doing Theology in Public: An Engagement with Economic Rationalism [online]. *International Journal of Public Theology*, **4**(4), 391–409. Available from: 10.1163/156973210X526373

DINHAM, A., 2020. Reimagining Religion and Belief in the Public Sphere [online]. *Modern Believing*, **61**(2), 141–151. Available from: 10.3828/mb.2020.9

DREWERMANN, E., 2009-. *Das Lukas-Evangelium. Bilder erinnerter Zukunft*. Düsseldorf: Patmos.

DUCKETT, S., 2022. A journey towards a theology of health economics and healthcare funding [online]. *Theology*, **125**(5), 326–334. Available from: 10.1177/0040571X221119276

DUSEK, J., ed., 2018. *The Samaritans in Historical, Cultural and Linguistic Perspectives:* De Gruyter.

DUŠEK, J., 2014. Mt. Gerizim Sanctuary, Its History and Enigmaof Origin. *HeBAI*, **3**(1), 111–133.

EBERTZ, M.N., 2011. Charita jako činitel německého sociálního státu. K náboženskému kontextu evropského vytváření sociální péče. *Caritas et veritas*, (2), 20–29.

EBERTZ, M.N., 2016. *Spiritualitäten als Ressource für eine dienende Kirche. Die Würzburg-Studie*. 1. Auflage. Würzburg: Echter.

ELLIOT, A., 2007. Doing Theology: Engaging the Public [online]. *International Journal of Public Theology*, **1**(3), 290–305. Available from: 10.1163/156973207X231635

ERASMUS, D., 2003-2016. *Paraphrase on Luke, 11-24*. Toronto: University of Toronto Press. Collected works of Erasmus. -48.

ERLEMANN, K. and I. NICKEL-BACON, 2014. *Gleichnisse, Fabeln und Parabeln. Exegetische, literaturtheoretische und religionspädagogische Zugänge*. 1. Aufl., neue Ausg. Tübingen: UTB; Francke, A. UTB. 4134: Theologie, Literaturwissenschaft.

FEITER, R., 2008. "Die Praktische Aktion bleibt zu wenig...". Zu einem Schlüsselsatz von *Deus caritas est*. In: G. COLLET, ed. *Liebe ist möglich, und wir können sie tun. Kontexte und Kommentare zur Enzyklika "Deus caritas est" von Papst Benedict XVI* Berlin: Lit, pp. 79–94.

FITZMYER, J.A., 1970–1985. *The Gospel according to Luke. Introduction, translation, and notes*. 1st ed. New York: Doubleday. The Anchor Bible. v. 28-28A.

FRANCIS, 2016. Amoris laetitia. Post-synodal apostolic exhortation on love in the family. Rome: Libreria Editrice Vaticana.

FRANCIS, 2016. Angelus. Saint Peter's Square, Sunday, 10 July 2016. Avaiable on https://www.vatican.va/content/francesco/en/angelus/2016/documents/papa-francesco_angelus_20160710.html

FRANCIS, 2020. *Fratelli tutti. Encyclical Letter on Fraterniny and Social Friendship from October 3, 2020.* Rome: Libreria Editrice Vatican.

FUCHS, O., 1990. *Heilen und befreien. Der Dienst am Nächsten als Ernstfall von Kirche und Pastoral.* 1. Aufl. Düsseldorf: Patmos.

FUCHS, O., 2004. *Praktische Hermeneutik der Heiligen Schrift.* Stuttgart: Verl. W. Kohlhammer. Praktische Theologie heute. 57.

GOLLWITZER, H., 1962. *Das Gleichnis vom Barmherzige Samariter.* Neukirchen: Neukirchener Verlag. (= Biblische Studien: Eine Schriftenrheie herausgeben von Otto Weber, Helmut Gollwitzer und Hans-Joachim Kraus). 34.

GOODMAN, N.P. and R.Q. HERZBERG, 2020. Gifts as governance: Church Welfare and the Samaritan's dilemma [online]. *Journal of Institutional Economics*, **16**(5), 703–714. Available from: 10.1017/S174413741900047X

GRAHAM, E., 2017. Reflexivity and Rapprochement: Explorations of a 'Postsecular' Public Theology [online]. *International Journal of Public Theology*, **11**(3), 277–289. Available from: 10.1163/15697320-12341496

HABERMAS, J., 2008. Notes on Post-Secular Society [online]. *New Perspectives Quarterly*, **25**(4), 17–29. Available from: 10.1111/j.1540-5842.2008.01017.x

HAMPLOVÁ, D., 2013. *Náboženství v české společnosti na prahu 3. tisíciletí.* Vyd. 1. Praha: Univ. Karlova, Nakl. Karolinum.

HASLINGER, H., 1996. *Diakonie zwischen Mensch, Kirche und Gesellschaft. Eine praktisch-theologische Untersuchung der diakonischen Praxis unter dem Kriterium des Subjektseins des Menschen.* Würzburg: Seelsorge-Echter. Studien zur Theologie und Praxis der Seelsorge. 18.

HASLINGER, H., 2009. *Diakonie. Grundlagen für die soziale Arbeit der Kirche.* Paderborn: Schöningh. UTB. 8397.

HENDRICKX, H., 1997. *Ministry in Galilee, Luke 3. 1–6:49 / Herman Hendrickx.* Collegeville, Minn.: Liturgical Press. The third Gospel for the third world. v. 2-A.

HOFFMANN, M., 2002. *Selbstliebe. ein grundlegendes Prinzip von Ethos.* Padeborn-München-Wien-Zürich: Schöningh. Abhandlungen zur Philosophie, Psychologie, Soziologie der Religion und Ökumenik Herausgeben von heinrich Petri. 50.

HOPPE, R., 2006. Von der Grenzenlosigkeit christlichen Helfens. Überlegung zum Gleichnis von barmherzigen Samariter (Lk 10,25–37). In: I. BAUMGARTNER, B. HASLBECK, and J. GÜNTHER, eds. *Wer hilft, wird ein anderer. Zur Provokation christlichen Helfens Festschrift für Isidor Baumgartner.* Berlin: Lit, pp. 23–33.

HOYECK, P.-A., 2021. Religion and Democracy: Jürgen Habermas and Charles Taylor on the Public Use of Reason [online]. *The European Legacy*, **26**(2), 111–130. Available from: 10.1080/10848770.2020.1824314

CHALMERS, M., 2021. Samaritans, Biblical Studies, and Ancient Judaism: Recent Trends [online]. *Currents in Biblical Research*, **20**(1), 28–64. Available from: 10.1177/1476993X211024247

CHAMBURUKA, P.M. and I.S. GUSHA, 2020. An exegesis of the parable of the Good Samaritan (Lk 10:25–35) and its relevance to the challenges caused by COVID-19 [online]. *HTS Teologiese Studies / Theological Studies*, **76**(1). Available from: 10.4102/hts.v76i1.6096

JANEBOVÁ, R. and B. CELÁ, 2016. Kritická praxe mezi „jinou" sociální prací a aktivismem. *Sociální práce*, **16**(2), 22–38.

JANEBOVÁ, R., 2018. Stává se sociální práce „soft cops" neoliberální společnosti? Rozporuplná identita sociální práce ve vztahu k jejímu poslání. In: Z. TRUHLÁŘOVÁ and M. PÍŠOVÁ, eds.

Sociální práce jako nástroj podpory sociální změny. Sborník vědeckých textů z mezinárodní vědecké konference XIV. Hradecké dny sociální práce Univerzita Hradec Králové. Hradec Králové: Gaudeamus, pp. 38–42.
JENS, W., 1973. Einleitung. In: W. JENS, ed. *Der barmherzige Samariter.* Stuttgart: Kreuz, pp. 9–18.
JEREMIAS, J., 1984. *Die Gleichnisse Jesu.* Kurzausg., 11. Aufl. Göttingen: Vandenhoeck und Ruprecht. Kleine Vandenhoeck-Reihe. 1500.
JOHN PAUL II, 1984. *Apoštolský list Jana Pavla II. o křesťanském smyslu lidského utrpení.*
JOHNSON, L.T., 2006. *The Gospel of Luke.* Collegeville: Liturgical Press. Sacra pagina. 3.
KEDDIE, G.A., 2020. "Who Is My Neighbor?" Ethnic Boundaries and the Samaritan Other in Luke 10:25–37 [online]. *Biblical Interpretation,* **28**(2), 246–271. Available from: 10.1163/15685152-00282P06
KERN, G., 2007. Parabeln in der Logienquelle Q. Einleitung. In: R. ZIMMERMANN and D. DORMEYER, eds. *Kompendium der Gleichnisse Jesu.* Gütersloh: Gütersloher Verlagshaus, pp. 49–58.
KÖNIG, F. and G.R. HOFMANN, 2017. *Die Kostenstellen der Barmherzigkeit. Caritative Dienstleistung im Spannungsfeld von Nachhaltigkeit, Professionalität und Finanzierbarkeit.* Freiburg im Breisgau: Lambertus. Sozialmanagement.
KÖRTNER, U.H.J., 2017. *Diakonie und Öffentliche Theologie. Diakoniewissenschaftliche Studien.* Göttingen: Vandenhoeck & Ruprecht. Neukirchener Theologie.
KRÄMER, M., 2016. *Die Entstehungsgeschichte der synoptischen Evangelien. Das Lukasevangelium.* 1. Auflage. Würzburg: Echter.
KÜBERL, F., 2013. Barmherzigkeit. Herzschlag der Caritas. In: E. KOLLER, M. ROSENBERGER, and A. SCHWANTNER, eds. *Werke der Barmherzigkeit. Mittel zur Gewissensberuhigung oder Motor zur Strukturveränderung?* Linzer WiEGe Reihe: Beiträge zu Wirtschaft – Ethik – Gesellschaft. Linz: Katholisch Theologische Privatuniversität Linz, pp. 13–23.
KUDER, U., 2015. Das Gleichnis vom barmherzigen Samariter in der ottonischen und frühromanischen Buchmalerei. In: C. STIEGEMANN, ed. *Caritas. Nächstenliebe von den frühen Christen bis zur Gegenwart: Katalog zur Ausstellung im Erzbischöflichen Diözesanmuseum Paderborn / herausgegeben von Christoph Stiegemann.* Petersberg: Michael Imhof Verlag, pp. 161–179.
LEHNER, M., 1997. Caritas ist Politik. *Theologisch-praktische Quartalschrift,* **145**(4), 391–397.
LEHNER, M., 1999–2000. Konkretion. Diakonie-Institutionen. In: H. HASLINGER and C. BUNDSCHUH-SCHRAMM, eds. *Handbuch praktische Theologie.* Mainz: M.-Grünewald-Verlag, pp. 410–421.
LUTHER, M. *Vom barmherzigen Samariter* [online]. Available from: http://www.sermon-online.de/search.pl?lang=de&id=2342&title=&biblevers=&searchstring=&author=0&language=0&category=0&play=0&tm=2
MANDL, A., 1959. *Srdce věci.* Manuscript, vyd. A. Mandl.
MARCIANO, A., 2022. Sado-masochism in Buchanan's Samaritan's Dilemma: A Constitutional Perspective [online]. *Homo Oeconomicus.* Available from: 10.1007/s41412-022-00126-7
MAURER, C., 1998. Wie entstand die „Caritaswissenschaft"? Ursprung und Entwicklung eines Konzepts und einer Handlungspraxis. In: M. MANDERSCHEID and H.-J. WOLLASCH, eds. *Die ersten hundert Jahre. Forschungsstand zur Caritas-Geschichte.* Freiburg im Breisgau: Lambertus, pp. 138–158.
MEISINGER, H., 1996. *Liebesgebot und Altruismusforschung. ein exegetischer Beitrag zum Dialog zwischen Theologie und Naturwissenschaft*: Universitätsverlag Freiburg, Schweiz; Vendenhoeck Ruprecht Göttingen. Novum testamentum et orbis antiquus. 33.
MERZ, A., 2007. Parabeln im Lukasevangelium. Einleitung. In: R. ZIMMERMANN and D. DORMEYER, eds. *Kompendium der Gleichnisse Jesu.* Gütersloh: Gütersloher Verlagshaus, pp. 513–517.
METZSCH, F.-A.v., 1998. *Menschen helfen Menschen. Der barmherzige Samariter als Leitbild und in der Kunst.* Neuhausen-Stuttgart: Hänssler. Hänssler-Bildband. 1998.
MIETH, D., 2012. Barmherzigkeit. In: T. SCHREIJÄCK and J. SAYER, eds. *Horizont Weltkirche. Erfahrungen-Themen- Optionen und Perspektiven Josef Sayer zu Ehren.* Ostfildern: Matthias Grünewald Verlag, pp. 176–194.

MICHÉA, J.-C., 2013. *Les mystères de la gauche. De l'idéal des Lumières au triomphe du capitalisme absolu.* Paris: Climats.

MOESSNER, D.P., 2016. *Luke the historian of Israel's legacy, theologian of Israel's Christ. A new reading of the 'Gospel Acts' of Luke / David Paul Moessner.* Berlin: De Gruyter. Beihefte zur Zeitschrift für die neutestamentliche Wissenschaft. 182.

MOLTMANN, J., 2018. *Über Geduld, Barmherzigkeit und Solidarität.* 1. Auflage. Gütersloh: Gütersloher Verlagshaus.

NAVRÁTIL, P., M. PUNOVÁ, P. BAJER, and J. NAVRÁTILOVÁ, 2014. *Reflexivní posouzení v sociální práci s rodinami.* Brno: MUNI Press.

NEUTEL, K.B. and M.B. KARTZOW, 2020. Neighbours Near and Far: How a Biblical Figure is Used in Recent European Anti-Migration Politics [online]. *Biblical Interpretation,* **29**(3), 358–380. Available from: 10.1163/15685152-2020003

NOLL, T., 2015. Das Gleichnis vom barmherzigen Samariter in der Kunst des 15. bis 20. Jahrhunderts. In: C. STIEGEMANN, ed. *Caritas. Nächstenliebe von den frühen Christen bis zur Gegenwart: Katalog zur Ausstellung im Erzbischöflichen Diösesanmuseum Paderborn / herausgegeben von Christoph Stiegemann.* Petersberg: Michael Imhof Verlag, pp. 336–347.

OPATRNÝ, M. and T. MORONGOVÁ, 2016. The Outsourcing of Neighbourly Love [online]. *Studia theologica,* **18**(4), 111–124. Available from: 10.5507/sth.2016.041

OPATRNÝ, M., 2010. Karitativer Arbeit. Interaktion der sozialen Arbeit und der Diakonie. In: M. LEHNER and M. OPATRNÝ, eds. *Theorie und Praxis der karitativen Arbeit. Einführung in die Problematik. praktische Reflexion und Anwendung.* České Budějovice: Südböhmische Univ., Theol. Fak, pp. 43–51.

OPATRNÝ, M., 2013. *Sociální práce a teologie. Inspirace a podněty sociální práce pro teologii.* Vyd. 1. Praha: Vyšehrad.

OPATRNÝ, M., 2020. "Caritas theory" as theological discourse within education in social work? [online]. *Journal of Religion & Spirituality in Social Work: Social Thought,* **41**(2), 1–25. Available from: 10.1080/15426432.2020.1780182

OPATRNÝ, M. and ŠIMR, K., 2023. To Build Bridges and To Leaven the Dough: Caritas and diakonia in the Perspective of the Radically Secular Czech Experience. In: EURICH, J., MOOS, T., HOFFMANN, B. *International Diakonia, in press*

PAETH, S., 2016. Whose Public? Which Theology? Signposts on the Way to a 21st Century Public Theology [online]. *International Journal of Public Theology,* **10**(4), 461–485. Available from: 10.1163/15697320-12341461

PANNENBERG, W., 1993. *Systematische Theologie.* Band 3. Göttingen: Vandenhoeck & Ruprecht.

PANNENBERG, W., 2009. *Systematic Theology. Volume 3.* Grand Rapids, MI: Wm. B. Eerdmans-Lightning Source.

PARSONS, M.C., 2007. *Luke. Storyteller, interpreter, evangelist.* Ada: Baker Book House.

PAYNE, M., 2005. *Modern social work theory.* 3rd ed. Basingstoke: Palgrave.

PEHE, J., 2020. *Nejkrvavější katastrofy moderní historie souvisí s nacionalizací levice* [online]. *Proto je - dnes mnohými vzývaný - konzervativní socialismus tak nebezpečný.* Deník N. Available from: https://denikn.cz/358528/nejkrvavejsi-katastrofy-moderni-historie-souvisi-s-nacionalizaci-levice-proto-je-dnes-mnohymi-vzyvany-konzervativni-socialismus-tak-nebezpecny/?ref=tit

PENG-KELLER, S., 2021. *Klinikseelsorge als spezialisierte Spiritual Care. Der christliche Heilungsauftrag im Horizont globaler Gesundheit.* Göttingen: Vandenhoeck & Ruprecht.

PETERS, T., 2018. Public Theology: Its Pastoral, Apologetic, Scientific, Political, and Prophetic Tasks [online]. Its Pastoral, Apologetic, Scientific, Political, and Prophetic Tasks. *International Journal of Public Theology,* **12**(2), 153–177. Available from: 10.1163/15697320-12341533

PETRÁČEK, T., 2020. *Kde byla církev v době krize?* [online]. Ukázalo se, jak je odtržená od potřeb lidí. Místo návratu k podstatě řeší, jak se přimknout k moci. Available from: https://archiv.ihned.cz/c7-66794270-rrpo7-e6ca65a451645ed?fbclid=IwAR2RXHzO06kQe5nxmFM7_j5o9D1_VuQW6xRmre4OXs9xE6Xvuqv_97hASxI

PEW RESEARCH CENTER, 2017. *Religious Belief and National Belonging in Central and Eastern Europe* [online]. Available from: https://www.pewforum.org/2017/05/10/religious-belief-and-national-belonging-in-central-and-eastern-europe/

PHAN, C. P., 2023. *Why Pope Francis sees the good Samaritan as the parable for our times* [online]. America: The Jesuit Review. 9 February 2023, 12:00 [viewed 21 February 2023]. Available from: https://www.americamagazine.org/faith/2023/02/09/good-samaritan-pope-francis-244684

POKORNÝ, P., 1997. *Theologie der lukanischen Schriften:* Vandenhoeck & Ruprecht.

POKORNÝ, P., 1998. *Vznešený Teofile. Teologie Lukášova evangelia a Skutků apoštolských*. 1. vyd. Třebenice: Mlýn.

POKORNÝ, P., 2004. Der Evangelist Lukas als Interpret älterer Bekenntnistraditionen. *Nachrichten der Akademie der Wissenschaften zu Göttingen aus dem Jahre 2004. Philologisch-Historische Klasse.* Göttingen: Vandenhoeck & Ruprecht, pp. 1–23.

PONGRATZ-LIPPITT, C., 2020. *Nationalists abusing Christian symbols 'greatest threat to EU'* [online]. *Czech priest warns of increasing xenophobia and populism as European elections loom.* Available from: https://international.la-croix.com/news/politics/nationalists-abusing-christian-symbols-greatest-threat-to-eu/10142

PUMMER, R., 2016. *The Samaritans. A profile.* Grand Rapids: William B. Eerdmans Publishing Company. 20.

READER, S.W., G.H. WALTON, and S.H. LINDER, 2022. Review and inventory of 911 Good Samaritan Law Provisions in the United States [online]. *The International journal on drug policy*, **110**, 103896. Available from: 10.1016/j.drugpo.2022.103896

RÜEGGER, H. and C. SIGRIST, 2011. *Diakonie - eine Einführung. Zur theologischen Begründung helfenden Handelns.* Zürich: TVZ, Theolog. Verl.

Sander, H.-J., 2005. Theologischer Kommentar zur Pastoralkonstitution über die Kirche in der Welt von heute Gaudium et spes. In HÜNERMANN, P. and HILBERATH, B.-J. *Herders Theologischer Kommentar zum Zweiten Vatikanischen Konzil*, Freiburg: Herder.

SCHAAB, G., 2008. Which of These Was Neighbour?: Spiritual Dimensions of the US Immigration Question [online]. *International Journal of Public Theology*, **2**(2), 182–202. Available from: 10.1163/156973208X290035

SCHILLEBEECKX, E., 1996. *Church. The human story of God.* New York: Crossroad.

SCHOTTROFF, L., 2005. *Die Gleichnisse Jesu.* Gütersloh: Gütersloher Verlagshaus.

SCHÜRMANN, H., 1994. *Das Lukasevangelium.* Freiburg im Breisgau: Herder.

SNYDER, T., 2018. *The road to unfreedom. Russia, Europe, America / Timothy Snyder.* London: The Bodley Head.

SÖDING, T., 2015. *Nächstenliebe. Gottes Gebot als Verheissung und Anspruch.* Freiburg: Herder.

SÖDING, T., 2016a. Barmherzigkeit – Gottes Gabe und Aufgabe. Neutestamentliche Orientierungen in einem zentralen Begriffsfeld. In: G. AUGUSTIN, ed. *Barmherzigkeit leben. Eine Neuentdeckung der christlichen Berufung.* Freiburg: Verlag Herder, pp. 19–34.

SÖDING, T., 2016b. Barmherzigkeit – Gottes Gabe und Aufgabe. Neutestamentliche Orientierungen in einem zentralen Begriffsfeld. In: G. AUGUSTIN, ed. *Barmherzigkeit leben. Eine Neuentdeckung der christlichen Berufung.* Freiburg: Verlag Herder, pp. 19–34.

SPEARE, R., 2020. Postsecularity prefigured. In: J. BEAUMONT, ed. *The Routledge Handbook of Postsecularity.* [S.l.]: ROUTLEDGE, pp. 409–421.

SPENCER, N., 2017. *The political samaritan. How power hijacked a parable.* London: Bloomsbury.

STAUB-BERNASCONI, S., 2018. *Soziale Arbeit als Handlungswissenschaft. Soziale Arbeit auf dem Weg zu kritischer Professionalität.* 2., vollständig überarbeitete u. aktualisierte Ausgabe. Opladen: Verlag Barbara Budrich; UTB. UTB Soziale Arbeit. 2786.

STEGEMANN, W., 2010. *Jesus und seine Zeit.* Stuttgart: W. Kohlhammer. Biblische Enzyklopädie. Bd. 10.

STEINKAMP, H., 1991. *Sozialpastoral.* Freiburg im Breisgau: Lambertus.

STEINKAMP, H., 1999. *Die sanfte Macht der Hirten. Die Bedeutung Michel Foucaults für die praktische Theologie.* Mainz: Matthias Grünewald.

STEINKAMP, H., 30 Jan. 2019. *Dienen? oder: die "Berührbarkeit" des Samariters?* Praha.

STÖGER, A., 1964. *Das Evangelium na Lukas.* Düsseldorf: Patmos. Geistliche Schriftlesung: Erläuterungen zum Neuen Testament für die Geistliche Lesung.

SVOBODA, R., 2012. Patrimonium pauperum. Sonda do problematiky křesťanské sociální a charitativní práce ve starověku. In: C. HIŠEM, ed. *Dejiny cirkvi v staroveku.* Prešov: M. Vaško, pp. 172–175.

TAYLOR, C., 2018. *A secular age.* 1st Harvard University Press paperback ed. Cambridge (Mass.): The Belknap Press of Harvard University Press.

THEIS, J., 2005. *Biblische Texte verstehen lernen. Eine bibeldidaktische Studie mit einer empirischen Untersuchung zum Gleichnis vom barmherzigen Samariter.* Stuttgart: Kohlhammer. Praktische Theologie heute. Bd. 64.

THEISSEN, G., 2008. Die Biebel diakonisch lesen. Die Legitimitätskrise des Helfens und der barmherzige Samariter. In: V. HERRMANN and M. HORSTMANN, eds. *Biblische, historische und theologische Zugänge zur Diakonie.* Neukirchen-Vluyn: Neukirchener Verl., pp. 88–116.

TRUNDLE, C., 2014. *Americans in Tuscany. Charity, compassion, and belonging / Catherine Trundle.* New York: Berghahn Books. New directions in anthropology. volume 36.

TWELFTREE, G.H., 2009. *People of the spirit. Exploring Luke's view of the church / Graham H. Twelftree.* Grand Rapids, Mich.: Baker Academic; London: Society for Promoting Christian Knowledge.

VERSTRAETEN, J., 2011. Towards Interpreting Signs of the Times, Conversation with the World and Inclusion of the Poor: Three Challenges for Catholic Social Teaching [online]. *International Journal of Public Theology,* **5**(3), 314–330. Available from: 10.1163/156973211X581560

VIO CAIETANI, T. de, 1639. *In quatuor Euangelia et acta apostolorum commentarii ...: tomus quartus.* Lyon: Sumptibus Iacobi [et] Petri Prost.

VITORIA, F. de, E. NYS, J.P. BATE, J.G. SIMON, and H.F. WRIGHT, 1917. *Francisci de Victoria De Indis et De ivre belli relectiones:* Carnegie Institution of Washington. Book collection on microfilm relating to the North American Indian.

WOLTER, M., 2008. *Das Lukasevangelium.* Tübingen: Mohr Siebeck. Handbuch zum Neuen Testament. 5.

WRIGHT, N.T., 2016. *Lukas für heute.* Gießen: Brunnen.

ZIMMERMANN, R., 2007a. Berührende Liebe (Der barmherzige Samariter). In: R. ZIMMERMANN and D. DORMEYER, eds. *Kompendium der Gleichnisse Jesu.* Gütersloh: Gütersloher Verlagshaus, pp. 538–555.

ZIMMERMANN, R., 2007b. Die Gleichnisse Jesu. Eine Leseanleitung zum Kompendium. In: R. ZIMMERMANN and D. DORMEYER, eds. *Kompendium der Gleichnisse Jesu.* Gütersloh: Gütersloher Verlagshaus, pp. 3–46.

ZULEHNER, P.M., 1997. *Ein Obdach der Seele. Geistliche Übungen - nicht nur für fromme Zeitgenossen.* 7. Aufl. Düsseldorf: Patmos-Verl.

ZULEHNER, P.M., 2006a. "Sah ihn" (Lk 10,31). Option für Überflüssigen. In: I. BAUMGARTNER, B. HASLBECK, and J. GÜNTHER, eds. *Wer hilft, wird ein anderer. Zur Provokation christlichen Helfens Festschrift für Isidor Baumgartner.* Berlin: Lit, pp. 131–139.

ZULEHNER, P.M., 2006b. *Gott ist größer als unser Herz (1 Joh 3,20). Eine Pastoral des Erbarmens.* Ostfildern: Schwabenverlag.